THE WORLD

A BEGINNER'S GUIDE

Göran Therborn

polity

First published in 2011 by Polity Press
Reprinted 2011 (twice), 2012

Polity Press
65 Bridge Street
Cambridge CB2 1UR, UK

Polity Press
350 Main Street
Malden, MA 02148, USA

ISBN-13: 978-0-7456-4343-4
ISBN-13: 978-0-7456-4344-1(pb)

A catalogue record for this book is available from the British Library.

Typeset in 10.5 on 12 pt Sabon by Toppan Best-set Premedia Limited
Printed and bound in Great Britain by the MPG Books Group

The publisher has used its best endeavours to ensure that the URLs for external websites referred to in this book are correct and active at the time of going to press. However, the publisher has no responsibility for the websites and can make no guarantee that a site will remain live or that the content is or will remain appropriate.

Every effort has been made to trace all copyright holders, but if any have been inadvertently overlooked the publisher will be pleased to include any necessary credits in any subsequent reprint or edition.

For further information on Polity, visit our website: www.politybooks.com

CONTENTS

LIST OF TABLES

LIST OF MAPS

PROLOGUE: IN THE BEGINNING THERE IS . . .

Most of us are beginners on the planetary terrain of humankind. We are much more familiar with our own country, occasionally with our own continental region, be it Africa, Europe, Latin America, North America or a part of Asia, but rarely all of it. And each and all of us are beginners in the twenty-first century, a century which promises at least one thing – that it will be very different from the past one. Therefore, this is a beginner's guide, written for all those of us who are curious about this world, those of us who do not already know everything we want to know, who do not know everything we need to know about the evil, the good and the salvation of this world. On offer is not a primary of mainstream wisdom, it is an individual scholar's vision, coming out of half a century of social study and carried by his personal passion for human freedom and equality, and for empirical evidence.

In this book, you will find a sociocultural geological map of the world, a compass outline of the fundamental drives of human society and a specification of how they operate in the world today, a picture of the current world stage with its major actors. You will be invited to a worldwide human life-course journey, from birth to after-life. In another sense, this is also a guide of beginning, of snapshots never shown before (outside my Cambridge classrooms), although pixelled together from the vast archives of human research and experience.

This is a guide to the world after the stardust of 'globalization' has settled, when the global vista is clearing up. What is opening up then is a new space of social imagination, no longer just national, no longer the North Atlantic region writ large as the universe, of a first or second, solid or liquid modernity, or of postmodernity. It is a finite planet of enormous variety, interdependent and intercommunicating. This new world is a world of plural civilizations, each with its living

ix

history, not the binary one of yesterday's North Atlantic leaders putting (our) civilization against the barbarians threatening it. It is a world of emerging powers and re-emerging cultures, and not just one of global markets, a world of alternative possibilities and of different life-courses.

Intellectually, this may the hour of global sociology, taken as scholarship, with its sensitivity to variety and limitations as well as to connectivity, and its refraining from policy pontificating. Half a century ago, I entered university, in Lund in Sweden, with a view to studying politics and economics, but in the process I learnt about sociology, as a more scientific approach, which may have reflected local circumstances more than a universal truth. Later on, in the Netherlands, I had a chair of political science, and political economy has always been prominent on my mind, although my favourite scholarly writers have mostly been historians, models of erudition-cum-style. Nevertheless, I think sociology offers the best vantage-point from which to comprehend the world as a whole, the past and the contemporary together. It is wide open to different expertise and disciplines, itself pluralistic, driven by an unbound, non-paradigmatic curiosity, and by an ambition of connecting as much evidence, as much human experience, as possible.

However, after all, academic disciplines are important only within the small compounds of academia, and this book is concerned with the world outside. It is written by a scholar-citizen to fellow citizens of the world. Suddenly, besides everything else we are, we have become fellow residents of a planet and members of humanity.

Finally, a word of thanks. I am a craftsman sociologist, neither an armchair theorist nor a research manager. Most of the empirical evidence on which this book is based I have dug out with my own hands, voraciously and gratefully picking up fruits from institutional data collectors as well as from scholarly colleagues of many disciplines. But I thankfully acknowledge the assistance of my student Maruta Herding on cultural exchange. I further want to thank all my students at Cambridge for a most challenging and stimulating teaching experience, and for intercultural learning. My editor and colleague, Professor John Thompson, is also one of my creditors, for his sharp critical acumen as well as for his generous support.

Cambridge, England / Ljungbyholm, Sweden

INTRODUCTION: HUMANKIND
AND ITS WORLD

Human society and human history can only be grasped by their contradictions. The twentieth century was homicidal, the worst since the sixteenth century and the European conquest of the Americas – as well as the peak of human net population growth. It produced the worst genocidal racism of human history, and it left us with a legacy of an awareness of one humankind existing in a common, finite world.

Human rights, the internet, 'globalization' and the Kyoto Protocol – all products of the last quarter of the previous century – have opened a new horizon of social understanding and of social action, i.e., humankind and its world. While we go on being, say, Chinese or Americans, Muslims or Hindus, workers or bankers, African women or European men, young or old, we have also become members of a common humankind and stakeholders in the same planet.

It was an extraordinary confluence of events. The post-fascist 1948 UN Declaration of Human Rights was an avant-garde publication of little importance for a long while. Its affirmation of the freedom to marry (or not), for instance, was systematically violated in most of Africa, Asia and the USA (inter-racial marriages), often in the rest of the Americas and in Eastern Europe, although there recent legislation had at least formally freed young people from parental control. Human rights began to emerge as a serious issue in the 1960s, thanks to Amnesty International, but reached the geopolitical mainstream only by the mid-1970s. The Western powers had them inserted in the Helsinki Accord of 1975, recognizing the post-Second World War borders of Europe, crucial to Poles and most other East Europeans, communist or anti-communist. In the Americas, human rights also became a key issue in the second half of the 1970s. In Latin America, they became a defence in defeat, after all attempts at progressive social change (outside Cuba) had been crushed by military dictatorships. In the USA, there was, for once, a positive resonance during the Carter administration. The completely unforeseen interlocking of

1

Cold War diplomacy and a US recognition of human rights in the Americas made human rights irremovable from the international political agenda, accepted in violation even by the Reagan and the two Bush administrations.

Segments of humanity have been in global, or at least transcontinental, transoceanic, contact for a long time. There were trading links between ancient Rome and India about 2,000 years ago, and between India and China. The foray of Alexander of Macedonia into Central Asia 2,300 years ago is evident from the Greek-looking Buddha statues in the British Museum. What is new is the mass of contact, and the contact of masses, mass travel and mass self-communication. Global TV broadcasting by satellite emerged on a large routine scale in the 1980s. The internet became public in 1991. Global chat and picture-exchange clubs appeared in the 2000s, soon acquiring tens, nay hundreds of millions, of members worldwide. The net and the satellites now reach almost every corner of the planet, whereas in my mid-life career (in the 1980s), one could hardly correspond with colleagues in Italy, because of the dreadful state of the Italian mail.

When the Cold War ended, 'globalization' became the most popular of social concepts, its usage exploding in the 1990s. It captured the moods of the time, in plural because it had both positive and negative vibrations. In both cases, it referred primarily to a global extension of what existed, capital and markets above all, but also cultures. Social change had ceased to have structural or cultural content, and had become only or overwhelmingly spatial. Anyhow, whatever critical quarrels one might have with globalization discourse, it was right in drawing attention to the new interdependence of humankind, through capital flows, commodity chains, foreign penetration of domestic markets, migration flows picking up and cultural exchange intensifying and cross-fertilizing.

The planetary environment of humankind first emerged into the limelight in 1972, with the *Limits to Growth*, put out by a tiny, rather aristocratic outfit called the Club of Rome. It had great resonance because of the oil crisis of 1973–4 in the wake of the US rescue of Israel in the Egyptian-Israeli Ramadan/Yom Kippur war of 1973. The United Nations took up the environmental challenge rapidly, with conferences in Stockholm in 1972 and in Rio in 1992, and with its attempt at global legislation in the Kyoto Protocol of 1997. Because of the refusal of the US Congress to participate, not much concrete action came out of Kyoto, but awareness of a common human environmental challenge from manmade climate change increased in the 2000s. Again, the UN effort at Copenhagen in December 2009 was largely unsuccessful in terms of action, but there was an almost universal consensus that there is one humanity facing a planetary environmental problem.

This is a novel situation in the history of humans, a mass awareness of a common humanity, electronically directly interconnected and a common target of satellite beams of communication, in one global economy, in one planetary environment. Among intellectual elites, visions of a world community have a history. Just in the European tradition, there is the 'world citizen perspective' (*welbürgerliche Sicht*) of Immanuel Kant and the Enlightenment, and even before that the medieval universalism of Dante and the sixteenth-century defence of Amerindian humanity by Bartolomé de Las Casas (see Bartelson 2009). But that was only single intellectual vision, and Kant's hope for a 'perpetual peace' was followed by the mass carnage of the Napoleonic wars, the last phase of the Franco-British world war.

The world as otherness has a long history of mass fascination with exploration and conquest. We are all indebted to the intellectual as well as the physical courage of the great geographers and cartographers, from Strabo and Mercator and on, of the great travellers and explorers, from Ibn Batuta, Marco Polo, Zheng He, Fernão de Magalhães, James Cook, Alexander von Humboldt etc, and we are also heirs to the more ambiguous legacy of the big conquerors, from Alexander, to Chingiz Khan and Hernán Cortés and their later followers.

The new challenge is to comprehend, and to be able to act upon, this new common human world. A very elementary start is to recognize that commonality necessarily entails neither sameness nor equality. Rather, any proper understanding of contemporary humanity had better be prepared for its diversity and for its inequality, not a priori less than that of the manorial village, the plantation, the Indian caste system or the current 'global city', all supposed to manifest a common society. But that is only a precaution against short-circuiting common awareness of existence and conditions for sameness or equality. The real task begins, then.

To get a handle on humankind and its world, for action as well as for understanding, we need to know something about the following. Why are we who we are? From where come our characteristics, our knowledge and our ignorance? It will be argued that these questions will require a recourse to *sociocultural geology*, of enduring, layered history, looking at enduring effects of ancient civilizations, multiple waves of globalization, different pathways to modernity. Our views of the world, our fundamental beliefs, aesthetic tastes, our languages, our ways and manners of social interactions, our politics and our sports interests can all be traced back to our historical formation.

Secondly, why do we and others act the way we/they do? I will argue that there are five irreducible drives of humankind which constitute the *world dynamics*. By no means do they exhaustively constitute the human condition, but they are propelling the social world. Where they will take us, neither God nor academia can tell. But they can be understood, and put to use.

Thirdly, there is the *world stage* of geopolitics and geoeconomics, but also of a media show. While world idols and celebrities do form a significant part of current humanity, focus here will be primarily on the small set of big collective players dominating the field of world power.

Then, there is the human *life-course*, our finite time on earth. We are living our lives in almost seven billion different ways, but we are all subjected to a pre-programmed life-course, truncated or extended, with its different stations, characteristic challenges and rites of passage, from birth and infancy to old age and death. This life-course, and its probabilities in the different parts of the planet and in different sociocultural milieus, are amenable to social comprehension and analysis. Current human courses of life are set out on the base of the geology of human history, propelled – or blocked – by the dynamics of the contemporary world stage.

Finally, we shall take stock of why we got where we are, and venture some answers to the unanswerable question: where are we going?

— 1 —

WHY WE ARE WHO WE ARE: A SOCIOCULTURAL GEOLOGY OF TODAY'S WORLD

Coming together as members of humankind, we need, in order to relate and interact properly, to understand our differences – and not just the obvious ones, i.e., that we do not look alike, and talk in different tongues. Our basic values and tastes differ and our conceptions of the world and our expectations of life are different, as are our sense of body, sex and family. While no social scientist or psychologist will ever be able to grasp the infinite variety of human individuality, our differences tend to be historically and geographically patterned, and are thereby comprehensible.

As humans, we descend from different historical cultures and experiences. Our first task in grasping the world of humankind is to get a handle on this historical descent and experience. The most promising, if so far hardly used, approach, then, is to look at contemporary human societies and configurations from a perspective of social geology. The sociocultural mould, in which we have been formed, is not just of yesterday. It had better be understood as layered by different social processes of different age.

Sketching the contours of a contemporary global social geology depends on world history, of which the 1,300 or so pages of a 'brief' world history by Felipe Fernández-Armesto (2008) are a wonderful start. But this book is neither dabbling in it nor competing with it. It is looking at the sedimentations of history from the special vantage point of the present. Our focus is not the historical record, but the historical DNA which we are carrying in our social and cultural make-up.

In this vein, I have found three extensive layers of human social formation, around the myriad of local strata, particularly pertinent. The most ancient we may, in accordance with much everyday language, call 'civilizations', in plural, spatially grounded cultural configurations of enduring importance, with 'classical' languages, texts and/or oral traditions, views of life and after-life, sense of beauty, notions of family, sex and gender.

Secondly, world patterns of society and culture history have been lastingly shaped by transcultural, transpolity, transcontinental processes, which we may term 'waves of globalization', even if, prior to 1492, they were not literally global. Thriving from long-distance travel, communication and exchange, these waves have by no means all been primarily economic in dynamics and significance. Religion and politics have also been at the forefront. These waves have further given rise to two important hybrid family-sex-gender systems, in Southeast Asia and in the Americas.

The third layer is 'modernity', the modern world. In the same way that art museums nowadays distinguish contemporary from modern art, so we should distinguish the contemporary from the modern world. The latter is a crucial historical layer of our formation, for two reasons. One is that modernity fought its way into cultural domination along different routes and across different constellations of proponents and opponents. These pathways have left their imprint on how much weight we give today to religion, to ideology, to class, to language. Secondly, the birth of the modern world was also the establishment of the current divide into what is now euphemistically referred to as 'developed' and 'developing', aka 'underdeveloped', countries. For almost all of us, being born in one or the other makes an enormous difference. Why that rift opened up and has divided the world for, by now, two centuries remains subject to seemingly interminable controversy. How it happened is somewhat less controversial. In the geological perspective of this book, the divide was established through the confluence of the roads to modernity and the fourth wave of historical globalization.

In other words, we are who we are because of the civilization and the family-sex-gender system in which we were brought up, because of our home's location in the recurrent historical waves of globalization, piled upon each other, and, finally, because of our society's experience of the struggles for and against modernity. Individualists are not wrong in adding that these are moulds that can be broken and rejected, but they are naive if they assume that their impact can be wished away.

The Rock of Civilizations

The global geological perspective adopted here focuses, and narrows, our look at civilizations, which may be approached in several different ways (see Braudel 1963/87; Fernández-Armesto 2000, Huntington 1996; International Sociology 2001). The comparative study of (Eurasian) civilizations had already become a 'fine art' in ninth-century Baghdad (Chaudhuri 1990: 67). What we are concerned with are large, enduring cultural configurations, pertinent to our contemporary world. Historically, they have been shaped by geospatial forces – Braudel's first rule of the grammar of civilizations was 'civilizations are spaces' – which now may elude the non-specialist. In such configurations we expect to find a cosmological and moral worldview, a pattern of symbolic imaginations, and, in literate civilizations, one or more classical languages and a classical canon, of cosmology, ethics, politics and aesthetics. Eventual clashes or dialogues between civilizations are out of focus here. To what extent they bear upon the dynamics of today's world will be considered below.

For this purpose we may identify five ancient major civilizations of enduring importance. This is not meant to be an exhaustive list; my only claim is that there is no other of as much or greater importance in terms of numbers of people encultured by it. It should be remembered that here we are not aiming at a brief historical summary of civilizations, or of any other layer of the world's sociocultural geology, but at grasping key features of their current significance.

The Sinic

Sinic civilization is the largest of all. Developed and centred in China, it spread far outside *Han* culture, to Korea, Japan and Vietnam. The adjective 'Sinic' is used in civilizational analysis precisely to convey this larger configuration. A recent scholar (Fogel 2009) has called it the 'Sinosphere'. Its Chinese core, developed around and between the Yangtze and the Yellow rivers, is the oldest of all major civilizations today. It is the only continuously surviving of the great ancient fluvial civilizations, including those of the Euphrates and Tigris, of the Nile and of the Indus. A civilization of dense population, fed by wet-rice and millet, governed by a large centre of political organization, only by exception divided among different rulers. A sedentary civilization, which more than 2,000 years ago as a defence against nomadic 'barbarians', built the largest construction in human history, the Great Wall.

The most distinctive feature of the Sinic worldview is a non-transcendental moral and social philosophy, usually summarized as 'Confucianism', without God or gods. The currently world-spreading Chinese cultural centres bear the name of Confucius (who died in 479 before Christ). Sinic civilization is distinctively this-worldly, without sacred texts of godly narratives and revelations. Human life runs along bloodlines, which it is a moral duty to keep and to venerate. House altars are devoted not to gods, but to one's ancestors. 'Filial piety', a son's love and respect of his father, is the prime social norm.

True, the tradition has recognized something extra-worldly and sublime: the emperor was the Son of Heaven ruling with a mandate from Heaven. But this heaven was nebulous, harbouring no commanding patriarch like the Jewish-Christian-Muslim God, no godly dramas and impersonations as in the Hindu world, nor the spiritual animation of extra-worldly Africa. The imperial mandate could be lost, but not because some divine law had been violated. 'Heaven sees as people see; Heaven hears as people hear', Mencius, the paradigmatic disciple of Confucius, explicated (Tu 1990: 119). The Master himself had established a this-worldly focus: 'When still unable to do your duty to men, how can you do your duty to the spirits?' 'Not yet understanding life, how can you understand death?' (Bodde 1981: 321). This moral philosophy has left ample room for different religious faiths – Buddhism and Taoism together with Confucianism constituting the 'three teachings' in China – as well as for all kinds of magical beliefs and practices. But always off-centre, as if in Europe and West Asia, Christianity and Islam had remained a popular undervegetation to a reigning Aristotelian philosophy.

To the contemporary world, Confucianism has left a legacy of secular politics, of meritocratic educational credentialism and patriarchal familism. While understandable pride in ancient power and glory sustained conservatism, political modernizers in the Sinosphere have never had to confront a powerful religious reaction – not the late nineteenth-century Westernizers of Japan, nor the Chinese, the North Korean or the North Vietnamese (the South was different) communists, nor the birth-controlling military men of post-Second World War capitalism in South Korea and Taiwan. The extraordinary Mandarin examination system, formally recruiting officials on a meritocratic basis of classical education, which was not fully institutionalized in Japan but which covered China, Korea and Vietnam, put a high value on education, and on education that was, in principle, accessible to everybody. Mass education emerged as a trump card of East Asian development in the twentieth century. To the family system, inherited and reproduced, we shall return below.

To the heirs of the Sinic civilization, a key feature of it is the language – that is, the written language, the ideographic Chinese script. This script is the classical language of this civilization. It was the common language of educated communication throughout the region at least until the Second World War, in spite of the fact that the spoken languages are mutually unintelligible, and that separate scripts had been developed in Japan, Korea and Vietnam. Communication in this classical Chinese script was known as 'brush talking' (Howland 1996: 44ff). The ideograms could be understood by educated people across national boundaries throughout the civilization, like numerals and mathematical symbols between, say, English and Russian. The Japanese and the Koreans developed their own, simpler syllable scripts, which in the twentieth century became dominant, and late nineteenth-century colonial French missionaries succeeded in converting the Vietnamese – who had also produced an indigenous lower-culture script of their own – to the Latin alphabet, supplemented with a set of diacritical marks.

Chinese characters, *kanji*, are still part of Japanese writing, and part of East Asian classical education. Upon the insistence of its main corporate donors, a major private university of Seoul, Korea University, where I taught in 2007, demands a knowledge of 2,000 Chinese characters for student admission. The script has also given rise to a special art form: calligraphy. While not unique, it is cultivated also in the Islamic civilization and it maintains an unrivalled position in Sinic civilization. The main monument of the Beijing Tiananmen, in front of the big Mao mausoleum, was a column to the 'Heroes of the People'. Its original inscription was in Mao's calligraphy, and the text alongside in that of Premier Zhou Enlai.

A classical education in Sinic civilization is nowadays usually as fragmented, intellectually as well as socially, as a classical education in Europe, but my Chinese students at Cambridge have studied Confucius. A proper classical Sinic education included, above all, the *Analects* of Confucius, and the Five Classics, the *Book of Documents* (on just government), the *Book of Poetry*, the *Book of Songs* (on emotions), the *Book of Rites* (on social relations), the *Spring and Autumn Annals* a state chronicle) (Tu 1990: 123ff). There were also the canonical *Book of Changes* and the *Book of Music* (Poceski 2009: 37).

Classical forms of architecture were consolidated during the Tang Dynasty (seventh to tenth century CE), but classical principles of

9

urban layout are much older. They still govern central Beijing, the Forbidden City and its surroundings, the layout of Kyoto and of central Seoul, and characterize the Van Mieu Confucian complex in Hanoi, nowadays often referred to as the Temple of Literature (Logan 2000: 26ff). Contemporary East Asian skyscrapers in their basically international style often add a roof reference to the East Asian canon – an upside-down reverence as classical Sinic architecture which was low-rise horizontal – and they regularly take *feng shui* principles of geomancy into consideration. Regional and national variants have developed across East Asia, but a 'neo-classical' building there remains recognizably different from, say, South Asian or European, neoclassicism.

The East Asia of Sinic civilization is a densely populated area, still largely governed by its ancient norms of obligation and harmony. Crime and family disruption are more marginal than in the rest of the world. Politics may be authoritarian and repressive of dissent, but social harmony and consensual decision-making remain important norms. Ancient historical traditions are kept alive, as in the imperial rituals of Japan, the recent museums of Seoul, the new monumentality of Hanoi, and in the recent Confucian robing of the Chinese state. In Pyongyang – in the early twentieth century known as the 'Jerusalem of the East' because of the successful proselytization by Scottish Presbyterians – there may be more rupture with the past, but in China Mao was proud of, and used, his classical education of history, poetry and calligraphy. He had read the 24 dynastic chronicles, covering all the emperors of China from 221 BC to 1644 CE several times, eagerly discussing them with his physician and private conversation partner. Before his numerous sexual encounters, he often gave the girls a classical Daoist sex manual, with ancient, rare characters, to read (Li 1994: 122ff, 358).

The identities produced by this civilization are not me-centred, but sociocentric or contextual. The languages of the area have several different words corresponding to the English 'I', used according to social context. In Vietnamese, when talking to one's parents and referring to oneself, the first pronoun should be avoided altogether, and, instead, expressions like 'your son/daughter' should be used (I owe this piece of knowledge to my Vietnamese former star student, Pham Van Bich; on Chinese, Japanese and Korean, see Nisbett 2003: 51ff, 178).

From ancient Greece to contemporary Euro-America, there is a focus on, a concern with, the acting individual, with agency and its constraints – recycled as agency and structure in 1980s sociological debates. Their East Asian counterpoint is a concern with interrelations, totality and the 'harmony' of the whole, in which all individuals and groups have their proper place, like a successful blend of herbs and spices in a good dish. And 'harmony' is a current explicit policy goal of the Chinese government. To Euro-American confrontation of right against wrong is counterposed East Asian avoidance of division, and adjustment. That is the civilizational heritage underlying, for instance, Japanese government policymaking and corporate board management, as well as ASEAN decision-making. The opaqueness of contemporary Chinese top-level decision-making had better not be abused for ungrounded exemplifications. However, there is another aspect of the latter which is visible. That is the long-term view, radical and patient at the same time, which characterized the modernist political planning of nineteenth-century Meiji Japan and which is characterizing the Chinese post-Mao era of socioeconomic reform.

In an impressive work – using a range of hard evidence running from ancient Chinese and Greek philosophy to contemporary comparative child development, psychology and managerial studies, via cross-cultural student experiments – the American psychologist Richard Nisbett has demonstrated how Sinic and European civilizations have generated distinctive ways of seeing and knowing the world. The differences were there among the great philosophers 2,500 years ago, and they are here among parents, toddlers, students and managers of the 2000s. Of course, the differences are probabilistic, and are not inscribed in every single Chinese, Japanese, European or American of European descent.

Europeans tend to see the world in analytical categories, East Asians in a web of relationships. A simple example, used by Nisbett in his experiments, which also caught this writer off-guard as Eurocentric, is to ask people which two phenomena belong together from a triplet – in one version, panda, monkey, banana. Europeans tend to group the panda and the monkey as belonging to the same category, of animals. East Asians, on the other hand, mostly opt for monkey and banana as related, monkeys eating bananas. Euro-Americans tend to see the world in either – or categories, whereas East Asians more often see it in contradictory dialectical terms, of x as well as non-x. Mao Zedong may not have been the great thinker his adulators once claimed, but his contribution to Marxism was precisely his Chinese sense of dialectics.

The Sinic civilization today holds an immense cultural pride in a rich, ancient, continuous civilization, which, after its decline and intellectual rejection in the late nineteenth and early twentieth centuries, is still there in modern, prosperous or rapidly growing countries. This pride is most general in China (cf. Jacques 2009: chs. 7–8), the centre of the civilization, whereas in Japan, Korea and Vietnam it is grafted onto national cultural traditions. Its main historical weakness has been its self-centredness, which finally led to self-isolation from the rest of the world, in turn causing a stagnation of science, technology and economy that, by mid-nineteenth century, had become nearly fatal. Its most important strengths are probably its tradition of large-scale collective work organization, of civic discipline, its high evaluation of education and learning and its secular framework, which provides little room and basis for religious conservatism and inter-religious strife.

The Indic

India and Indic as well as Hindu all derive from the river Indus, in today's Pakistan, but none of them has any known direct connection with the Indus valley civilization, which disappeared about 4,000 years ago. Indic civilization began emerging 500–1,000 years later, developed by peoples coming from the northwest of Iran and Central Asia, 'Aryans' – from whom the current name of Iran stems – through today's Afghan passes and by the five-rivers country, Punjab. From its northwestern beginnings it fanned out eastwards, along the plain of Ganges – which has become a holy river of Hinduism, on which lies also what is perhaps the main religious centre of this polycentric faith, Varanasi (or Benares) – reaching southern India much later.

Indic has a similar relationship to India as *Sinic* has to China, extending conventional India south- and eastwards, to current Sri Lanka, to Bali and Java, and to what is now Myanmar/Burma, Thailand, Laos, Cambodia and into southern Vietnam. It also grew north, into and across the Himalayas, into Nepal and Tibet, whose Lamanism is an offshoot of Indian Buddhism. The European expression 'Indochina' captures the meeting-ground of Sinic and Indic civilizations. It is the southwestern end of Chinese characters, architecture and chopsticks, and the mainland eastern end of Sanskrit inscriptions and sculptural Indic temples, which reached into the Cambodia of the Angkor Wat temples, Laos and southern Vietnam under the Champa of the first half of the second Christian millennium, and of reading the *Mahabbarata* and the *Ramayana*, still part of the royal rites of Thailand (Coedès 1966, 1968).

Cognitive psychologists have discovered some similarities of causal attribution, emphasizing context more than actor's disposition, between East and South Asian cultures, in contrast to Euro-American ones (Nisbett 2003: 114ff), and there may be others, e.g., a holistic worldview in which individuals are embedded in larger contexts (Singh 2002: 32ff). In different ways, both civilizations have been able to tolerate and to manage religious pluralism, although in both cases these have been occasionally violated by bigoted rulers. The secular Confucian tradition of moral and political philosophy left a space open for different personal beliefs and practices – Daoist, Buddhist, Shintoist, Christian. Infinitely polytheistic Hinduism, on its side, could easily coexist with Jainist, Buddhist, Jewish, Christian, Muslim, Sikh gods and beliefs.

But the Indic and the Sinic are also civilizations in some respects poles apart, in spite of their geographical proximity and of their Buddhist cultural exchanges 1,500–2,000 years ago.

First of all, while Sinic civilization is predominantly this-worldly and secular, the Indic is soaked in religion. The religiosity of Indians was a story already in the Hellenistic world, and at least apocryphally in classical Greece. An early fourth-century CE bishop told this anecdote: An Indian asked Socrates to define his philosophy and got the answer: 'It is a study of human reality.' Whereupon the Indian visitor burst into scornful laughter: 'How can a man study human reality while ignoring divine reality!' (Braudel 1963/1987: 66).

Arguably the most distinctive feature of Indic civilization, common to Hinduism and to Buddhism, is the notion of transmigration or rebirth of souls, and the idea that the lives of their incarnations are determined by deeds in a previous life. This provided a firm and deep religious foundation of a hierarchical social division, of *varna*, originally not very different from similar conceptions in East Asia or in Europe. In the Indian version there were four major rungs, the priestly Brahmins (also written Brahmans), the ruler-warrior Kshatriyas, the farming or trading Vaisyas and the Sudra servants and labourers. Below the latter there emerged a stratum of 'untouchables', whose duties included performing the most polluting tasks, like taking care of latrines or skinning dead animals. Gradually, a large number of inherited occupational *jatis* or castes were distinguished. Caste members all had to marry within their caste, and social interaction between castes was governed by religiously anchored rules of purity and pollution. A Brahmin could not accept food or drink from lower castes; an untouchable had to keep out of the way of all others, never letting his or her shadow fall upon them, etc.

13

Much of the rigid caste hierarchy and its 'pollution' taboos have now been eroded. Independent India has given disadvantaged, 'scheduled' castes privileged access to public employment. Democratic politics has brought forward prominent *Dalit* ex-untouchable politicians, from the extraordinarily brilliant Dr B. R. Ambedkar, a father of the Indian Constitution, to the mass-appealing prime minister of Uttar Pradesh, Mayawati, who, although she has been democratically elected – three times to date – is not unlike a nineteenth-century plebeian Caribbean *caudillo*. Former untouchables may now enter or approach many, if not all, village stores, and many village wells, if far from all. Although the marriage ads of the Delhi papers were still grouped by caste when I studied them a few years ago, there was also at the end a small section, 'Caste does not matter'. However, caste hierarchy, which spread also to South Asian Muslims, is still an important legacy of Indic civilization. While its hierarchy may be being eroded by the politics of numbers, caste identity and caste associations constitute obvious targets of political mobilization. And, for everybody to see, your caste is given by your name. (The literature on caste in India is huge. A few of the recent important works I have consulted include Yadav 2006; Rao 2009; Thorat and Newman 2010).

Mahatma Gandhi was an extraordinary embodiment of his culture, and an extraordinary political leader of his people. He was not representative statistically, but he was a major modern incarnation of Indic civilization, demonstrated by his iconoclastic attempts to get those from higher castes to clean Congress Party latrines. With his highly charged symbolic politics, his repudiation of industrial developmentalism, and his dramatic body asceticism, he would have been inconceivable (or dismissed as a freak) in any other part of the world.

India is still a stage of extraordinary religious performances, of naked, wandering *sadhus* or holy men, of *devadasis*, prostitutes dedicated (by poor parents) to their vocation as children in temple ceremonies, of Tantric awakeners of spirits from skulls, and of many more – performers who have little to do with the more familiar modern world of business, film or medicine (Dalrymple 2009). True, India embodies everything and its opposites too. Atheism also has a significant place in the overwhelmingly lush vegetation of Indic beliefs. A major regional political party, the DMK of the southern Tamil Nadu state, has been even more militantly secularist than French state *laïcité* or Turkish Kemalism, not only banning, in 1967, gods and goddesses from schools and public offices of the state, but also staging 'superstition eradication' conferences (Smith 2003: 147). The culture venerating its numerous ascetics also produced the world's most famous erotic manual, the *Kamasutra*, and built the world's most sexually explicit temple, Khajuraho. But religious rites, at home as well as in temples or in the sacred river of the Ganges, remain important parts of Indian life. The subcontinent and its island appendix Sri Lanka, for all their diversity, are also sites of intercommunal religious violence, driven not only by *Hindutva* militants, but also, in Sri Lanka, by Buddhist zealots and, in Pakistan, by intra-Islamic conflict.

The East Asian Mandarins had to compete for their status as the guardians of knowledge in the world's first meritocratic system, whereas the Brahmins inherited their knowledge, which was to be off-limits to non-Brahmins. India and South Asia still have a high rate of illiteracy alongside a very developed system of higher education, churning out loads of IT engineers as well as masses of intellectuals.

Sinic civilization had a single political focus: the emperor and his empire. The Indic never had an established imperial centre. What is now the Indian Union was never politically united before 1947, and the largest political units of the subcontinent were all headed by non-Hindu rulers. Ashoka (third century BC) was Buddhist, the great Mughals of the seventeenth century CE were Muslims of Turkic-Mongol descent – 'Mughal' is a Persian word for Mongol – and their British nineteenth–twentieth-century successors were Christian. The great Mughal rulers of the seventeenth century CE were paramount on the subcontinent, but were never continental unifiers nor uncontested. The British rule combined areas of direct colonial rule, centred in Calcutta, Delhi, Bombay and Madras, and including most of today's Pakistan and Bangladesh – and of current Burma – with 'protected' princely states, of which Hyderabad, Mysore and Rajputana were the most important. It was a set of religious conceptions of life, and of before- and after-life, with its *dharma* obligations and its *kama* deeds and rituals, which polytheistically unified Indic civilization, through the Brahmins, who had ritual priority over the rulers, their temples and their knowledge of sacred rules and rites, conveyed in the subcontinental elite language of Sanskrit.

Today, most of the enduring features of the civilization of India may derive from Brahminic Hinduism, and there is a powerful political current, which emerged in national government office a few years ago, asserting its Hindu character. But to substitute Hindu for Indic civilization would be unhistorical. It is not just a polytheistic civilization; it is poly-religious, in a complex, interwoven way which Hinduism alone among religions could manage. Buddhism grew out of

15

Hinduism, as did Jainism and Sikhism. Jewish, Christian and Parsee minorities have more than a millennial presence in India. Major Muslim rule in India began in the early eleventh century, under Mahmud of Ghazni (in today's Afghanistan), was succeeded by the end of the twelfth century by a Sultanate in Delhi and became paramount in the sixteenth century with the Mughals. It has been estimated that a fourth of the subcontinental population converted to Islam, mainly low-caste people, while the Muslim elite tended to come from outside, from Afghanistan, Persia, Central Asia (Singh 2002: 66ff). Caste penetrated Indian Islam, Sufism attracted Hindu interest, while the converted Muslims tended to keep their pre-Islamic culinary tastes and festival practices. But the crucial point in this particular context is not the truth of historical multiculturalism. It is the abiding weight of an ecumenical religiosity, from the Buddhist emperor Ashoka, emblematically referred to in the Indian flag, 2,300 years ago, and the 'good Muslim' Mughal ruler Akbar 400 years ago, to the twentieth-century moral and intellectual models, Tagore and Gandhi, a tradition to which the Nehru-Gandhi dynasty of independent India has always paid respect (cf. Sen 2005: ch. 13).

Sanskrit is the classical language of Indic civilization, cultural as well as religious, like Greek and Latin, almost like the latter no longer a living language – with a few local exceptions (Goody 2010: 161n) – but currently taught at Indian universities and favoured, together with other features of Hindu-interpreted Indic cvilization, by the BJP federal government of the beginning of the millennium. While the language is maintained mainly as an exclusive sacred language by the Brahmin caste, 'Sanskritization' has become a concept of modern Indian sociology, denoting a kind of collective caste mobility upwards by imitating the manners and rites of higher castes (Srinivas 2002: chs 12, 13).

The Indic classics were compiled between 2,500 and 3,000 years ago – nobody really knows when, and the dating is still hotly controversial, among historians as well as ideologues. In contrast to the Sinic and the European, Indic civilization had little historiography. Its classics form a huge corpus, from the hymns and liturgies of *Vedas*, the philosophical *Upanishads*, the Code of Manu with its elaborate family norms, economic and erotic manuals, to the popular epics of *Ramayana* and of *Mahabharata*, the latter said to be 'India's equivalent to the *Iliad*, the *Odyssey*, and the Bible all rolled into one', 15 times the length of the Bible (Dalrymple 2009: 90), and the mythological and genealogical *Puranas*. Contemporary schoolteaching appears erratic on classical literary education, but the epics constitute a widespread cultural reference and were run on Indian television in the early 1990s, to rapt, almost total, audiences.

Classical Indic architecture, mainly in the form of temples, rose in the period of the Gupta dynasty, fourth–sixth centuries CE, and seems to have peaked in the eleventh and twelfth centuries (Harle 1986/94: Part II; Speir 1973: 458f; Keay 2000: 212ff). The Taj Mahal and other spectacular sepulchral buildings were produced by Mughal rulers half a millennium later, bringing Persian and Central Asian models to magnificent florescence.

The West Asian

West Asian Muslim civilization is more delimited than the whole *Dar-ul-Islam* (House of Islam) with its many believers from other civilizations, not unlike the European in relation to Christendom. 'West Asian' corresponds to the Sinic and the Indic, there seemingly being no possible similar derivation from Arabic. Its origin and core are the Arab peninsula with the holy cities of Islam, Mecca and Medina. But it formed a much wider cultural area, with northern nodes at Damascus and, later also, Istanbul, establishing major western cultural centres in Córdoba in today's Spain, in Fez in Morocco, in Tunis – all now either gone altogether or, since long ago, of minor importance – and in Cairo. To the east it flourished in Baghdad, in Persian Isfahan, Shiraz, and on to Bukhara, then later to Samarkand in today's Uzbekistan, now rather sad shadows of their past existence, waiting for tourists.

The deserts and the oases, the city merchants and Bedouin nomads, and the caravans connecting them, constituted the ecological basis of this civilization, in a way similar to the dense wet-rice settlements of the Sinic. A dialectic between nomadic desert and sedentary urban cultures characterized for a long time the recorded history of Central and West Asia, and unsurprisingly forms the focus of the work of the region's greatest social scientist, Ibn Khaldun, who argued that 'the desert is the basis and the reservoir of civilization and cities' (1377/1967: 93). The deserts, the narrow river-paths through some of them (the Nile, Euphrates and Tigris, Amu-Darja and Syr-Darja), the arid mountains, the oases, the cities with their specific cultures are all still there, grounding the culture, from Morocco, *Makhzen* (the West) to its natives, to Iran, and into Central Asia, and above all in at the very centre, the Arabian peninsula. Key parts of the sociology of this civilization were a combination of a hedonistic urban mercantile society and a stern nomadic one, of both caravan traders and mounted warriors. They still seem to capture a great deal of the culture area.

However, while not coextensive with the House of Islam, this has become a religiously defined civilization. Historically, it was an area of two magnificent riverine civilizations, one discontinuous, between and along Euphrates and Tigris in today's Iraq, the other along the Nile with a long, linked line of Pharaonic dynasties. It also included the great enemy of classical Greece, the Persian empire. But Islam broke with them all, in a manner Christianity never did with ancient Greece and Rome. The pre-Islamic civilizations constitute no 'classics' of West Asia, only origins of museal objects, increasingly appreciated for the tourist money they can attract.

The Islamic *tabula rasa* with previous civilizations of the area does not derive from a more hermetic theological closure than that of Christianity, but from historical contingency. In West Asia there was no Roman empire bridging paganism and monotheism. Arabia of Muhammad was a society of tribes. But there was Persia, whose grand political traditions later seeped into the splendid Muslim polities of Damascus and Baghdad. More importantly, when Persia had become conquered for Islam, by Arab warriors, a new distinctive Persian culture developed, and Persian became the main literary language of the Islamic world, outside Arabia, and the high court language from Mughal India to Ottoman Turkey (Lewis 1964/1994: 13; see also the splendid overview of the three great late Muslim empires by Stephen Dale 2010). This Persian high culture included great medieval poetry, of Hafez, Rumi, Said and others, in which wine flows profusely and in which the goals of erotic desire are often titillatingly vague – a woman? a man? God? These poets, more or less coeval with Chaucer, are accessible to and appreciated by many readers today, and monumentally commemorated in contemporary Iran – at least, this was the case in the early 1990s when I was there.

This is a proudly, self-consciously Islamic civilization, which, of course, befits an area housing the most holy sites of Shia Islam – Karbala and Najaf in Iraq, and Qom in Iran – as well the holiest cities to all Muslims – Mecca and Medina in Saudi Arabia. Its core worldview and values derive from the salvation religion of Islam. The Koran is the sacred, constitutive classical text, knowledge of which is a necessity of Muslim education. Full oral mastering of the text is still a pupil's proud achievement.

But the Koran is also the basis of the classic canon of civilizational art. Calligraphy is an Islamic, as well as a Sinic, art, but in the former mainly manifested in Koranic quotations decorating mosques and possibly other public buildings, or in hand-written Korans – an art undisturbed by printing presses until the nineteenth and twentieth centuries. Recitations of the Koran are still very popular cultural events, comparable to European song festivals.

Arabic is *the* classical language, as the language of the Koran. Persian and Turkic – ancient variants of modern Turkish – did survive as major interstate languages, Persian as the court and secular literature language, and Turkic as the military language of the once formidable Ottoman and Mughal armies. But both were written in Arabic script, and Persian still is. Nowadays Persian is almost wholly forgotten among South Asian intellectuals (as my distinguished American-Iranian colleague Said Arjomand has sadly told me), marginalized by imperial English from the second third of the nineteenth century, although you still get a fair way with Persian in Afghanistan. The ancient Turkic connection may have got a little new leverage in Central Asia after 1991, but in West Asia Turkish has become a language for Turks only, since the 1920s in a Romanized script.

A proper Muslim has to learn the Koran in Arabic, not in translation, as is perfectly legitimate for a Christian learning the Bible. There are now authorized translations of the Koran, but they are mainly meant for interested outsiders. Like Greek, and in contrast to Sanskrit or Latin, Arabic is, of course, a living language, common to the area from Iraq to Morocco, from Syria to Sudan. But like the ancient Greek language of Plato, the classical language of Koranic Arabic is no longer spoken. It is a high formal standard which must be learnt, and is used on solemn religious and official occasions. Among educated people, the classical idiom may be used as a means of communication between, say, Iraqis and Moroccans, who would otherwise not comprehend each other.

The teaching of Arabic and its grammar is a central part of a classical Islamic education. Alongside the Koran and the *hadith* (chronicles of the Prophet and his deeds and sayings), there is a classical jurisprudence, of religious origin and importance, divided, since the eighth and ninth centuries into five major schools, four Sunni and one Shia. While encroached upon by modern state legislation, most strongly in secularized states like Tunisia, these more than millennial schools of jurisprudence are still pertinent to matters of family and marriage, as I learnt when studying the twentieth-century family patterns of the world.

Islam does not have a bureaucratic hierarchy like Christianity, but nor is it as amorphous as Hinduism. There is one centre of pilgrimage, Mecca. De facto, there is a universal centre of (Sunni) Islamic learning, the al-Azhar in Cairo, attracting theological students not only from the whole West Asian and North African region, but also from, e.g., Malaysia and Indonesia. Its *sheikh* or head is a major authority. Islamic countries also usually have a *mufti*, a chief religious judge, although it is currently neither a very powerful nor a very respected position, as it is often seen as no more than a mouthpiece of the Egyptian or the Saudi government. Iranian Shi-ism is more strictly organized – even regardless of the theocratic set-up of its Islamic Republic – with its mandarin hierarchy topped by Grand Ayatollahs, and its own international centre of learning, at Qom in Iran.

West Asian Islamic architecture got its classical forms from the ninth century CE Abbasid Iraq, later, in the fifteenth and sixteenth centuries, branching off into alternative models by the constructions of Ottomans in Turkey and the Safavids in Iran, from where the Timurid rulers of Bukhara and Samarkand and the early Mughals fetched their model architects and builders. Mosques are the aesthetically dominant, most ambitious buildings, often with *madrasa* school complexes, and as a rule more ornate and elaborate than the citadels of political power. The Mughals developed in another direction, making imperial tombs their most splendid monuments, a rather un-Islamic custom which did not commemorate great rulers. The Delhi tomb of Humanyun remembers a weak defeated emperor, and the Taj Mahal was built in memory of a queen (Hattstein and Delius 2005; Dale 2010: 147ff). Interestingly, classical Arabic is a major, if not the only, reference in the monumental architecture of the new twenty-first-century Malaysian capital Putrajaya.

The European

Europe is a promontory of Asia, outside the wide arc of fluvial civilizations, from the Nile to the Yellow River, clearly very backward 3,000–4,000 years ago. It is surrounded by seas, where, first in the Aegean Sea and later in the Mediterranean as a whole, there developed 'thalassocratic', sea-ruling powers of enduring significance, which were also interconnected, joining Athens and Rome, although the Roman rule of the whole Mediterranean was primarily based on landed armies. The main navigable rivers linked the sea to the interior: the Rhine, the Danube, the Elbe, the Volga and many others. Naval power, later enhanced by ship artillery, became the outward thrust of Europe, from the Portuguese of Henry the Navigator and the Spanish led by the Genovese Columbus, via Jan Pieterzoon Coon of the Dutch East India Company, to James Cook and the British Royal Navy. Seaborne European conquerors and explorers succeeded the horse-riding nomad land warriors of Eurasia, the Arabs, the Mongols and the Turks.

The most distinctive, and the constitutive feature of European civilization is its dual basis, in pagan polytheistic antiquity and in Christian monotheistic religion, a universalistic mutation of West Asian Judaism. While West Asian Islam basically rejected its cultural predecessors as the era of ignorance, Christianity built upon its pagan base, originally by necessity perhaps, being unable to muster a military force of its own.

A European civilizational formation is, then, a dual one. On one hand, you have to know the meaning of the cross, the story of Jesus and Mary, and what Christmas and Easter are in the Christian calendar. You have to know what the Bible is, and at least something of its contents. You are supposed to be able to distinguish Orthodox Christianity from Catholic and from Protestant Christianity, and perhaps even among the latter's Anglican, Calvinist and Lutheran branches.

On the other hand, you ought also to know who Zeus (or Jupiter) was, but only as an educated person, by no means as a worshipper. Having a European culture also means knowing something about the *Odyssey* and the *Iliad*, about Socrates, Plato and Aristotle, about Julius Caesar, Augustus, Hadrian. If claiming a higher education, you are most often expected to have read something, at least in translation, of Homer, Plato, Virgil, Horace and Ovid, and to know something about Greek drama and Roman law.

Classical European architecture is first of all identified in the ancient Greco-Roman temples, with their colonnades and straight triangular roof fronts, sometimes with a Roman dome, reproduced in modern times as republican neoclassicism in the USA and as imperial in Russia. Though never called neoclassical, the historical European tradition also includes the Christian Gothic cathedrals, reaching towards heaven as an assembly of believers, rather than as a dead Pharaoh or as sites of sacrifice like the Mayan and the Aztec pyramids. Modern iconic buildings of Europe often opted for the neo-Gothic, the British Parliament and the Vienna City Hall among them. And neo-Gothic became a favourite style of nineteenth-century US colleges.

Christian Europe never dismissed the pre-Christian era as one of darkness and ignorance, and for good reasons. After initial persecutions, Christianity became the official religion of the Roman empire, proclaimed from the imperial throne. Unlike Islam, it never had to defeat militarily the powers that be, from the outside. The final victory of Christianity was the outcome of a war between two Roman imperial pretenders. The church saw itself as, and was de facto, the main cultural passage from antiquity to the post-ancient feudal Middle Ages (see Anderson 1974). The Catholic Church established Aristotle as *the* authority of secular knowledge, and a European dual jurisprudence of canonical and secular law, both on a Roman basis (see Berman 1980). Indeed, it could legitimately see itself as the heir to the Roman empire, since Constantine had made Christianity the imperial religion in 330. No new sacred language was asserted: Latin was the language of the Roman church, and Greek that of the Byzantine. Only after the fall of the latter did Church Slavonic become the language of Orthodoxy.

Ancient Greece and Rome were adopted as parents of Christian Europe, and forever provided the standards of European classicism. Reading 'Classics' in modern Oxbridge means reading Latin and Greek, including the history and the literature of Greek-Latin antiquity. 'Classicism' in European architecture means one following, or at least being inspired by, that of Greece or Rome. Classical literature in Europe comprises the traditions from Homer to Ovid.

Christianity, like Islam and Buddhism, but in contrast to Judaism, Confucianism or Hinduism, is a salvationist religion of universal vocation. Harnessed to European and, later, North American imperial power, it has been a formidable arm of conquest, as well as a powerful engine of expansion. This universalist vocation has more recently been sustaining Euro-American secular crusades, in the names of 'enduring freedom' or 'human rights'.

That Christian crusades and Islamic *jihad* should clash in the modern world was hardly predetermined, but once the religious *jinns* were let out the modernist bottle, you could expect them to collide, and their conflict to resonate through the magnifying drums of geopolitical divisions, between the American empire and its dependencies.

The relationship of secular classicism – the ancient gods soon became mainly literary figures – to the religious tradition of Christianity has sometimes been conflictual, but in being so has provided a fruitful, opening tension in European culture. That was the case, rather accommodatingly, of the Renaissance and the humanism of Erasmus and others, and, more frictional, during the Enlightenment of Voltaire, Gibbon and Winckelmann. But even more important, before that, the dual traditions of Christian religion and Roman law gave rise to a legal doctrine of separate spiritual and temporal powers, encapsulated in the supreme and separate figures of pope and emperor (Berman 1980).

While taking a position of caution in relation to the ample discussions of 'the values of European civilization', a couple of points should be singled out. Europe developed a distinctive political culture, which included principles of election (or lottery) for office, popular representation as the proper basis of taxation, and citizenship. Others coexisted with them and often overrode them, but they were never extinguished, and in medieval Europe the two highest offices were formally and regularly elected, those of pope and of emperor. 'Democracy' is, after all, an ancient European word. At a time of acute fiscal crisis, the French absolutist monarchy had to summon the representation of the Estates-General for 1789. More important for most people, though, was the notion of the citizen as a person with rights, an idea going back to the free men of the Greek *polis*, but crucially codified in Roman law and extended throughout the empire. This legal conception of individual rights was not developed in the other civilizations.

European civilization captured the Americas. The US kept both the pre-Christian classical architecture, interpreted as republican rather than imperial by Jefferson et al., and the Christian faith, first of all in Protestant form. Latin America also kept its faith, but Catholic Christian in this case, and experienced the built world more in Baroque terms.

The sub-Saharan African

Africa seems to be the origin of us all. Predominant paleoanthropological knowledge appears to converge on a common African ancestry of the human species, from which we fanned out, populating the earth. (A plausible non-expert overview is given by Chanda 2007: ch. 1). But origin does not necessarily mean continuity, or even meaningful linkage. Against all the white supremacists, or 'Western civilizationists', many of us today will no doubt proudly claim that we are all Africans. But that is a stand for human respect. Here we have to do, primarily, with the differentiation of humanity.

Sub-Saharan African civilization differs in kind, and not only in its characteristic features, from all the others. It is an oral civilization, without any canonical texts, a family of cultures without a historical core, without a single religion or any classical language. How can it then be a major civilization, or even one civilization? An amateur historian has to be very careful here, and what V. Y. Mudimbe (1988) has called 'the invention of Africa' had been a tortuous, complicated and quarrelsome colonial and nationalist enterprise. But if we want to keep the number of currently pertinent civilizations down, a case can nevertheless be made for treating sub-Saharan Africa as one. The African Union comprises also supra-Saharan North Africa, but that is modern geopolitics. It has been argued, though, by a very respected but little followed scholar, the Senegalese Cheikh Anta Diop, that 'Egyptian antiquity is to African culture what Graeco-Roman antiquity is to European' (the argument is laid out in Diop 1967/1993). Without taking a position on whether the ancient Egyptian civilization was 'Negro' (*nègre*) or not, for our purposes here it is sufficient that there seem to be no continuous links to Pharaonic building, worldviews or scripts south of the Nile and the big desert, although traded objects have been found (Braudel 1987: 194). In so far as there is a common African civilization of contemporary relevance, it is sub-Saharan.

The ecological parameters have always been difficult. They were clearly delimited, by two big deserts, the Sahara in the north and the Kalahari in the south, and by two oceans, the Atlantic to the west, and the Indian Ocean to the east. Neither boundary was impenetrable in ancient times, but together they put Africa outside the main Eurasian routes of exchange. Even more important was probably the difficult geography of the continent itself. The spatial centre could never become a social centre of it, made up of dense tropical forest, infested with insects and parasites, and without any natural lines of radiation. None of the great rivers was navigable from the sea to the interior, cut off by rapids and cataracts, the most central, that of the Congo, being the most notorious. The great cultural and political sites of Africa, from Timbuktu and Djenne to the Great Zimbabwe, have been on the savannah margins, or close to the west coast, like Ife and Benin.

Nevertheless, there is, first of all, a linguistic unity in diversity, stretching from Gambia and Senegal on the northwest coast down to the Cape in the southeast, the Niger-Congo language family, of which the core Bantu subgroup is assumed to have fanned out from what is now the Nigeria–Cameroon border. This unity excludes a vast linguistic horseshoe north, west and east of the Sahara, populated by Afro-Asiatic speakers, Arabic, Berber, Amharic, Somali – once including Pharaonic Egyptian. Furthermore, some Nilo-Saharan language communities south of the desert are outside, like the Hausa of northern Nigeria and the Masai and the Luo of northern Kenya, and in

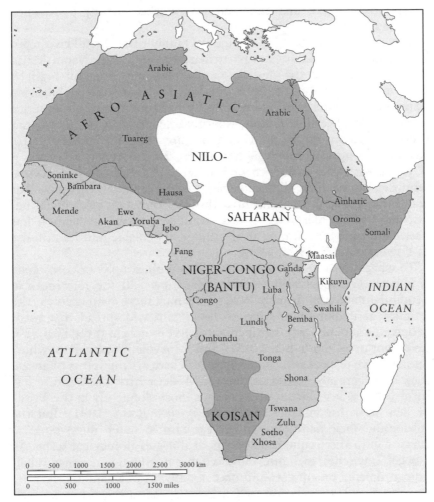

Map 1 Families of African Languages

the southwest the rather few survivors of the Khoisan linguistic family (Collins 2006: 11ff ; Iliffe 2007: 11).

Across the ecological variations outside the deserts in the north and in the southwest, with tropical forests, savannah grasslands, the fertile hills of the Great Lakes, and rivers of limited navigability, most of sub-Saharan Africa had a very important common characteristic. Land was abundant, but labour was scarce. This was compounded by the fact that its agriculture was based on a hoe, not a plough, except in Ethiopia, and the land was worked mainly by women (Boserup 1970).

This situation produced a distinctive family pattern, still characteristic of sub-Saharan Africa, a particularly strong value given to fertility – now affected by modern family planning, but still high by current global standards, four children being an official Nigerian norm. And, related to this, a practice of mass polygamy, now unique in the world (Therborn 2004), recently celebrated by South Africa's President Jacob Zuma, marrying a third wife in January 2010. According to press reports he has, so far, 20 children.

The great Africanist anthropologist Jack Goody has in several works emphasized the difference between Africa and the 'Bronze Age civilizations' of Eurasia, and how this, not only less mechanical but also less rigidly hierarchical, less stratified African civilization has been manifested in, among other things, its cuisine and its non-use of flowers (Goody 1993, 1998).

To what extent there is a common Bantu philosophy or cosmology is a hotly contested topic (see the overview and the references in Mudimbe 1988 and Appiah 1992), on which there is no need to take a stand here. But there seem to be certain widespread themes of beliefs of contemporary significance. There is a rich, diversified spiritual world, of both malevolent and benevolent spirits, to which humans owe respect and ritual sacrifice. There are the spirits of ancestors, and there are spirits of nature. Modern African literature has turned their voices into script, perhaps most eloquently in the works of Ben Okri, for instance his *The Famished Road* (1991). But the spirits and their handling are present also in much more tangible ways, e.g. in the frequent diagnosis of illnesses in magical terms, in a belief in witches, including child witches in Nigeria, in armed rebellions protected by amulets and occasionally, as in Uganda, driven by a spiritualist interpretation of Christianity, as in the priestess-spirit Alice Auma 'Lakwena' (the Messenger) and her successor Joseph Kony leading the 'Lord's Resistance Army'.

'Africa' is, like 'Asia', a European invention, but that does not detract from the heuristic value of taking note of a sub-Saharan African civilization. Christianity and Islam have become the dominant religions of modern Africa, but both have to accommodate tenacious African sex-gender-family patterns, Christianity to polygamy and Islam to women in the public economic sphere, for instance.

Artistically, the widespread ritual use of masks and dance is also a noteworthy feature of the continent. Nowhere else can you see traditional worthies (chiefs), politicians, and clergy dance solo or collectively in public.

Finally, at the end of this look at civilizations, it should be remembered that the above is not meant to be a Hall of Fame of the Greatest. It is simply a list of the largest, as they loom in the twenty-first century. Compared to them, the Maya and other Amerindian civilizations or the ones of Southeast Asia, for example, are smaller, but not necessarily less important.

All civilizations have been deeply concerned with family-sex-gender relations and have left their lasting imprints upon them today. But in the course of extensive family research I found out that there are, alongside the five civilizational ones, two major contemporary family systems of a hybrid character, resulting from later waves of globalization and routes to modernity: the Southeast Asian and the American Creole systems.

Family-Sex-Gender Systems

We are all of us not just heirs of, but also, as a rule, participants in what we may call a family-sex-gender system, of descent, kinship and coupling, sexual practices and social gender relations. The main family-sex-gender systems of the world derive from the five main civilizations, and may even be seen as a central element of the latter, often the most continuous through centuries, even millennia. They are therefore treated here under the general heading of civilizational heritage. But the contemporary world also includes two more major systems, which are civilizational hybrids coming out of waves of globalization, a Southeast Asian system and an American Creole pattern, which merit a separate overview. It was a major finding of my family research that all seven systems are still operating, mutated but not convergent (Therborn 2004; the sections that follow are based on that book).

The Confucian East Asian family

This covered the vast area historically marked by Sinic civilization – Japan, Korea, and Vietnam, as well as China – and of course included regional and national variations. Classical Confucian patriarchy had been modified in Japan and softened in Vietnam, and was by 1900 endorsed in its most orthodox form in Korea.

The relation between father and son is the most important of the five relationships in human life, and filial piety the cardinal virtue, to which all other family and social norms are subordinate. Marriage is a contract between families, dissoluble by mutual agreement or by the husband. Like everywhere outside Western Europe, marriage was historically virtually universal. By and large it still is, outside some metropolitan cities, like Tokyo and Singapore. Bigamy was illegal, but 'concubines' had a formal family status as second-rank wives, and their children were legitimate. Sexual intercourse has always been a morally legitimate male pleasure. The patrilineal joint family was the Chinese ideal, while the stem family – with younger married sons expected to branch off – was the main Japanese one. Patrilineal ancestors are owed veneration, traditionally with a house altar and in collective, lineage ancestor halls, practices that are now returning in parts of China. Ancestral graves are very important family sites, and Tomb Sweeping Day is still a major event in today's Chinese calendar.

Parental respect and obedience are central norms of the Confucian family. The enormous political and economic changes of this region have challenged and altered, but not wholly done away with, Confucian generational relations. The current Chinese norm of one-child families has led to a great strengthening of the family position of the child. Seniority and gender strongly affect social relations, both inside and outside the family, but there is no norm of female seclusion.

Confucianism lends itself easily to a paternalist familism of politics and of organizational authority, including corporate ones. As such, it could even seep into communist language, especially in Vietnam under 'Uncle' Ho Chi Minh, more formally referred to as 'great-grandfather', where the main allies were referred to as Elder Brother Soviet Union and Elder Sister China (Marr 1981: 132n; Bayly 2007: 187).

The South Asian Hindu family

I call it South Asian because in many ways this system also affects non-Hindu, including Muslim, families of the subcontinent, although its distinctive norms are Hindu. Marriage here is a sacred obligation, which everybody has to fulfil. A truly proper marriage is the gift of a virgin by one patrilineal family to another, which historically has meant that girls were married off before puberty – around 1900, this was, on the average, at the age 10 or 11. A Hindu widow cannot legitimately remarry, even if a virgin child, although secular law of independent India allows it. The marriage age edged upwards in the twentieth century, spurred by colonial legislation, but in rural South Asia half of all girls marry before the age of 18. In northern India, marriage took place, and still does, out of the village, which is very alienating for the young girl, separated from her parents and from her peer friends. A widespread topic of sad songs.

Marriage is in principle indissoluble, and, certain Brahmin groups apart, it is monogamous. Marriage arrangements are governed by rules of caste endogamy and lineage exogamy. Inherited caste has moulded social interaction, also among Muslims and Christians, and has remained of importance, if not all-pervasively, also in current times. The bride is expected to bring a dowry, the size and the actual implementation of which for her family is a frequent bone of family contention. In conservative high-caste Hinduism, there is the norm of *purdah*, of female seclusion.

The historical family ideal, still in existence, is the joint patrilineal family, including married sons, with property held in common. This is normally a large family world for children to grow up in. Girls are often neglected, as they are destined soon to leave their family of origin. An important historical bond has been that of mother and son, and mothers are today usually the most important matchmakers for their children.

In terms of gender, South Asia is permeated by misogyny and maltreatment of women, to which we shall return later, looking at human life courses. But like the old Europe of powerful queens – Elizabeth I, Maria Theresa, Catherine II – dynasty can trump gender. In the last three or four decades, South Asia has been led more frequently by female political leaders than any other part of the world, through the Bhuttos of Pakistan, the Nehru-Gandhis of India, the Bandaranaikes of Sri Lanka, and the daughter and the widow leading the two bitterly rival parties of Bangladesh. Sexually, it has become very prudish in modern times, as seen in the asexual Bollywood movies, and enforced by police harassment of couples sitting close or holding hands in public, as witnessed in Delhi in the early 2000s (here I am indebted to the firsthand observations of my anthropological colleague Dr Perveez Moody).

The Islamic West Asian/North African family

Islam, like Christianity, is a world religion, spread across continents. But outside its historical homelands, the Islamic family institution has been importantly affected by other cultures, and subjected to other regional processes of twentieth-century change.

While Islamic marriage is a contract, and not a sacrament, all kinds of family matters and gender and sexual relations are extensively regulated by holy law. An important, albeit now diminished, peaceful division within Islam runs between five major schools of Islamic law, all of them about 1,200–1,300 years old, four Sunni and one Shi'a, prevailing in different parts of the vast Muslim world. This law does not only express a general principle of male superiority – like the Pauline tradition of Christianity – but specifies it in a number of precise rules, of male guardianship, of delimited polygny, of divorce by male repudiation, of the patrilineal appurtenance of children. However, it is also concerned with the protection of women as individuals, of daughters' inheritance rights, which are half of sons'. It classically recognized female property rights, including property rights and legal capacity of married women, long before these were recognized in the nineteenth century in Christian Europe. Sexuality as such in the Muslim world is not seen as a morally reproachable indulgence, but it is taken as a serious threat to the social order. Therefore it has to be strictly regulated by a marital order. Female pre-marital virginity is held to be part of family honour. Remaining single, or having children outside marriage, are not considered to be legitimate options in the life-course.

Children grow up in large patriarchal households, which historically and in the countryside still today are part of larger kinship units of patrilineal ancestry, clans and tribes. The pride in the first-born son is indicated by an Arabic naming custom, according to which his mother can be known as Umm (the mother of . . . [the boy's first name]), like Umm Kulthum, the immensely popular mid-twentieth-century Egyptian singer. Abu (father of . . .) is less widely used, but occurs. Yasser Arafat's generation of Palestinian leaders used it for *noms de guerre*, which have stuck to their public roles, such as Abu Mazen, the, in Arabic, most frequently used name of the current President of the Palestine Authority.

Families are closely knit, with a high frequency of marriages between cousins. Child marriages (without sexual consummation) are religiously sanctioned, but have now become rare, after a brief revival in the first years of the Iranian revolution. Polygamy was always confined to the rich, and has also become rare, and is now usually legally dependent upon explicit consent by the first wife. Rates of divorce, previously quite frequent and easy for a husband, have decreased. Children of divorced parents always stay under their father's guardianship, which, in modern intercultural marriages, is an issue of bitter contention, while the custody of children, up to a certain age, can be given to the mother.

The Christian-European family

This system is basically Christian, with some support from Germanic monogamy, much more than it is Greco-Roman. It has been exported to European settlements and Christian converts overseas, but more often than not in mutated forms. Hence its composite label, denoting its Christian formation in Europe. Its distinctive features include bilateral descent – meaning that your mother's family is almost as important as your father's – the principle of free choice of marriage partner, including the legitimate option of not marrying, monogamy, no special moral obligation to ancestors, and a critical moral evaluation of sexuality. The most unique European feature was its conception of marriage, of pre-Christian roots but crystallized by the church, although in practice very often sinned against. Marriage should be a matter of choice, by a man and woman wanting to unite, and marriage should be monogamous. Marriage as, in principle, a matter of individual choice was unique to Europe. It was pushed by the Catholic Church, and reasserted by the Counter Reformation *Concilium* at Trento in the 1560s. Marital individualism is a Catholic not a Protestant norm.

Christianity had a negative appreciation of sexuality, and with respect to children a crucial distinction was made between those of marital legitimacy and illegitimate ones. However, its flexibility on marriage and non-marriage did imply a certain accommodation of 'illegitimate children', particularly of high-ranking fathers. The principle of counting kinship on both the mother's and the father's side implied a certain gender balance and a potential of greater child autonomy. Girls were not expected to 'disappear' into another family after marriage. Cousin marriages were not allowed to Catholics, making parental control more difficult than in Islamic countries.

But also in Europe, the historical family was patriarchal, normally run by fathers and husbands, although their powers were more circumscribed than in pre-Christian Rome. In Scandinavia well into the nineteenth century everybody had a *patronymikon*, i.e., a second name showing that you were the son or the daughter of your father. Icelanders and Russians still use that name norm.

Within Europe, there is a cultural East–West divide going back to the early Middle Ages, 1,000 years ago or more, along a fault-line running from Trieste to St Petersburg. It is traceable back to the

31

frontiers of early medieval Germanic settlements. With non-negligible simplification – overriding significant exceptions in Latin Europe – the line divided a Western variant of a norm of neolocality, whereby a new household was established upon marriage, from an Eastern one of patrilocality, whereby a new couple usually settled with the parents of the groom. West European children then usually grew up in nuclear families. East of the line, people married young and, almost universally, west of it the average age was some years older, with at least 10 per cent, often more, never marrying. The divide survived both the coming and the going of communism.

Inside Western Europe, there was an important south–north divide, which ran through central France. North of that line, children and young people, including those from property-owning farming families, left home early, by puberty or by the end of their schooldays at least, working as servants in other households until marriage or inheritance. South of the line, youngsters tended to remain with their parents until marriage. The divide, now most visible between Italy and Spain on one hand and Central and Northern Europe on the other, still persists.

The nineteenth century was a period of great disruption of European family life, due to massive proletarianization and urbanization. Between a third and half of all children born in the major, and many smaller, cities on the European continent were born outside marriage. Tens of thousands of babies were left to foundling homes, where the rate of mortality usually far exceeded 50 per cent. Successful industrialization gradually restabilized family patterns. From the late nineteenth century on there was also a growing public concern with abused children, and public authorities were given powers and duties to intervene to protect children in malfunctioning families.

The sub-Saharan African set of family systems

This is more like a grouping of family-sex-gender systems. But it has a characteristic unity, in spite of religious pluralism (including Christianity and Islam) and huge ethnic diversity. It has a distinctive marriage pattern, of polygny, a specific relationship of kinship and fertility, and of a family devotion to ancestry. It includes both matrilineal – mostly in middle Africa – and patrilineal descent. African marital alliances are formed by the groom's family paying wealth or services to the bride's family, and property is inherited from one generation to another, as a rule only among members of the same sex. Having girls is a source of family wealth, in contrast to the South Asian rules of marriage.

Africans value fertility highly, as a key human life goal, in a broader, more general sense than the classical Confucian emphasis on not breaking the ancestral line. Although there are in Africa, like everywhere, norms of legitimate and illegitimate sexuality, a distinction between legitimate and illegitimate children has hardly ever been important. Sexual freedom and restrictions vary among the peoples across the continents, but on the whole African sexuality has been less corseted than in historical Eurasia. Polygny as a mass practice – also in predominantly Catholic countries like Rwanda and Burundi, is a unique feature of the African family. It derives from women's key historical role as agricultural labour. The conjugal bond is usually relatively weak, and husband and wife (or wives) often have separate means of livelihood, be it subsistence land plots or female trading. Mother–children relations are embedded in and somewhat blurred by larger kinship relations. African children are often out-sourced to relatives, many growing up without either parent. The African family system further includes a great respect for age, elders and ancestors, including a great importance accorded to collective rites of passage into adulthood, and to age groups as bases of rights and solidarity.

In spite of the possibilities of sexual adventures for teenage girls, including linking up with economically generous 'sugar daddies', and despite the economic independence of hard-working married women, the African family-sex-gender system remains remarkably strongly male-ruled, above all in the Muslim savannah belt south of the Sahara and in the religiously mixed but largely Christian eastern and southern Africa.

The world also has two interstitial or hybrid family systems of major importance, namely the Southeast Asian system and an American Creole pattern, as outlined below.

The (religiously pluralistic) Southeast Asian family pattern

This is a pattern of family relations stretching from Sri Lanka to the Philippines, including Myanmar, Thailand, Laos, Cambodia, southern Vietnam, Malaysia and Indonesia. Buddhist family insouciance and flexible Malay customs have here come together in mellowing the normative rigidities of other Asian family norms. These include bilateral kinship ties, a range of marital choice, whether in partner selection or, as among Muslim Malays, in divorce. In the 1950s, Muslim

Malays held the still unbeaten world record of divorce, then open to women as well. When the British arrived in Burma in the nineteenth century, they were struck by the informality of marriage, similar to today's cohabitation, as Buddhism did not provide any marriage rites.

Although Malay girls were historically under heavy pressure to marry, young teenage girls in Southeast Asia have a better deal than in the mainstream patriarchies of Asia. This is still part of Asian patriarchy and male dominance, but significantly less stern and rigid than in East, South and West Asia, now more obediently Catholic in the Philippines than in secularized Europe, but with more gender leeway than in classical European Christianity.

The American Creole family

In the Americas, from the US South, through the Caribbean down to Rio de Janeiro in Brazil, and in the Spanish mining and hacienda areas from Mexico to Paraguay, there developed a bifurcated or dual family system, which may be called Creole. It came out of the American socioeconomic history of Christian European patriarchy running plantations, mines and landed estates with African slave labour or Indian servile labour. Slaves were not allowed to marry, but were encouraged to breed, and were accessible to white male predation. The scarcity of Spanish women and the absence of a taboo against inter-ethnic sexual relations created a substantial mestizo population in Latin America, uprooted from Indian communities and never fully accepted by the whites.

The ensuing Creole duality included, on the one hand, a strictly patriarchal, ruling white high culture and family pattern, often with female seclusion, a rigid variant of the European family. On the other side of the colour line, there developed an informal black, mulatto, mestizo, and (uprooted) Indian macho-cum-matrifocal family pattern, with weak or absent fathers. In the Caribbean, particularly, informal sexual unions developed into a mainstream lifestyle. Jamaica has never had a majority of its babies born within marriage. Children tended to grow up in families of mothers and grandmothers.

Historical Creole white patriarchy has blended into mainstream white American culture, and post-Civil War Reconstruction and black migration to the industrial north of the US tended to stabilize African American family patterns, which previously had been a product of poverty as well as of racist exploitation. But with the ghettoization and relative impoverishment of many African Americans in recent decades, the black Creole pattern is returning in North America, and persisting in the Caribbean, in Brazil and in poor parts of Hispanic Indo-America. It is a family-sex-gender system of male dominance and privilege, but not patriarchal – as fathering is marginalized in the system – sexually highly charged, and with its strongest kinship bonds along female lines: grandmother–daughter–granddaughter.

Sediments of Six Waves of Globalization

Whatever our location, whoever was our ruler in the past, what we are, what we believe, what we remember today: all were affected by forces larger than our land, by historical waves of globalization. By a wave of globalization is here meant an extension, acceleration and/or intensification of important social processes to at least a trans-continental – not necessarily planetary – stretch or impact. And an extension/acceleration/intensification which can be delimited in time. These processes, practices and beliefs do not usually either originate or disappear with the wave, which rises, rolls forward and reclines – but the water is there all the time. For an understanding of the contemporary world, I am arguing that we need to take notice of at least six such waves.

Others might be added, one serious candidate being the rise of the Eurasian Mongol empire in the thirteenth century, but they have left fewer enduring sediments of human history than the six to be touched upon here. The main historical effect of the shortlived but breathtakingly wide Mongol rule of Eurasia was probably to facilitate the rise of Europe – after its peace had resulted in infected rats being spread into Europe, carrying bubonic plague and killing off about a third of all Europeans in the second third of the fourteenth century (McNeill 1979: 158) – by destroying Baghdad, then the centre of Islamic civilization, and by speeding up technological transfers from China. The *Völkerwanderungen*, the migration of peoples, beginning with the ancestors of us all moving out of Africa, on the other hand, have left enduring legacies in the peopling of the earth with humans. But early migrations are *sui generis* moves of populations rather than extensions or intensifications of social processes, while later migrations form part of economic, political and cultural waves.

The making of world religions and the demarcation of civilizations, fourth–eighth century CE

Civilizations, as we have already defined them, are broader than the rule of a chief or the blessing of a priest. In some sense, then, they are creations of a first transcultural, transpolity wave. But while civilizations may share a core worldview and certain values, by waves of globalization we are referring to processes of spatio-temporal change. In a kind of heuristic logic, civilizations are here taken as a starting-point of social geological analysis, with the extension of their core decided by the first historical wave of globalization.

The first wave of globalization was a transcontinental spread of religions, creating what we now, more than 1,000 years later, call 'world religions'. In a remarkably short time, 400–500 years, all the heartlands of all the world religions were established, and still exist today. The boundaries of contemporary civilizations have been extended, contracted or blurred since then, but the cores remain the same. I think this period of historical diffusion is more interesting than the so-called 'axial age', a notion developed by the German philosopher Karl Jaspers, and in recent decades deployed by the great Israeli sociologist Shmuel Eisenstadt (2006), of the coeval but coincidental founding of the great religions.

Christianity became the official religion of the Roman empire by the end of fourth century, and from that base area it gradually won over the rest of Europe. Before it managed that, it established itself in Armenia and Georgia, and in what is now Ethiopia. At about the same time as Christianity conquered the Roman empire, Buddhism got its breakthrough in China, arriving from northern India along the Silk Road, and from there it moved on to Korea and to Japan. Somewhat later, in the eighth century CE, it captured Tibet (Cousins 1985: 320, 331). But in the area of Sinic civilization, Buddhism, along with other religions, always remained subordinate to the political rulers. To current Burma and Thailand, it travelled also by sea, already firmly implanted in Sri Lanka, and further southeast into the Malay archipelago, erecting the magnificent temple of Borobodur in Java (Coedès 1966, 1968).

In this period, Buddhism also lost for good its original home base in India – apart from some post-independence conversions of so-called 'untouchables' – with Sri Lanka instead becoming the kind of international centre from which, later, a reformed Buddhism captured the masses of Southeast Asia. In India, Buddhism lost out to the vast, polymorphous constellation known as Hinduism, from which it had originally sprung, a loss that involved a reassertion of Brahmanic authority and of caste hierarchy.

Hinduism was also part of the first wave of globalization, spreading southeast to western Indochina and to the Indonesian islands. It tended to emerge in the wake of Buddhism, but outside India it subsided as a separate religious practice, although it is still practised in Bali, for instance. It seems to have been mainly a court religion, legitimating divine kingship. The sacred language of Hinduism, Sanskrit, became also the main literary and political language of South and Southeast Asia (Pollock 1998: 48ff). Hinduistic rites, epics and political traditions became part of Javanese life well into the nationalist era (Anderson 1996), and they remain part of Thai royal court practices (Peleggi 2007). The official name of the kings of the reigning Chakri dynasty of Thailand is Rama, currently Rama IX, from the Hindu god and the hero of the Ramayana epic.

Islam was the fastest of all religions. It often travelled by night, on horseback and by camel, through the vast deserts between the oases and the patches of fertile land of the 7,000 kilometres between western Morocco and the Ferghana Valley in today's Uzbekistan. A hundred years after the death of Muhammad, in 632 CE, Islamic rulers governed a huge territory from Spain along North Africa, Egypt, Palestine, Arabia, today's Iraq – whereto its political centre was soon relocated, moving from Mecca to Baghdad via Damascus – and Iran, to the Indus valley of contemporary Pakistan and to Bukhara and Tashkent in Central Asia. To begin with, these were victories of Arab Bedouins defeating over-extended sedentary empires – Byzantium, Sasanid Persia – exhausted after recent ferocious wars between them. However, these Bedouins were not just warriors ready to assimilate the culture that had been defeated by the much richer sedentary populations. They were believers of a new religion, victorious messengers of God, and their conquest gradually came to acquire religious significance. (Kennedy 2007; Lapidus 2002: 30ff). Seaborne traders and missionaries had brought Islam to the East African coast and, in the ninth century, to Chinese Guangzhou or Canton (Welch 1985: 127ff; also see Barnes 2008 ; Fernández-Armesto 2009: ch. 9).

The establishment of what we now call the world religions also meant the eclipse of other religions. Above all, pagan Greco-Roman polytheism, including its late emperor cults, and, more gradually dualistic Persian Zoroastrianism. That is the official religion of two of the three greatest Eurasian empires on the eve of the wave.

This first historical wave of globalization spread much more than religions. It also had a lasting impact on the civilizational areas. This was the period in which the dominant East Asian civilization became Sinic, rather than just Chinese, which in northern Vietnam and parts of Korea involved both a strong cultural import and a preservation of distinctiveness under Chinese imperial rule, for a millennium in the former case (Huard and Durand 1954:47ff; Eckert et al. 1990:

Map 2 Muslim Arab Conquests, 632–750 CE

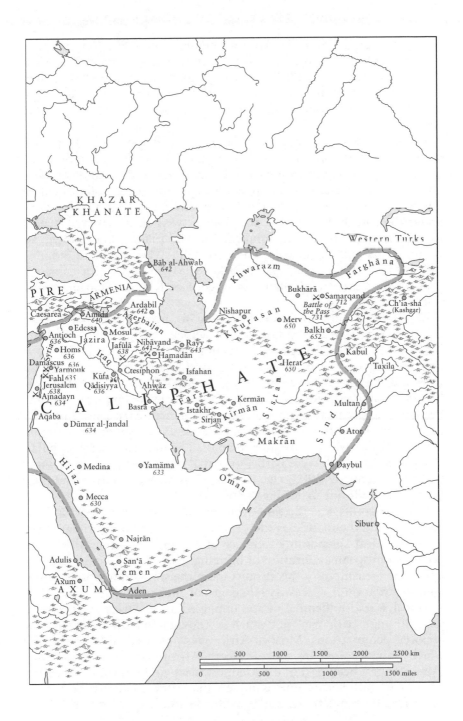

KHAZAR
KHANATE

Western Turks

PIRE

ARMENIA

Bāb al-Ahwab
642

Caesarea

Ardabil

Azerbaijan

Amida
640

Nishapur

Khwarazm

Bukhārā

Farghāna

Samarqand
712

Ch'ia-shá
(Kashgar)

Khurasan

Battle of
the Pass
731

Antioch
636

Edessa

Mosul

Jazira

Merv
650

Balkh
652

Homs
636

Jafūlā
638

Nibāvand
641-2

Rayy
643

Iraq

Kabul

Damascus 636

Hamadān

Taxila

Yarmouk

Ctesiphon

Isfahan

Herat
650

Fahl 635

Kūfa

Jerusalem
.638,

Qādisiyya
636

Ahwāz

Sīstān

Ajnadayn
634

Basra

C A L I P H A T E

Aqaba

Dūmar al-Jandal
634

Kermān

Istakhr

Sirjan

Kirmān

Multan

Sind

Ator

Makrān

Hijaz

Medina

Yamāma
633

Oman

Daybul

Mecca
630

Sibur

Najrān

Adulis

Sanʿā

Yemen

Aẋum

AXUM

Aden

| 0 | 500 | 1000 | 1500 | 2000 | 2500 km |

| 0 | 500 | 1000 | 1500 miles |

ch. 4). Ideograms and the classical literary canon of China became the high culture of Korea, Japan and northern Vietnam. The Silla kingdom in Korea established a Confucian College in 682. The first two capitals of unified Japan, Nara and Heian (or Kyoto) were built from the Chinese model of Changan (today's Xian) (Coaldrake 1996: chs. 3–4).

Sanskrit, the sacred language of northern India, became the political and literary idiom of Dravidian southern India as well, indicating a semi-continental expansion of Indic civilization, thousands of kilometres from the Indus. The great Chicago Sanskrit scholar Sheldon Pollock has given us the best qualified summary: '[S]uddenly, from about the fourth century on, inscriptions written in Sanskrit began to appear with increasing frequency in the places now known as Burma, Thailand, Cambodia, Laos, Vietnam, Malaysia, and Indonesia' (Pollock 2006: 123; cf. Pollock 1996). Indian script came to provide the basis for the later emergence of Khmer, Thai, Lao and Burmese alphabets.

The Arabic alphabet conquered Persian and Turkic, giving West Asian civilization a common script, which, because alphabetical, could never become an ecumenical script like the Chinese. In the West of Asia and in North Africa, this was the time when Iraq, Syria, Palestine, Egypt and current Libya, Tunisia, Algeria and Morocco became Arab countries. Iraq was part of the Persian empire, speaking Persian and Aramaic. Syria, Palestine and North Africa were part of the Roman-Byzantine empire, with Greek as the language of high culture. Arabic was hardly spoken at all. The majority of the population of the Maghreb were Berbers, a tribal society with a non-Semitic language (Kennedy 2007: chs. 2–4, 6). Persian high culture and language survived, but in Arabic script.

In Europe, this was the time when a post-Judaic sect of West Asia could assume the mantle as the depository of and the legitimate heir to the cultural splendour of Greece and Rome, bringing about the peculiar European civilization of bringing 'pagan' and secular culture under the lordship of a salvationist monotheism, and adopting Latin and, in Byzantium, Greek as languages of the church.

This first mid-millennial period impinged upon African civilization too, although perhaps – not much is known – mainly as externally imposed delimitations. Most of Africa was not reached by the wave, which only watered its shores. North Africa had, well before the Common Era, been part of the Mediterranean and not the continental African world. The Islamic conquest made the Mediterranean link more fragile, but left the Saharan divide for later crossings, never

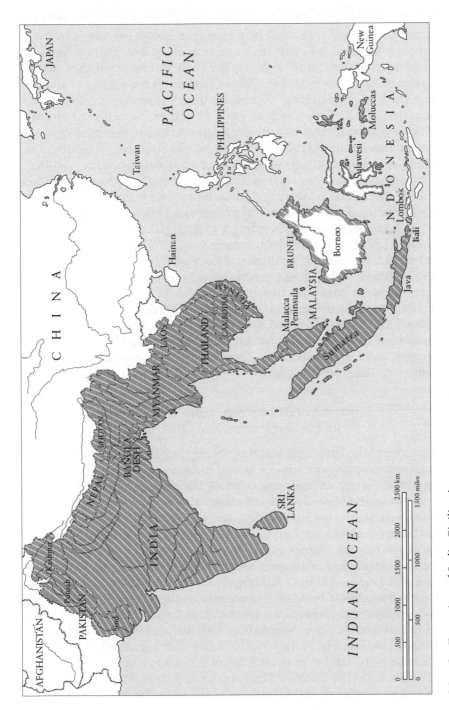

Map 3 Extension of Indic Civilization

41

dense, for natural reasons. The Christian triumph in today's Ethiopia contributed to, or was part of, a new boundary drawing of a Eurasian plough agriculture and a more Eurasian polity, connected to the Egyptian Copts through the Nubian corridor. One might say that the first wave of globalization consolidated the isolated specificity of sub-Saharan Africa. The Americas were, of course, not affected at all.

After this enormous expansion, religious change slowed down, and several transcultural religious languages, like Sanskrit, (Buddhist) Pali, and Greek and Latin, began losing ground to vernaculars (Pollock 1998: 50ff). The heartlands of all the world religions had been established, the main civilizational boundaries had been staked out and inside them a distinctive culture of language, beliefs, family norms and style of ruling, ritual and building had emerged. The wave receded.

But today's religious world map was, of course, not yet fully drawn. In the ensuing centuries, Russia and Northern Europe were Christianized. Armed horsemen brought Islam to northern India, trans-Saharan caravans began to implant it in the Sahel, making Timbuktu a major cultural centre, and seafaring traders took it to Indonesia. A new form of Buddhism spread from Sri Lanka and caught on in Indochina. The Americas were included only with the second wave of globalization, and most of central and west Africa only with the fourth wave.

European colonialism, from the sixteenth to the early seventeenth century

This was the first planetary, literally global, wave. With the conquest of the Americas – a world hitherto unknown on the other continents – the circumnavigation of the world, by the Magalhães expedition in 1519–22, was complete, and empires were established that stretched across two oceans, connecting the Philippines to Spain via Mexico, across the Pacific and the Atlantic. Its most visible legacy is, of course, the Europeanization of the Americas, in terms of language – Spanish, Portuguese, English, French, even Dutch (Surinam and the Dutch Antilles, although now being pushed aside by the largely Hispanic Creole of Papiamentu) – the Christian religion and the civilizational canon. It also includes, in Latin America and in parts of North America (e.g. Manhattan, Philadelphia, Québec), European urban planning. The Philippines have now lost almost all their Spanish language – to later American English – but have kept, as a majority religion, a fervent Catholic faith and a Latin American type of landed oligarchy. Traces of colonialism in Africa and Asia from this time are marginal, although they are visible from slaving forts in today's Ghana to Portuguese churches in Goa and Macao. The colonial legacy was recently reaffirmed when independent East Timor decided to make Portuguese the country's official language.

The Americas soon came to enrich the African as well as the European diet, less so the Asian although some influences were manifest, for example new seeds that were taken into Southeast Asia. From the New World came potatoes, maize, manioc, tomatoes, chilli peppers, peanuts, pineapples and avocadoes, etc., not to speak of sugar, tobacco and coffee from European plantations there (cf. Kiple 2007: ch. 14).

The European conquest of the Americas put European powers at the cutting edge, ahead of their conceivable Asian rivals, first as an enormous source of silver, then the global currency, and soon in the form of slave-worked plantations, of sugar, tobacco, cotton, etc. – an unrivalled base of profit accumulation. Much later, when Europe in the twentieth century got exhausted from ruling and warring the world, the USA would proudly take over the torch of European civilization as 'Western', claiming to be 'the indispensable nation' of it (according to Clinton's Secretary of State Madeleine Albright).

This was the beginning of a European military rule of the oceans. The Chinese abdicated from the high seas in the 1430s, and the Ottoman navy was crushed in the Mediterranean battle of Lepanto in 1572. Commercial shipping across the Indian Ocean and through the archipelagos of the western Pacific was still dominated by regional traders – Arabs, Bugis, Chinese and others. European colonialism was to remain for a long time, but its expansion resided for a while, and the mother continent became absorbed in its devastating Thirty Years War (1618–48). The wave subsided.

One important aspect of European colonialism which began in this period, and then continued to accelerate, was the slave trade involving the capture and trans-Atlantic transportation of Africans to sugar and other plantations of the Americas. In the first wave of the slave trade, about 1.5 million Africans were shipped to the Americas. By 1900 about eleven million had been transported in all, with a peak in the eighteenth century of six million (Collins 2006: 137; cf. Blackburn 1997).

The Franco-British world war, 1750–1815, and the rise of a European superpower

Though hardly commemorated as such, this was the first world war of human history – World War Zero. That the antagonists were two

European powers indicates that military supremacy had by the mid-eighteenth century decisively gone to Europe, even though cultural and economic hegemony were still about a century away. The war was fought in North America, in North Africa and West Asia, in India and, of course, in Europe. It included occupation of the South African Cape and of Java, and rival naval expeditions in the Pacific and around Australia.

It was actually a series of wars, each with its own immediate rationale, including, from 1792, the French Revolution. Basically, however, it was a battle for European and global hegemony fought out by the two major imperial powers of the time. In this respect it was very similar to the twentieth century's First World War. Though the decisive battles were fought in Europe, at Trafalgar, Leipzig and Waterloo, the most important theatres of war were in India and in North America. In neither was the ultimate French defeat a foregone conclusion: the French were well positioned in North America inside the Eastern seaboard, from Québec to New Orleans, and in both areas aligned with native forces.

British victories over the French in India and in Canada were enduring victories of the English language and English law, although Louisiana and Québec still keep traces of French law and administrative practices. And they laid the grounds for the beginnings of South Asian cricket. French-aided US independence was a setback for the British, but exhausted France, incapable of recapturing Saint-Domingue from the Haitian revolution, could not make much out of it. Instead, the French sold off cheaply a huge chunk of mid-western North America, from the Canadian border to the Mexican Gulf, and later had to admit that it was the former colonialist enemy and not the supporter of national independence that had been able to strike up a 'special relationship' with the emerging North American giant. Napoleonic annexation of the Netherlands spawned lasting British retaliation on the now helpless Dutch empire. It brought the British to South Africa, to Ceylon and to the foundation of Singapore. While most of the British have now gone, the English language, and the middle- and upper-class option of an English education, are still there.

However, the effect of World War Zero was something else as well: the emergence of the British empire as the world's first superpower, i.e., a dominating supra-regional world power, in spite of its loss of the 13 colonies of North America. The sun may never have set upon the Spanish empire, from Madrid to Mexico and the Philippines, but the Spanish in their maritime lanes were of little significance to the landed Ming, the Mughals, the Safavids and the Ottomans, and the

British were recurrently robbing them – a kind of naval highway banditry. World power had now definitely become a European contest, and the British defeat of the French, of the Napoleonic post-revolution as well as of the *ancien régime*, decided the contest.

While the coming world power was discernible, the Franco-British world war did not create the modern split world of development and underdevelopment. By 1750, the real wage of a Chinese or a Japanese farm worker was at least on a par with, and probably higher than, that of an English worker, which was almost twice that of a northern Italian. Indian farm wages had begun to fall behind the English, but skilled workers in Agra in the 1750s had higher real wages than most European ones, half again as much as a Viennese worker, for instance, and more than an Oxford worker, although not quite up to London and Amsterdam standards (Allen 2005: tables 5.2, 5.5). In 1793 the last of the great Chinese emperors, Qianlong, sent a visiting British ambassador back with a letter to King George III: 'We have never valued ingenious articles, nor do we have the slightest need of your manufactures' (Spence 1990: 120).

By 1820, more than half of the world's goods were still produced in Asia, and only about a fourth in Europe (Maddison 2001: 263). Mughal India was disintegrating politically and losing out economically, but China had a very successful eighteenth century, economically and politically. The Southeast Asian archipelago was growing economically, largely driven by an expanding Chinese economic presence, and cultural vibrancy, rather than stagnation, seems to have characterized both Northeast and Southeast Asia in the eighteenth century (Reid 1997). Safavid Persia was collapsing, and the Ottomans were forced to begin a retreat from Europe, but there was still no global set and match.

Generalized imperialism, and the creation of development and underdevelopment, 1830–1918

Drug-trafficking, as it would now be called, was a European wedge to world power, breaking into the last major non-European premodern power. The British wars of the 1840s to force China to import opium from British India broke the Chinese empire and its East Asian hegemony. Even before that, control of the opium market of emigrant Chinese labourers had become a key lever of colonial control in Southeast Asia (Trocki 1997: 98–9). The contemporary equivalent would be a Chinese war to open the US market for Chinese-owned Latin American factories of cocaine.

Usury with seizure of property was another important mechanism. It brought to heel the Ottoman empire and its autonomous dependencies. In 1869 the *dey* of Tunis had to declare bankruptcy, as did the Ottoman Sultan in 1875, and the *khedive* of Egypt in 1876. The European big powers, headed by Britain and France, took control of state finances – there was no IMF at the time. 'The greatest threat to the independence of the Middle East was not the armies of Europe, but its banks', a latterday Oxford historian has concluded (Rogan 2009: 105). Threatened regimes tried to modernize, which could be very expensive, especially if infrastructural investment was combined with ostentatious image-making of city and palace. The old tax systems could not cope with these new sudden demands, but loans were available, ungenerously but easily – until the bubble burst.

Superior weaponry was crucial – armoured steamships against China and (by the French) against the polities of the Western Sahel, magazine rifles and machine guns in the general conquest of Africa. These colonial wars were similar in their enormously disproportional killing capacity to the US invasions of Afghanistan and Iraq of this century or to the Israeli war on Gaza in 2009, often exceeding the Israeli killing ratio of 100:1 (cf. Curtin 2000: ch. 2). True, at that time there was more of an arms market, and on one single occasion an African ruler managed to defeat a European invader. In 1896 the Abyssinian emperor Menelik decisively beat the Italians at Adwa, preserving his country's independence until 1936, when the Italians, under fascism, struck again. When weapons alone no longer could make it, the colonial politicians gathered enough domestic political momentum to be able to overwhelm recalcitrant natives with larger military manpower, as the Americans did in the Philippines and the French in Morocco.

This is, of course, not an explanation of the development of the North Atlantic area and of the underdevelopment of (most of) the rest of world. It is only a summary of its most crucial mechanisms of tilting world power. It is not an attempt at explaining the bases of the decisive inequality of strength in the moments of confrontation, related, of course, to the North Atlantic surge of industrial capitalism. Weakness invites viciousness, while strength commands respect. Here we are concerned with explaining the present, rather than the past.

This wave, which started with the French invasion of Algeria in 1830 and the British opium wars against China in the 1840s, and ended in the hecatomb of the First World War, is the most complex (cf. Bayly 2004; Darwin 2007; Hobsbawm 1987; Pomeranz 2000).

It was the wave which created the twentieth-century world of developed and underdeveloped countries, and it was the first time that Europe exceeded Asia in economic product. The Asian share of the world product fell from 56 per cent in 1820 to 36 per cent in 1870, continuing down to 22 per cent in 1913, and 16 per cent in 1950. By 1960, an unskilled Indian worker's real wage was lower than in 1595, indeed 20–25 per cent lower (Allen 2005: 121). Between 1870 and 1913, Europe produced a little less than half, 45–47 per cent, of global GDP. The German share in 1913 was twice that of Latin America and three times that of the whole of Africa (Maddison 2001: 263). The Enlightenment universalism of Leibniz, Voltaire, Kant, Raynal or, as cultural equal diversity, Herder, gave way to European racism and particularism, later on draped in Social Darwinist evolutionism (cf. Kiernan 1969).

The wave had at least four crucial thrusts. One was a new surge of conquests – sustained by industrial muscle and new weaponry, armoured steamships with heavy artillery, Gatling and Maxim machine guns – generalized from Europe to Japan and the USA. American warships in Edo Bay in 1853 forced Japan to modernize, as a result of which Japan soon interpreted modernity as a vocational call to imperialism, successfully attacking China in 1895 and annexing Taiwan, then taking Korea in 1910. A 'scramble for Africa' was unleashed among the European powers, and the continent was divided up between them at the Berlin Conference in 1884. In 1898 the US attacked the remaining Spanish colonies of America and Asia, annexing Puerto Rico, colonizing the Philippines and establishing a protectorate over Cuba.

Secondly, in the second half of the nineteenth century there was a revolution in global communication and transport. In communications there were the inventions of the telegraph and telephone, and the deploying of trans-oceanic telegraph and telephone cables. In transport there arrived ocean-going steamships, carrying cheap North American grain and, with freezing technology, New Zealand lamb and Argentine beef to Europe.

That in turn, thirdly, had a boosting impact on world trade and world investment, protected by imperial powers and facilitated by an international gold standard. World capitalism accelerated. After 1820, world trade took off on a large scale, decelerating slightly, but from a much higher base, from 1870 (Maddison 2007: 81). After Britain's 1846 repeal of its Corn Laws, free trade became a model of the world, though it was later qualified by continental European agricultural protectionism.

Finally, this was a wave of migration of unprecedented size, facilitated by the transport revolution and promoted by the states of the Americas and by plantation owners and colonial officials of the British empire, from Trinidad to Malacca and Fiji. (Potts 1990: chs 3–5). Masses of adventurous young poor of Europe, China, Japan and India took their chance, although East Asians were soon barred from and booted out of Australia and North America.

The main enduring legacy of this wave is the contemporary world division of developed and underdeveloped countries. This trend began to be undermined by the post-Second World War growth of independent China and India and of most of Asia, and it is now challenged, but far from eradicated, by the recent surge of China and India. Part of the legacy is also the anticolonial movement of the twentieth century, which in spite of its victories of decolonization is still visible in the UN Group of 77.

Secondly, modern Africa was shaped by this wave of globalization. The latter gave the former its present national boundaries, wisely accepted by the African Union in spite of their blatant inadequacy by European standards of language and ethnicity, as well as its educated language and culture, French in Senegal and Congo, English in Nigeria and Zimbabwe, for instance. Given the narrowness of higher education, some postcolonial switches might be possible, as in current Rwanda run by Tutsis brought up in Anglophone Uganda joining the British Commonwealth. Christianity, through missionaries, became a force of African modernity, educating many of its future nationalist leaders, including, lately, extremely controversial figures like Robert Mugabe of Zimbabwe.

Then it all ended with the imperial powers falling out among themselves in the bloodiest war ever fought: the First World War. This was followed by a low ebb of nationalist economic deglobalization, which, in terms of trade, direct investment and migration, was not overcome until the very end of the twentieth century.

Globalized politics, 1919/1941/1947–89

While, economically, deglobalization was ruling the waves, a new global politics was emerging. It was adumbrated in 1919 by the foundation of the Communist International, the Comintern, followed by the Anti-Comintern Pact of 1936 between Germany, Italy and Japan, with an agenda of a globalized imperialism. Although the Comintern never became the high command of world revolution it set out to be, it did bring a model of European revolutionary politics to China and Vietnam, where it mutated into epochal Asian revolutions. In 1941 the German-Italian-Japanese pact materialized in the Japanese attack on Pearl Harbor in American Hawaii, and the ensuing German and Italian declarations of war against the USA. They were then already at war with the Soviet Union. This was the Second *World* War, with its three main 'theatres', in Europe, in the Pacific and in China, following upon the intra-European war of 1939–41. In the end, all three anti-Comintern powers were smashed. But at the end of the day, and of temporary tactical alliances – the US and UK being no less anti-communist – a new globalized politics ensued almost seamlessly.

It pitted the two main victors of the Second World War against each other – the USA and the USSR, the 'empire of liberty' and the 'empire of justice', as the Norwegian historian O. A. Westad (2005) has called them. It was a novel form of global politics, in its combinations of ancient big power politics and clientelism with global agglomerations of political parties and social movements, driven by intense ideological commitment and dedication. True, some similarities may be found with the post-1789 phase of the Franco-British world war, particularly in the 1790s.

It was an epoch of Asian and African emancipation from European colonialism, the emergence of new nation-states, the current UN set-up. Sometimes the Europeans abdicated with some style, as the British in India, or after having killed off the enemies of local conservatism, again the British, this time in Malacca. In Africa both the British and the French had to deal and manoeuvre in devious ways, but always to get out. There were some spectacular colonial defeats, of the French at Dien-bien-phu in Vietnam and a decade later in Algeria, of the Americans, who took up the French mantle, in Vietnam, and a humiliating backdown, of the British and the French at Suez, in the face of American disapproval. The smaller powers, Belgium, Netherlands, Portugal and Spain, were either roundly defeated or scared off, like the Belgians and the Spanish.

As any fighting took place only at, what was seen as, the margins and with proxies on one side or the other, the post-1945 era has become known as the Cold War. The perceived central point was Berlin, split in two. The final post-1945 act of the Chinese Revolution was mainly treated as an internal Chinese affair, until the communist victory, when the question 'Who lost China?' – i.e., 'Who delivered our China to them'? – became a hot domestic issue in the USA. But it did include very bloody localized wars, in Korea and Vietnam in particular, but also in Africa and Central America. It ended with the abdication global ambition by the Soviet Union in 1989, and by its implosion and final disappearance in 1991.

Globalized mid-twentieth-century politics has left enduring cleavages of nation-states, apart from its more ephemeral political hopes and ideological experiments. The disastrous defeat of Germany and Japan in the war generated strong and lasting pacifist and post-nationalist currents in those countries, which continued to prevent even their most pro-American politicians from fully taking part in any American wars. For the French and Germans, the Second World War was their third devastating war in less than a century, which provided a major impetus to seeking European integration in order to forestall a fourth round.

The Second World War ended in Europe with the continent divided between the American and the Soviet armies, with capitalist reconstruction in the West and imposed communism in the East. A result of this, still audible in the European Union, is that after the end of communism, East European anti-communists tend to be much more deferential to the USA than are West Europeans. Their national suffering as a result of the 1939–41 non-aggression pact between Germany and the Soviet Union has led to a particular anti-Russian bitterness among Balts and Poles. Katyn, where thousands of Polish officers were killed by the Soviets in 1940, is seen as a defining moment of modern Polish history. In his recent film about the massacre, Andrzej Wajda has again proved himself the national bard of post-communist Poland. By belatedly admitting Soviet responsibility for this horrendous Stalinist crime, Russia in 2010 took an important step towards a post-ideological Russo-Polish reconciliation.

West Asia and the Arab world were enduringly traumatized by the establishment of a Jewish state in Palestine, as a transplanted, posthumous outcome of the European genocide of Jewry. The new state has been recurrently at war with its neighbours, in 1948, 1956, 1967, 1973, 1982, 2006 and 2009. Through the US–Israeli alliance and its proximity to major Western oil interests, this local conflict has acquired global significance.

The post-Second World War challenge and fear of communism in East Asia, North and South, had important consequences beyond the victory of the communists in China and North Vietnam. It led to radical land reforms by conservative regimes in Japan, South Korea and Taiwan, while the military defeat of communist guerrillas, from the Philippines to Thailand, consolidated authoritarian rightwing politics there. Supplying the enormous American war machine in

Korea and in Vietnam opened US markets and stimulated a boost of economic development.

South Asia was outside that zone, and was instead traumatized by the Partition of ex-British India and the ensuing communal massacres and border disputes. But its long economic stagnation under British rule was succeeded by growth, and India under Nehru became a leader of the decolonized world.

Post-war decolonization left a demarcation between former colonizing and former colonized nation-states, once symbolized in the latter coming together at a famous conference in Bandung in Indonesia in 1955. Traces of it are still discernible in the Non-aligned Movement (of mainly ex-colonized states), and in the UN Group of 77 (actually about 130 countries) and their voting records. The very interdependent decolonization process in sub-Saharan Africa gave rise to a significant postcolonial pan-Africanism.

Self-assumed globalization and its shifting meanings, 1990–?

It was the sixth historical wave which gave globalization its name, in a conceptual explosion from the late 1980s (Chanda 2007: 245ff; Osterhammel and Peterson 2005). This was the period when time imploded into space – when a new future became an extended, 'globalized' space – with the collapse of the Soviet Union and China's turn to the capitalist road following upon the defeats of West European labour, of Latin American revolutionaries and of African socialism in the late 1970s–early 1980s.

Utopias of emancipation, perspectives of transformative change were eclipsed all over the globe. In this context, 'globalization' appeared as the only future on the horizon. As a purely spatial concept, it denoted modernity's flight into space. Although globalization always had its leftwing dystopian critics, as a view of the world it was part of the rise of a forceful rightwing conception of modernity and modernization, universally known as 'neoliberalism', politically spearheaded by British Thatcherism. Because of the peculiar pathways of fashionable intellectual debate, this new rising manifestation of modernism was never attacked by the postmodernists of the 1980s and 1990s (see, e.g., Anderson 1998; Bauman 1992; Lyotard 1984; Rosenau 1992; Seidmann 1994).

Spatiality has the two-dimensional character of flatness, of surface. It carries none of the burdens of substance, depth, conflict or contradiction, in other words, of dialectics. That is why 'globalization' lent itself so cheaply to both critique and adulation. Spatiality is devoid of substantial content. The new goal, always crucial to any kind of modernism, is no longer 'progress', and certainly doesn't include leftwing projects of 'emancipation'. Progress means that something is getting better, i.e., it denotes some quality of substance. Globalization signifies that impact and/or connections are being extended. Progress has a forward direction, whereas globalization is just extension, without any particular direction. But both concepts refer to some compelling force transcending individual action, to something rational that individuals play *with*, and not against.

Globalization was the buzz word of the 1990s, and, in an unconscious way, it captured well the peculiar mix of fast change and deep freeze that characterized the last decades of the twentieth century and the very first years of the twenty-first. The world was changing – fast – but not in any structural or cultural sense. On the contrary, the events of 1989–91 were supposed to solidify the structure and the political culture of the world, those of triumphant capitalism. But the pace of global capitalism, and of global culture more generally, was accelerating, and those who did not swim with the stream were likely to sink like a stone. All economic activities, except rich world agriculture, were, or would soon be, pushed into a steel bath of global competition. Financial tricksters amassed enormous fortunes by creating their own surreal economy that soared above the other one, still known as 'the real'. New electronic media wrapped up the globe in fast communication.

The predominant perception of this sixth wave of globalization was that it was unique and unprecedented, and that its most important manifestation was an extension of markets, of opening-up of capital movements and of trade in merchandise and in services. Globalization was global competition. Socially, there was also a recognition of rising global connectivity, through media of communication and through cultural migration. In retrospect, if still provisionally, a somewhat different picture is emerging.

The inflated, ahistorical view of unprecedented activity is increasingly abandoned, even though this writer's long waves' view of world history by no means represents conventional wisdom. Capitalist development is seen less in terms of spatial extension, and more in a structural relocation of profitability, from industry and services to finance. Communications developments are coming to the forefront. Finally, and most importantly, is a growing recognition that what we are living in this wave is much more a global shift of gravity or centrality than a global extension. Looking backwards from 2010, globalization does not look so much an extension of US capitalism as a delimitation of it, by the rise of China and India.

Two main currents have driven the familiar, latest wave of globalization. One is the revolution of electronic communication, centred on the internet as a globally accessible means of communication, as worldwide mass self-communication. It began in the 1980s, and gathered momentum in the 1990s (Berners-Lee 1999). By 2007, almost a quarter of humankind was using it (Tryhorn 2009). Satellite television and digital channelling have also transformed the global mediascape.

The other driving current has been capitalist finance, since the mid-1980s geared up as a worldwide electronic casino, where enormous sums of fictitious money are traded, in currency betting and in guesses on the future, so-called derivatives. In recent years the world's top derivatives trader has been the French bank *Société Générale*. In January 2008 the outside world caught a glimpse of the stakes at the financial casino tables, when it was found that a junior trader had caused the bank to lose 4.9 billion euros. His total outstanding bets, in the bank's name, amounted to 50 billion euros, about the total national income of Vietnam (*Financial Times* 28/1/ 2008). It seems that the man's objective was neither to steal nor to damage, but to show his superiors his trading ability. Little wonder there was a financial crisis around the corner.

A neoliberal ideology, nourished by the 1970s crisis of post-war Keynesianism and by the capitalist victory in the Cold War, has added an impetus of free capital movements and free trade. A post-1960s delegitimation of racism together with new possibilities of transport have given the 1980s–90s economic polarization of the world a migration outlet. Foreign-born residents are now on a par with their share of world population a century ago.

In terms of trade, global capital flows and faith in financial capitalism, at least, it may now already be argued that 2008 saw the petering out of the latest wave of globalization. World trade contracted strongly in 2008, and so did cross-border capital flows (IMF 2009). What that will amount to in the longer run is much too early to tell. The editors of the American weekly *Newsweek* and the director of the World Economic Forum were already convinced by the turn of 2009/10 that it will not much matter (*Newsweek* 2010).

However, even if the crisis of 2008–9 should turn out to be little more than a dip in an ongoing global surf, the meaning of it is beginning to change. The wave is taking a direction unnoticed by the globalization discourse of the 1990s. It is no longer, only or mainly, an extension of markets, of virtual networking, of compression of time–space. It is also, and perhaps above all, an epochal global shift of economic and political (in that order) gravity, from Euro-America back to Asia, East and South. In 2007, China became the third largest economy of the world, and in 2009 the world's largest exporter and largest automobile market (*International Herald Tribune* 11/1/2010, p. 13). In 2010, it is on track to replace Japan as world economy number two. In the global crisis summits of 2008–9, the G8 group of countries – the largest Western economies, Japan and Russia – was no longer held to be strong enough to call the shots, and the G20, including China, India, Brazil and other countries outside the North Atlantic, was called upon. What little climate deal finally came out of the UN Copenhagen meeting in December 2009 was hammered out between the USA and China, and seconded by Brazil, India and South Africa.

Pathways to Modernity and Their Legacy

Nowadays, we are all 'modern'. But we became modern in very different ways, forming yet another layer of our cultural constitution. *Modernus* and *modernitas* are words of medieval Latin meaning 'present', as adjective and as noun. They were usually deployed in contrast to 'ancient' and 'antiquity', the classical Greco-Roman epoch of European civilization. As such, the concept developed primarily as an aesthetic category and for evaluative purposes: what is better, the ancient or the modern? (Gumbrecht 1978; Graevenitz 1999).

In English language social discourse, 'modernity' was a rare concept until the challenge of postmodernism in the 1980s. I have found it useful to designate a *cultural orientation*, not any particular sort of social institutions, but an orientation that turns its back on the achievements and rules of the past, embracing the new present with a view to constructing a novel, this-worldly future. A modern perspective in this sense entails a linear conception of time instead of a cyclical one, and a sense of forward direction, of an 'arrow of time', instead of a decline from a golden age. Modernity, then, is an epoch, a society, a culture, a polity, in which a modernist, future-directed time orientation is hegemonic. It is a torchlight concept in a search of epochal moments of social and cultural change. As a time orientation it has a clear empirical meaning, and as a general concept it is applicable to politics and economics as well as to art and cognition.

When, where and how did modernism become hegemonic? Can it get lost? Has it happened several times in history? Like everything human, a modernist hegemony can certainly get lost, and there was a recent postmodernist attempt to bring that about. It did not succeed, but it stimulated an awareness of and a debate about modernity. The way in which the concept is used here implies that there may have been modernities in the past which have disappeared. But whether human history can be read that way, I have to leave for another book. Here, I start from the question of *how* modernism became a hegemonic orientation in various parts of the world. Again, my main concern is not so much the historical process as its enduring consequences today.

The rise of modernist orientations can best be studied empirically with respect to specific practices, such as cognition, art, economics and politics. There is no reason to expect changes in such fields to be synchronic. The contrary should be expected. In Western Europe, there was a breakthrough of a scientific modernity in the first half of the seventeenth century, theorized in the works of Francis Bacon and Descartes, breaking with the classical authority of Aristotle, and soon institutionalized in the British Royal Society and the French Academy of Science. The modern cognitive development was strengthened by the discovery of a New World, unknown to antiquity, but it seems to be an unwarranted Americo-centrism to claim that the latter was decisive. The breakthrough came principally in physics and its philosophy, not in anthropology and botany.

In late seventeenth-century France there was a major aesthetic battle, 'the Quarrel of the Ancients and the Moderns', mainly in literature – it was won by the moderns, but in France that 'modern' age of Louis XIV later became known as 'l'âge classique', the classical age, and literary modernism is usually dated from almost two centuries later, the time of Charles Baudelaire. It is only by the mid-eighteenth century that an evolutionary conception of means of livelihood is asserted, and the rise of a new post-agrarian 'commercial' economy is heralded by the Scottish Enlightenment, in John Millar's *Origins of the Distinction of Ranks* and in Adam Smith's *Wealth of Nations*.

Political theory was still mainly backward-looking in the eighteenth century. The concepts of 'reform(ation)' and 'revolution' still referred to a glorious past of purity and freedom – like the English 'Glorious Revolution' of 1688 – and in a sense rightly so, given the return meaning of the prefix 're'. Alternatively, revolution could refer to cyclical motion, as Copernicus' work on planetary motion *De*

Revolutionibus planetorum, or in the main article on *révolution* in the French *Encyclopédie,* the *summa* of Enlightenment knowledge, which deals with the revolution of wheels in clocks and watches. It was the French Revolution that obliterated the meaning of the prefix and turned revolution and reform into keys to the future. Soon after this, the campaign for parliamentary reform in Britain showed that 'reform' too had lost its backward-looking connotation (Therborn 1989; cf. Kosellek 2002: ch. 10).

A breakthrough of modernity may then occur at different times in different fields of the same culture area. But from a perspective of social hegemony and of an understanding of the social geological formation of the contemporary world, it seems that it is the victory of a future-oriented conception of politics, as a concentration of a society's collective force, which is crucial.

The modern political rupture with the past took different forms and occurred at different times in different parts of the world. In an empirical work on the history of the right to vote (Therborn 1992), it dawned upon me that all these differences may be summed up in four major pathways into modernity, defined by the conflict lines for and against the new. They can be distinguished in general analytical terms, and therefore used not only to sort groups of countries but also as ideal types, two or more of which may have been taken by a particular country.

The questions to be asked then are these. How was the new, future-oriented political culture generated? Internally, in the given society, or imposed or imported from outside? Who were the forces of the new? A new stratum within the given society, an external force or a part of the old internal elite? Where were the main forces, and the perceived Others of anti-modernity, of traditional authority, submission or barbarism?

The answers to those questions, the four major pathways to modernity, are not just stories of the past, they are part of the geological formation of contemporary society.

Internalist Europe

The French Revolution of 1789 and the years that followed heralded the political breakthrough of modernity in Europe, even if it was in an immediate sense defeated by the counter-revolutionary alliance at Waterloo, which resulted in a short-lived monarchical restoration and a continental big power constellation of reaction: the Holy Alliance. As we noticed above, it was the French Revolution which gave us the modern meaning of revolution and reform. Despite its temporary defeat, it also meant a decisive victory for a new principle of political legitimation, the nation, the people, which in a more gradual way had also emerged in British parliamentarism. 'Only after 1789', says my great political theory colleague John Dunn, 'did any human beings begin to speak about democratizing the societies to which they belonged' (2005: 17; emphasis omitted).

The Revolution was by no means a purely endogenous European outcome. It was embedded in the Franco-British world war, the third wave of globalization, with its disastrous effects on French state finances, which in turn triggered the sequence of events leading to the Revolution. However, it was a completely internal European conflict, pitting the French forces of revolution and reaction against each other. The latter were aided by their powerful equivalents in other European countries, and the former tried to create allies of their European friends.

The new European politics returned after the defeat of the 1789–99 Revolution, from the French July 1830 revolution onwards, in a very meandering way, but only fully succeeded in 1917–18 with the fall of the Romanov, Habsburg and Hohenzollern empires. Throughout this time, the central conflict of political authority was internal to European civilization; colonial exploits did not decide anything. US intervention in the First World War certainly affected the outcome of the war, but the handling of the defeats was decided in Austria and Germany. All over Europe, modern conceptions had to fight their way through internal conflict, without support or models from abroad, against domestic forces of local traditional society. In its violent forms, this European pathway was the road of revolution and civil war.

Outside Europe, external models, threats and forces were always central, negatively or positively. The history of modernity can never properly be reduced to cultural history. It was also a history of world power. The scientific and industrial curiosity of, say, the seventeenth-century Royal Society or the eighteenth-century Birmingham Lunar Society was not simply diffused around the world. It became part of a European standard, which spread with the much more tangible arguments of naval artillery and the Gatling machine gun.

The New World and its othering

Among the European colonial settlers, ideals and models of a new society were inspired by the European Enlightenment, and, in the

North American case, by the political philosophy of 1688 and the British radical critique of the eighteenth-century Hanoverian monarchy of Britain. However European-inspired, and however European-aided – France supporting North American independence and later opening Hispano-American opportunities by defeating the Spanish monarchy – the forces of modernity were American, products of the transplanted settler society. They did not just import the European Enlightenment or British Protestant dissent, they made their own contributions to it.

Independence was the defining moment of American political modernity, when it came into its own. Though the notion of 'revolution' has stuck, from the USA to Argentina, and although the metropolitan power had considerable support, in the USA, Mexico and Peru in particular, American independence was not a European-type revolution or civil war. It ensued from wars of secession. The others of settler modernity, the enemies of modernity, were basically outside settler society, the corrupt and backward metropolitan governments to which the loyalists hung on, the barbarian or savage natives, and the brutish slaves. Inside it, there was hardly any anti-modern authority. The Catholic Church of Latin America, on the whole, wisely refrained from backing the colonial power, and North America was largely created by Protestant dissent. New World modernity was a modernity of settlers and of slave plantation owners, with downtrodden non-moderns nearby, the natives, the slaves and the ex-slaves. Traditional authority was the colonial metropolis and its governing representatives sent from overseas.

The New Worlds of overseas settlement include some noteworthy subvariants, although this is not the place for doing them analytical justice. One is made up of what before post-Second World War decolonization was usually known as the 'white Dominions', the gradually independent but imperially loyal states of Australia, Canada, New Zealand and South Africa, which volunteered – albeit not without internal opposition – to fight for the British empire in both the First and the Second World War. A vivid illustration of this loyalty – and of the intellectual poverty of utility-rational choice – is that the main commemorative event of Australian nationhood is ANZAC (Australian and New Zealand Army Corps) Day and ANZAC monuments, paying homage to the Australian sacrifices for the empire at Gallipoli – more than two oceans away on another continent – during the First World War. Nevertheless, for all their imperial loyalty, the white Dominions set out on their own settler course to modernity, quite distinctive from that of the motherland.

Israel, the Zionist conquest of most of Palestine, is another, small subvariant, but with wide international repercussions. Like once white South Africa, it faces an Other (of Palestinians), which has been strengthened, culturally and socially, by constant settler violence and humiliation.

Singapore, finally, is worth noticing as the only non-European New World, being mainly Chinese in an inter-Asian ethnocultural mix. The city was a colonial creation, but there was nobody there to be colonized, nor was the colony built by slaves and indentured labourers. New World settlers pay homage to their *conquistadores,* ex-colonies do not. The business class of Singapore Airlines is called Raffles Class (after the imperial founder of the city). No Air India executive would come up with the idea of calling its class of privilege, say, Curzon Class.

The colonial trauma: Identifying with and rebelling against the aggressor

Colonialism by modern states, such as by nineteenth- and twentieth-century European states, meant an imposition of modernity from outside, after having defeated native traditional authorities. In the colonial zone, modernity arrived literally out of the barrels of guns. Colonial modernism was usually confined to the direct colonial administration itself, to the building of separate colonial cities – ideally separated from the native cities or neighbourhoods by the standard distance of a mosquito's flight capacity (3–500 meters; I learnt this from a thorough, if somewhat defensive exhibition on Belgian Congo at the Royal Africa museum in Brussels) – and to the extraction and export of commodities. Occasional interventions against sex-gender-family practices repugnant to Christian Europeans – e.g., widow immolation in India, child marriages and polygamy – were usually ineffective. On the other hand, after having defeated or subordinated the traditional authorities, the colonial powers went to shore up and make use of them, as sheepdogs for the everyday running of the colonized. Ethnic boundaries and traditional norms were rigidified by procedures of classification and codification (see, e.g., Mamdani 1996: 50ff).

While modern European colonialism had little modernist impact on the mass of the colonized populations and their mode of living, it did open up new opportunities to a minority. Port, road and railway construction and operation, mining, plantations and the little manufacturing there was all provided new jobs and spawned new collective social relations to an emergent but small and delimited working class. Cash crops gave rise to a class of colonized farmers and planters. The imperial armies needed native soldiers, and made large recruitments, in India and throughout the colonial zone during both world wars. Finally, and politically most significant, modern education facilities, although strictly limited, and catering to a colonial need of clerical help, generated a new colonized elite.

Most systematically and most successfully, this was done in British India, according to the aim of the creator of the system, T. B. Macaulay, of creating 'a class of persons Indian in colour and blood, but English in tastes, in opinion, in morals, and in intellect ... who may be interpreters between us and the millions we govern' (Keay 2000: 431). It worked wonderfully, until the early 1940s, when the Congress Party started its 'Quit India' campaign. And after independence, the beneficiaries continued to be proud of their Macaulayan education: 'Its beneficent results [in the modernization of India] ... deserve the highest praise', a prominent legislator, civil servant and diplomat wrote in 1960 (Panikkar 1960: 22–3).

The new working class created modern associations, trade unions and mutual help organizations, and modern collective action, of strikes and demonstrations. The planters came to support a moderate national conservatism. The soldiers were, on the whole, amazingly loyal to their colonial masters – the 1857 mutiny in India was a rare exception – though, particularly after their eye-widening experiences during the First World War, they could constitute pressure groups against colonial discrimination. But it was the tiny new educated elite, the *évolués*, as the French masters called them, which turned their modern political education – about nations, peoples, rights – against their masters and created anticolonial nationalism. Patrice Lumumba, the first and short-lived Prime Minister of Congo, is an emblematic example. This is the road to modernity by *anticolonial rebellion*. In Burma from the 1930s, the nationalists proudly began to refer to themselves as *thakin*, 'master' (Callahan 2009: 36).

The first successful anticolonial revolution was the slave rebellion of Saint-Domingue in 1791. The original colonized population had been eradicated, leaving behind only their name of the island, Haiti, to imported slaves, who managed to overthrow their masters in the wake of the turmoil of the French Revolution. More or less unique among the slave colonies, French-ruled Saint-Domingue had a substantial and propertied class of mulattos and enfranchised blacks. The colonial denial of any of the Revolution's new political rights to the mulattos and the freed blacks ignited the rebellion. Against all odds,

Haiti survived a major attempt by the French in 1802 to recapture the island and to reimpose slavery. Though the Haitians were tough fighters, battle-hardened from being enlisted into inter-imperial struggles on the island between the French and the Spanish, their decisive ally was *Aedes aegypti*, the yellow fever-carrying mosquito, which killed off most of the French troops.

The first post-colony was crippled by its birth traumas. Its first leader was captured by the French and sent to die in a cold dungeon in the Jura, the very able, ex-mid-level plantation manager and later commander of first Spanish and then French colonial armies, Toussaint L'Ouverture. The long decade of wars generated a brutalized military elite, lethally divided between mulattos and blacks. The new country inherited an ex-slavery culture, where work and initiative beyond subsistence were seen as stratagems of oppression. The 'Black Jacobins' have not left much of a constructive legacy, but in these globalized times, there is a gradually spreading recognition that we, the privileged *Nachgeborenen* (late-born), owe them our respect as pioneers. Haiti is one vantage point from which to look at the challenge of postcolonial modernity. (The classic work on the topic is James 1938/1989; for a great overview by a current historian, see Blackburn 1988: 190ff, ch. VI; on the epidemiological side of it all, there is the penetrating analysis of McNeill 2010: 236ff).

The anticolonial modernism of the colonized – a perspective also adopted in late twentieth-century Latin America, rejecting settler creolity – was very conducive to radicalism. The colonized moderns, the generation of Nehru, Sukarno, Ho Chi Minh and Nkrumah, were probably the people most acutely living the contradictions of liberal European modernity. On the one hand, they had identified with the modern aggressor, the colonial power, learning his language, his culture and his political principles of nation/people, rights and self-determination. On the other, they experienced the denial of rights and self-determination to their people, the haughty face and the iron fist of liberal imperialism. Socialist radicalism, communist and non-communist, was a pervasive characteristic of post-Second World War anticolonial nationalism.

The adaptive openings and closures of reactive modernization

In a fourth major pathway of reactive modernization, modernity was imported by a part of an internal elite perceiving their realm as being under acute foreign threat, and imposed from above on the population, still following traditional orientations. Here modernity develops as pre-emptive reaction. This modernist project was aiming at enhancing the population's capacity to defend an existing state. Initially, it was generally conceived only in military terms, of acquiring modern arms, arms technology and military organization, but in cases of enduring importance the programme was soon widened to embrace economic technology, education, transport, public health and political institutions. A new and stronger form of social cohesion was a central aim, seen as key to the overwhelming strength of the threatening imperialist powers (see further Therborn 1992; Curtin 2000: chs 8–10).

The chances of success of such a transformation from above would be slim without an alteration of the *ancien régime* itself, and without some good luck of geopolitical context in the age of belligerent rival imperialisms (cf. Reid 1997). The Ottoman and the Qing empires failed, as did the Joseon monarchy in Korea, and the Siam and, especially, Abyssinian monarchies did not get very far. Only the Japanese project was fully successful, starting out from a much higher general level of economic and educational development, benefiting from its proximity to a historically much resource-richer and now weaker neighbour, China. But also from its independence of traditional court intrigue by entrenched conservative factions – a plague in all the failing monarchies – and without a powerful clergy, a main force of reaction in the Muslim states. The so-called Meiji imperial Restoration did not mean that the emperor and his court got to rule, but led instead to a modernizing faction of a reshuffled aristocracy and gentry.

While today only Japan and Thailand (ex-Siam) are directly continuing examples of reactive modernization or of modernity by pre-emptive reaction, the legacy of the Japanese pioneers – whose naval defeat of the Russians in 1904 enthused Asian and African patriots from Korea to Egypt, where the then leading nationalist intellectual Mustafa Kamil published a book on it, *The Rising Sun* (Hourani 1983: 205; also see Aydin 2007: 78ff) – is much more widely spread. It was attempted by the king of Afghanistan in the 1920s, and by emperors Memelik and Haile Selassie of Abyssinia. The current monarchies of Arabia and the Gulf belong to the same group, although their enormous wealth has allowed them to preserve much more of pre-modern indigenous institutions. The negotiable geopolitics of oil has meant that their pre-emption has been directed at least as much against domestic radicalism as against foreign threats. Japanese modernization from above inspired the post-Second World War emergence of national development states in East Asia, beginning in Korea and Taiwan, facilitated by the inclusive character of Japanese colonialism, and later emulated in Singapore, Malaysia and elsewhere, with a focused, consistent modernist developmentalism combined with close attention to national cohesion.

Before the contemporary national development states, state-led social transformation from above had been started with great vigour and ruthlessness by Mustafa Kemal in Turkey and by the Bolsheviks in Russia, in particular the building 'socialism in one country' project of Josef Stalin. Both Stalin and Kemal Atatürk tried to create strong, modern states against an immediate background of foreign military interventions breaking up the old imperial state and lethally threatening the successor regimes. Since these transformations were pushed by new, revolutionary regimes, their effects were different, disruptive of the social fabric rather than transforming-cum-tightening it, while at the same time inadvertently reproducing pre-modern beliefs and practices at the rural bottom. The Afghan communists, another radical modernist minority, tried a similar path in the 1980s. They were destroyed by a formidable coalition of enemies, of domestic patriarchal-cum-tribal reaction and a broad counter-revolutionary alliance of international Islamist warriors, American weapons, Saudi money and Pakistani secret services, against whom their Soviet support was ultimately counterproductive.

Hybrid paths: Russia and China, above all

As was said above, the roads to modernity can be seen as abstract types, implying that we may find countries taking two or more roads. The contemporary world has two major hybrids in this respect, Russia and China, the countries in which the two major revolutions of the twentieth century took place (see further Anderson 2010). More fine-grained analyses will no doubt discover more, including large tracts of the once Ottoman Arab lands, Egypt in particular, part of failed reactive modernization, more colonized than late Qing China but never fully, as Algeria was. Malaysia is another example of a hybrid path with distinctive features. The Malay sultanates were never fully colonized, and independent Malaysia has to be understood against a mixed background of ex-semi-colony and reactive modernization. From the former stems its multiethnicity, from the latter its autocratic Malay modernizing conservatism. Characteristically, the main monument of independent Kuala Lumpur is not to independence and the struggle against colonialism, but to the victory of the 'Emergency', the British suppression of the post-Second World War communist insurgency. South Africa started out as an American-type settler state, but was finally cut down to an ultimately failed colonial endeavour. An important part of pre-Independence India was made up of imperially 'protected' and supervised princely states. But, at least from an outsider's global perspective, they seem to have left little significant legacy to postcolonial India, except for the entangled conflicts of Kashmir.

Russia is a European power, and its revolution in 1917 was very much in the European modernist trajectory of the French Revolution of 1789, a reference constantly on the minds of the revolutionaries of 1917, of the uprising in February as well as of that in October. The Bolshevik Revolution was a European-type insurrection by an urban industrial working class, organized and rallied by a party that developed as a section of the international European labour movement.

However, Lenin and the other Bolshevik leaders were well aware of the fact that they and their following constituted only a minority in a mainly rural and agrarian country. Their modernist reading of historical development entitled them nevertheless, as they saw it, to start a profound social transformation from above. One of its first examples was a radical, anti-patriarchal piece of family legislation in October 1918. Originally, Lenin saw the Russian Revolution as a contingent ignition of an international revolution soon to break out, in Germany above all, the heartland of the European labour movement. It did not happen that way, and from the late 1920s the Soviet Union under Stalin embarked upon a ruthless and violent economic transformation from above.

Russia was European, but a backward part of Europe, never part of the latter's classical antiquity and kept down during the Middle Ages by Mongol rule. Reactive modernization from above had started already in the decades around 1700 in the reign of Tsar Peter I, generally known as Peter the Great. In spite of advances, it never caught up with Western Europe. Crystallized in the pan-European epoch of absolutism, Russian reactive modernization never made it to a consolidated constitutional phase. Devastating military defeats, in 1905 and in 1916–17 opened the gates to revolution.

Stalinism increasingly linked up with Tsarist history, from deportations to Siberia to claiming lost imperial lands like the Baltics and Bessarabia (current Moldova), conceiving the Second World War as 'the Great Patriotic War', repeating the 'Patriotic War' of 1812, against Napoleon. The blending of brutal communist modernism with Tsarist imperial *grandeur* was muted after Stalin. But a new blend has emerged in recent years, under Putin, of imported capitalist modernism draped in imperial pseudo-Tsarism, displayed in the gilded Kremlin pomp, in the new huge statue of Peter the Great in Moscow and in the return of the Orthodox Church into state ceremonies and rituals. Russian modernity has been driven by imported models imposed from above, as well as by internal evolution and revolution.

China is a more complex case of modern hybridity, involving aspects of reactive modernization, colonial identification with-cum-rebellion against the aggressor and an important import of European class politics. That its ancient wisdoms and splendour could no longer measure up to an increasingly encroaching world slowly, gradually and partly dawned upon sections of its ruling stratum and of the intellectual mandarinate, particularly after the British forced the country open to drug-trafficking in the two opium wars of the 1840s–50s. Its enormous scientific and technological creativity in the centuries before 1600 CE was not revived, and new models had to be imported. Attempts at reactive modernization by the late Qing dynasty were thwarted by court intrigues, spun by the Empress Dowager Cixi, and by violent imperialist interventions, British, German, Japanese and French. The Republic after 1911 certainly did try, but never got very far, deeply internally divided as it was, and besieged by foreign powers.

The hybridity of China's twentieth-century road to modernity stems above all from two features: the country's ambiguous national status and the character of its most successful political import. From the last nineteenth-century decades of the Qing dynasty and during the Republic, China was neither independent and sovereign nor a colony – or, rather, it was both at the same time. There was a Chinese state, without a viceroy or a governor-general above it. But foreign powers held a number of 'treaty ports', most importantly Shanghai, and had asserted various extra-territorial rights in the country. A major source of public revenue, the customs, was run by a foreign imperialist consortium. In true colonial fashion, modernist Chinese students and intellectuals went to Tokyo to learn.

Anti-imperialist nationalism, in the face of a long series of foreign humiliations, created the first modern political party, the Guomindang, and modern mass movements in China. Of landmark importance was the May Fourth [1919] Movement against the post-First World War settlement handing over the colony of defeated Germany, Tsingtao, to Japan. Out of this anticolonial nationalism came a

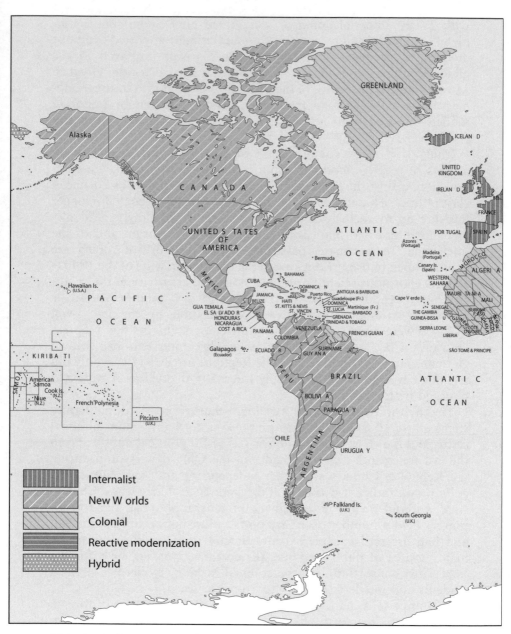

Map 4 Pathways to Modernity

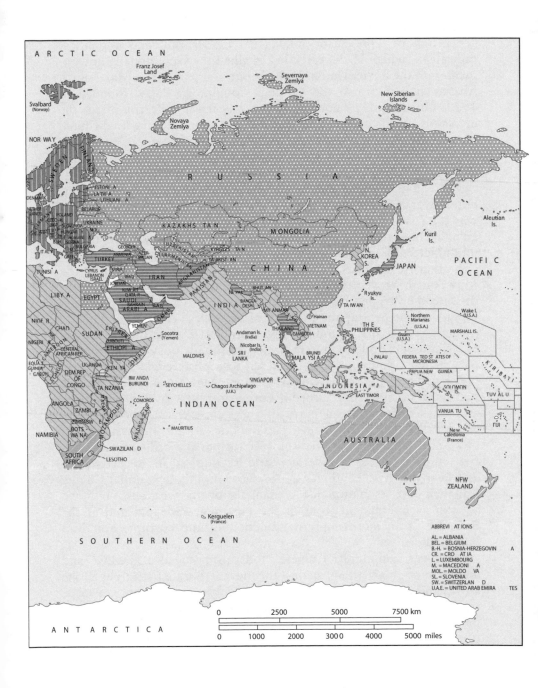

ARCTIC OCEAN

Franz Josef
Land

Severnaya
Zemlya

New Siberian
Islands

Svalbard
(Norway)

Novaya
Zemlya

NOR WAY

SWEDEN

FINLAND

R U S S I A

Aleutian
Is.

ESTONI A
LATVI A
LITHUAN I A

DENMARK
NETHER-
LANDS

BELARUS

KAZAKHS TA N

MONGOLIA

Kuril
Is.

UKRAINE

POLAND
CZECH
SLOVAKIA
MOL

GEORGIA

UZBEKISTAN

KYRGYZ S
TA N

N.
KOREA
S.

JAPAN

PACIFI C
OCEAN

ITALY

GREE

ARMENIA
AZER-
BAIJAN

TURKMENISTAN

TAJIKST AN

C H I N A

TURKEY

CYPRUS
LEBANON
ISRAEL

SYRIA

IRAQ

IRAN

AFGHANISTAN

Ryukyu
Is.

TUNISI A

JORDAN

KUW AIT

PAKISTAN

NE PAL

BHUT AN

TA IW AN

LIBY A

EGYPT

SAUDI
ARABI A

BAHRAIN
QATAR
U.A.E.

I N D I A

MY ANMAR

Hainan

THE
PHILIPPINES

Northern
Marianas
(U.S.A.)

Wake I.
(U.S.A.)

NIGE R

CHAD

YEMEN

Socotra
(Yemen)

BANGLA
DESH

THAILAND

VIETNAM

CAMBODIA

Guam
(U.S.A.)

MARSHALL IS.

NIGERI A

SUDAN

ERITREA

Andaman Is.
(India)

SRI
LANKA

BRUNEI

MAL A YSI A

PALAU

FEDERA TED ST ATES OF
MICRONESIA

CAMEROON

CENTRAL
AFRICAN REP.

DJIBOUTI

ETHIOPI A

MALDIVES

Nicobar Is.
(India)

EQUA-
GUINEA
GABON

UGANDA

SOMALIA

KEN YA

RW ANDA
BURUNDI

SEYCHELLES

Chagos Archipelago
(U.K.)

SINGAPOR E

I N D O N E S I A

PAPUA NEW GUINEA

KIRIBATI

DEM REP.
OF
CONGO

TA NZANIA

EAST TIMOR

SOLOMON

ANGOLA

ZAMBI A

COMOROS

INDIAN OCEAN

TUV AL U

FIJI

ZIMBABW E
BOTS -
WA NA

MOZAMBIQUE

MADAGASCAR

MAURITIUS

AUSTRALIA

VANUA TU

New
Caledonia
(France)

NAMIBIA

SOUTH
AFRICA

SWAZILAN D

LESOTHO

NEW
ZEALAND

Kerguelen
(France)

S O U T H E R N   O C E A N

| 0 | 2500 | | 5000 | | 7500 km |
| 0 | 1000 | 2000 | 300 0 | 4000 | 5000 miles |

A N T A R C T I C A

generation of iconoclastic intellectual modernism, and a political radicalism, which in the early 1920s allied the Guomindang government with the Soviet Union. Directly out of a part of the May Fourth Movement came also the Chinese Communist Party, founded in 1920. On the other hand, as China was never fully colonized, the ideologies of the colonial powers did not penetrate much of China, outside the swinging circles of Shanghai or the few pupils of American missionaries, and there was no colonial power in full control able either to crush or to co-opt the anti-imperialist movement.

The colonial/anticolonial road was central to Chinese modernity, but it was not the only one, as in, say, India or Nigeria. There was the road of social revolution. The ancient empire had fallen to an indigenous revolution in 1911, after a massive, ultimately defeated, mid-nineteenth-century upheaval, the Taiping rebellion. In Shanghai and other treaty ports a modern working class had emerged. In the May Fourth Movement it came forth as a national political force, in the *samba* or 'triple strike' of students, merchants and workers against Japan and the pro-Japanese Treaty of Versailles. The radical Chinese turn to the Soviet example after May 1919, and the import of Soviet advisers and Comintern organizers, made possible the forging of a strong Communist Party and led to a protracted revolutionary process. The Chinese communists under Mao's leadership became successful because they turned a European-type working-class party and class politics into a party of rural class struggle, and, above all, because they wedded their class politics to anti-imperialist, first of all anti-Japanese, nationalism. (See further the brilliant comparative study of class, modernity and revolution in St Petersburg and Shanghai by S. A. Smith 2008). The Guomindang under Chiang Kai-shek lost its nationalist credentials by its weakness, political as well as military, in front of the Japanese, and appeared as the defender of an increasingly malfunctioning and corrupt capitalism and landlordism.

In power, communist Chinese modernism staged a massive (and widely unpopular) attack against the most elaborate patriarchy of the world and created mass education and healthcare systems, as well as trying to build a socialist economy. Maoism continued to reproduce its hybrid background. Mao was a social revolutionary, in the Cultural Revolution vandalizing most of his own institutions of power. He was also a great admirer of the ancient Chinese imperial civilization, and his deal in 1972 with US President Nixon was a masterstroke of modernized imperial diplomacy. He is now mostly remembered and venerated – to an extent without comparison with

Lenin and Stalin in Russia – for his third role, as an anticolonial national unifier and liberator. The 'Four Modernizations' drive by his successors was a late, but powerful repetition of reactive modernization.

Legacies of the Routes to Modernity

Through colonial settlement, colonial rule and colonial threat, Europe left its imprint on the whole modern world (cf. Bayly 2004; Curtin 2000). But the world cannot be understood from the Western tip of the Eurasian continent. Even worldwide Europe-generated concepts like representative government and nation have acquired different meanings and rationales in other parts of the world. Key notions of social analysis, like religion and class, have vastly different significance in different parts of the modern capitalist world. The pathways to modernity have left enduring, though not perpetual or unchangeable consequences.

We can discern at least four lasting effects. One refers to the conception of the nation and its relation to language and culture, another to notions of government and of political rights, to political culture and behaviour, discourse, cleavages, organization. A third is modernity's consequences to religion, the major form of pre-modern culture. Finally, there are effects on social relations, on authority, deference, inequality, collective identity. We shall here hint at some of their concrete forms.

The different modern nations

The nation, through its marriage to a state, provides the most important collective identity of today. Only occasionally and among minorities is it trumped by any other identity, while there are, of course, always individual options. Islam is today the only religious identity which, in certain minoritarian milieus of some significance, can override a national one, and it is even then mainly blended with some anti-imperialist internationalism (cf. Haynes 1998; Roy 2004: 65ff). But in a polarized situation, like the rise of Bangladesh out of East Pakistan, only a small minority of Muslims stuck to a supranational religious allegiance (Khondker 2006). Occasionally, there are tiny, courageous human rights groups standing up against their own nation, in today's world most impressively, if ineffectively, in Israel.

The nation and the nation-state were European inventions, which, like representative government, spread around the world. But a similar concept took on different meanings, and was deployed for different reasons, with different consequences. I am not referring to divergent scholarly definitions and historiographic debates. (A swift introductory overview of the controversies around nation and nationalism, with brief contributions of some of the main figures, is given by Ichijo and Uzelac 2005). Here, a 'nation' is simply taken as a constructed political subject, in the name of which a right to some form of recognition and self-government – by no means necessarily a sovereign state – is claimed.

In a global perspective, two aspects of the European nation stand out. One is its anchorage in a popular and territorial history, distinguished from the landed property of princely power. The other is its heavy, distinctive cultural load, with spoken language at its core. The political dimension of the nation – important to the notion of 'freeborn Englishmen' – was most developed in the French republican current from the Revolution, as a nation explicitly open to non-natives. However, after the Revolution's embrace of all sympathizers, a mastering of the French language became required of all citizens of France, generating a large-scale programme of turning 'peasants into Frenchmen', as Eugene Weber's beautiful book names it (1979). The creation of national languages, i.e., through standardization among several dialects and by grammatical and orthographic codification, became a major task of European small nation intellectuals of the nineteenth century, from the Balkans to Norway. Where possible, minority languages were driven out of national culture.

The settler states of the Americas had to create new nations, which mythologically and emblematically of course drew upon historical examples as symbolic resources – ancient European republicanism in the case of the US, historical Catholic experiences and pre-Columbian, e.g., Inca and Aztec, high culture in Hispanic America – but which claimed no ethnocultural territorial history, and which shared their language with the colonial metropolis.

Most distinctive of the New World, however, was its conception of the nation as a club, to which desirable members could and should be recruited. Targeted immigration from Europe was a major dimension of nation-formation. 'To govern is to populate', a prominent mid-nineteenth-century Argentine politician and politician, Juan Bautista Alberdi, said (Chanda 2007: 165). Particularly in Latin American, Brazilian as well as, for instance, Argentine, discourse, this club member recruitment was explicitly referred to as 'whitening' or 'civilizing' the nation (Zea 1965: 65ff, 103ff; cf. Amnino and Guerra 2003). For a long time, only people of external, European descent were regarded as full citizens of the new nations of the Americas and Australia.

Nations of the colonial zone constitute a third variety. There were no historical territories, no singular historical peoples, only colonial boundaries. In a rare wise decision, African nationalist leaders decided to accept them all, however arbitrary and culturally divisive. Ali Jinnah did not, and British India, larger than any pre-colonial state of India, broke up into India – which Nehru refused to call Hindustan – Pakistan and Bangladesh, through terrible pogroms and wars of divorce.

The colonial language is arguably the most ostentatious legacy of the colonial pathway to modernity, with its ensuing complicated and hierarchical relations of nation and culture. The result was multilingual nations – Nigeria has 400–500 languages, according to different estimates (Simpson 2008: 172), and India has at least 122, according to a recent linguistic census analysis (Mitchell 2009: 7). The only exceptions developed in areas of developed pre-colonial interlingual trade, in the Indonesian archipelago, where a Malay lingua franca developed – in the mid-twentieth century renamed *Bahasa Indonesia* by the nationalists (see Anderson 2006: 132ff) – and in East Africa, in Tanzania and Kenya, where, less successfully, Swahili, the Bantu language developed out of the Arabian trade, was adopted as the national language, but along with English and local vernaculars (Githiora 2008; Topan 2008).

The European view, common both to the French and the German conceptions of a nation, though for different reasons, that a nation is defined by its language could not be applied in the ex-colonies. When it did, as in Pakistan, it had disastrous results, from 1952 bitterly dividing the Bengali East to the Urdu-promoting leaders of West Pakistan, where the Mughal hybrid of Urdu was not the majority mother tongue either (Rahman 2000).

A general legacy of anticolonialism is a strong nationalism as the decisive modern mass politics, which takes different forms from the various roads to independence but without any systematic internal cleavages. Postcolonial culture also tends to be starkly divided between elite and mass culture. Elite culture is usually conducted in the language of the former colonial power, a language which the majority of the population does not understand. In the capital city, the colonial divide is usually reproduced, the postcolonial elite taking over the official buildings and the private mansions and villas of the colonizers. Colonial administrative practices tend to be kept, although they are often subverted by corruption and/or a lack of state resources.

Traditional authorities and rituals tend to persist, drawing upon both their colonial institutionalization and their national credentials. In spite of their use in colonial indirect rule, traditional leaders were often incorporated into modern anticolonial nationalism. The founding programme (from 1948) of the radical Convention People's Party in Ghana, for instance, demanded, as its first objective, 'Independence for the people of Ghana and their Odikros [traditional rulers]' (Poe 2003: 96). Modern Malay nationalism, as the national Tunku Abdul Rahman museum in Kuala Lumpur narrates, started after the Second World War as a protest against British plans to reduce the powers of the traditional rulers and to institute an equal colonial citizenship for Malays, Chinese and Tamils alike. But independent India did away with the princely states of India.

The great linguistic diversity of most postcolonial states has meant a widespread maintenance of the language of the former colonial masters as the official or officious language of politics and business. Basically, the postcolonial nation is a colonial product, which implies a tendential reproduction inside the nation of the colonial divide of colonizer and colonized.

The nation of reactive modernization is the pre-modern realm, and is defined by the writ of the prince, the emperor, the king or the sultan. This was how the successful modernizers of Meiji Japan saw it, as did the less successful rulers of Siam and Abyssinia, and the soon defeated modernizers of Joseon Korea, Qing China and of the Ottoman empire. It was a historical legacy of rule, synonymous with its ruling dynasty, who often, though not in Japan, gave the realm its everyday name. The modern task here was not national emancipation, but the building of the realm into a nation. In Japan, this was greatly facilitated by the high ethnic homogeneity of the country, and the low salience of intertwined religions. The most important measure of national unification was the abolition of the feudal daimyo domains, returning their lands 'to the emperor'. The Meiji modernizers built a modern Japanese nation around the symbol and mystique of the Emperor, whose status, not his power, was more and more exalted as the modernization process progressed, culminating in the 1930s and during the Pacific War. As the pillar of national culture, the emperor survived the 'unconditional surrender' of 1945. His preservation was the last and only Japanese condition which the Americans finally accepted.

In Japan and Thailand of the twenty-first century, the monarch is a sublime national icon, in comparison with which even British monarchical deference and protocol pale into civic celebrity. The great modernizer of Siam, king Chulalongkorn, Rama V, has even become a figure of religious devotion, as I could notice at his equestrian statue in Bangkok in 2007.

National language and culture were not front issues. They were given by the realm, although the status of Sinic civilization culture came to suffer from the recurrent defeats of China. In the multinational and multicultural empires, of the Ottomans for instance, there was no national idiom to promote.

Representations of representative government

The European questions of modern representative government were: Shall government represent the people, or is government a divine right of kings? Who have the right to represent the people? How many political rights should be accorded the people and their representatives?

In spite of the inclusion of democracy and other forms of deliberative government in Europe's revered antiquity, in spite of the Roman law concept of *representatio*, spreading from business to politics, and in spite of the medieval traditions of representative government, with the two highest offices, of Pope and Emperor, elected, those questions took a very long time to be finally answered. In fact, it took 350 years, from the English Civil War of the 1640s to Swiss universal suffrage in 1971, the democratization of the Iberian peninsula in the mid-1970s, and the belated communist acceptance of competitive elections by the end of the 1980s. Even the principles of popularly elected government and of 'democracy', allowing for ambiguities of interpretation, took a long time to conquer the European mainstream, until the end of the First World War by the former, and until the defeat of fascism in 1945 by the latter.

Why it took so long, and so many revolutions, is a story too complex even to be summarized here. But underlying the whole process was that modern representative government in Europe concerned the fundamental internal socioeconomic ordering of society, around which there were many conflicting interests, well organized: the old ones from European medieval traditions and new ones from a rapidly evolving industrial class society. From the European pathway followed political systems of demarcated social cleavages and elaborated ideologies, deriving from fundamental internal conflicts and the motivation of opposite positions.

Traditional authorities, which finally lost in their frontal battles against modernity, were then seriously weakened or extinct.

Monarchs have become mere symbols, and accessible public figures, e.g., the traditional aristocracy, have either disappeared or, as in the UK, have been reproduced as royal decorations only (although a few immensely rich landowners of urban land remain – e.g., the Duke of Westminster).

We can still see politico-ideological effects, in a left–right party system with identifiable roots in the class structure, in class-structured economic organizations and institutions, of trade unions, employers' associations, and of unions' and employers' public bodies. Further, in a still living history of ideological -isms and programmes, almost all such -isms, from legitimism to anarchism and communism, are of European coinage. Only fundamentalism is not – it is a US invention, originally denoting Christian variants in the Bible Belt of the South.

In the New World of the Americas, rights and representations of the people were asserted in the wars of independence. Here the crucial questions were: Who are the people? How should political rights be implemented?

Were slaves, ex-slaves and Indians part of the people, whose rights the enlightened declarations of independence and new constitutions boldly proclaimed? No, obviously not. Conqueror–settler secession gave rise to a political culture of a uniquely huge gap between political rhetoric and political practice. The former was universalistic – freedom, rule of the people, rights of man, equality of men, the latter particularistic (sexist which for a long time was a universal particularism) and also fundamentally racist and institutionally manipulative. No one has better expressed this yawning gap in American political culture than George Washington, the national hero of the USA. During the war of independence, upon hearing that the last British governor was promising to set slaves free for supporting the British, Washington described him as an 'arch traitor to the rights of humanity' (Schama 2006: 18). Despite the defeat of the southern slave-owners in the American Civil War, racial universal suffrage was not established in the USA until 1968–70, after almost two centuries of independence.

Latin Americans were, on the whole, less rabidly racist than North Americans, but slavery persisted longer in Brazil (until 1888) than in the US, and explicit exclusion of illiterates from the right to vote was maintained in Chile, Ecuador and Peru until the 1970s, and in Brazil until 1989. The Australian Labour Party adhered explicitly to the slogan 'Keep Australia White!' until the 1970s.

The bifurcated political culture took several forms. One, by no means unique to the Americas, but there uniquely important as a focus of contention, was the rigging of elections. Therefore, the longest, bloodiest and most socially profound of revolutions in the hemisphere, the Mexican Revolution of 1910, started under the modest banner of 'Effective suffrage and no re-election' (of the President), and the landmark of democracy in Argentina came with the (President) Sáenz Peña Law of 1912, which established the notion of a secret ballot. The one-party US South did not officially legislate that Blacks had no political rights, but relied on devious subterfuge and practices to ensure it.

In the new settler worlds of the Americas, first of all, modern thought became the conventional mainstream after independence, fundamentally challenged only by Catholic clericalism, in Colombia and some other parts of Latin America. Secession leaves few internal cleavages, particularly if its opponents migrated out – to Canada from the US, to Spain from Peru – or were won over during the struggle for independence, as in Mexico. Nothing, or very little, was left of traditionalist politics and ideology. Liberalism – in a broad sense of defence of private pursuits, private property and private belief, in other words of liberty, and of commitment to science and progress (to reason) – has had a much wider intellectual hold than in Europe. Because of the much lower salience of ideological divides, Marxist thought and politics have occasionally been much more easily tacked onto mainstream political currents, such as US New Deal liberalism, Creole populism in Cuba, Guatemala and Argentina in the 1940s, or to Chilean radicalism and leftwing Christian democracy in the 1960s and 1970s. Or they have blended more easily with leftwing Christian movements, as in the Brazilian Workers' Party (PT) and the coalition behind the presidential election of Lula.

In the colonial zone, the key question of representative government was the representation of the colonized in the government of their country. Gradually, this was conceded by the British and the French (except in Algeria), but rejected by the Portuguese and by the African settler regimes of South Africa and Rhodesia. In the latter cases, independence as a result of war – or protracted struggles and international sanctions – but in the former, it came through constitutional negotiations. Independence was not a direct democratic conquest – it was rejected by referendum in all French Africa except Guinea in 1958 – but a deal negotiated by a political elite who had come to the fore through an electoral process, with variable constituency arrangements, as the legitimate representatives of the colonized people.

Representative government in the colonized zone centred around the rights of the colonized to represent their land; there was little about the rights and relations of the people vis-à-vis their representatives in government.

Politicians' representation of the people has tended to be tenuous and indirect in postcolonial politics, usually heavily overshadowed by executive power. Even an impressively resilient democracy such as the Indian has a political dynasty at its centre – the Nehru-Gandhi dynasty leading the dominant Congress Party. Political cleavages are rooted more in the pre-modern ethnic, religious and linguistic heterogeneities of the nation than in the class structure.

Shrewd rulers of countries of reactive modernization, of Meiji Japan, for instance, or the Young Ottomans in Istanbul, noticed that the powerful, threatening imperial powers had constitutional representative governments. This was interpreted as a key to their force and cohesion. So, in this fourth pathway to modernity, popular political rights and representative government emerged as a response to the question: How can national cohesion be strengthened?

The Japanese government in 1881 announced its plan to create a constitution by 1889 and to hold elections (with a very restricted suffrage) in 1890 – and it kept its promises. Rights of representation were given from above with a view to having 'the people satisfied and able to cooperate actively with the administration, in order to reach the goal of modernization and full national sovereignty' (Mason 1969: 24). Democracy, however, ensued only after national defeat and disaster, in the 1940s. In Turkey not even national disaster was enough. Following the crumbling Ottoman empire, there emerged a much more vigorous and forceful modernization from above under Kemal Atatürk, with more political participation, but no democracy.

Reactive modernization from above left little space for dissent. By definition, it meant an instrumentalization of nation, politics, science and progress with a view to preserving a regime under real or imagined external imperialist threat. Since liberty, equality and fraternity were in the mainstream reception predefined as means of the regime and its strengthening, their intrinsic social contradictions were kept out of sight or sidelined from the beginning. This did not, of course, prevent radical currents from entering, with modern ideas in general, into Japan, Siam, Turkey and the non-colonized Arab world, and later liberal dissent into the Soviet Union. But they encountered a more barren soil, as well as repressive vigilance, than in Europe or the Americas.

The whole idea of reactive modernization was to preserve traditional authority under new conditions. From such a route to moder-

76

nity, to the extent that it was successful, followed a deeply intertwined blend of modernity and tradition, of hierarchy and deference together with community, a pride in native tradition combined with a modernist curiosity for novelty. A pervasive small 'c' conservative nationalism has overwhelmed weak and/or volatile political-ideological cleavages. Deference to rank and seniority is still important in Japanese and Thai society.

The Modern Fate of Religions

Religion is everywhere an ancient, pre-modern institution. The rules and rites of the sacred were at the core of most pre-modern societies, and very much so of Europe. But in the breakthrough to the modern political era, religion played very different roles.

In the internal conflicts of Europe the established Christian churches, Protestant as well as Catholic and Orthodox, were on the losing side of anti-modern tradition. The pattern was set by the English Civil War and by the French Revolution, in spite of the fact that the early Revolution also counted men from the lower clergy in its early front ranks, like Abbé Siéyès and Abbé Grégoire. In the nineteenth century, the papacy became the centre of European anti-modernism. Protestantism dissolved into fission, between conservative High Church, and often moderately progressive dissent, a major basis of Anglo-Saxon and Germanic liberalism (cf. Porter 2000: ch. 5), while Latin European and Latin American liberalism tended towards anticlerical secularism. But there did also develop a reactionary Protestant fundamentalism, best represented by the Calvinist Dutch Anti-Revolutionaries, who started out as enemies of the French Revolution and remained so of all subsequent revolutions, including the anticolonial revolution of the 'East Indies'.

This anti-modernist stance cost the European churches dearly, and Europe is today the most secularized part of the world. But there have been exceptions, where the church became the main spokesperson of the nation against foreign, usually modernizing, powers. This happened in Catholic Croatia, Ireland, Lithuania, Poland, Slovakia, the Orthodox Balkans and Protestant Northern Ireland.

In the Americas, the dissenting Protestants of New England saw themselves as building a new social world, 'a city upon a hill', as well as being a vanguard to heaven. There was no established high church identified with British rule. North America today is the rich world centre of religiosity. It has pioneered a fusion of Christianity and capitalist enterprise, in 'theologies of success', and in television-beamed religious enterprises of personal pastoral promotion and devotional merchandise. It has also spawned a violent fundamentalism without any Christian equivalents anywhere else, but similar to recent militant Islamism. American crusaders attack abortion clinics, in particular, and the doctors who work in them, occasionally resulting in murder.

In Hispanic America, nationalism was often led by priests, like Hidalgo and Morelos in Mexico, receiving its formulations from them (Brading 1998: 43ff; Demélas 2003: 353ff). Mexican nationalists fought under the banner of the Virgin of Guadalupe, who first appeared in 1531. The church had been harassed by Spanish Bourbons of the second half of the eighteenth century, and was no colonial bulwark of royal Spanish power. The Enlightenment had influenced part of the clergy, who often also identified more with the Indians than with the Spanish power, like the Jesuit missions in Paraguay. Though European-inspired anticlericalism later reached the region, religiosity has remained a central feature of Latin American social life.

Belief in God remains constantly stronger in the USA than in Europe, more so in the USA than in Ireland, not to speak of Great Britain, stronger amongst Brazilians than amongst the Portuguese, stronger amongst the descendants of New Spain than those of Old Spain, stronger amongst Argentines than either Italians or Spaniards, stronger amongst Canadians than either the French or the British (Inglehart et al. 2004: F questions, esp. F063; cf. the similar results of Höllinger and Haller 2009: table 14.1; Rossi and Rossi 2009).

In the colonial zone, missionary religions, Christian much more than Muslim, have been conveyors of modernity, of modern education and healthcare, in particular. Many of the anticolonialist leaders, particularly in Africa, were educated in missionary schools. Native organized and codified religions, like Buddhism, Hinduism and Islam, on the other hand, have benefited from nationalist promotion. Unorganized African religion has been able to draw upon nationalist respect of traditional chiefs and customs. Colonial and ex-colonial societies have never been secularized. The modern ex-colony is today among the most religious parts of the globe.

In pre-modern East Asia, religion was always clearly subordinated to the secular rulers, and usually to a this-worldly official ethical culture, which might be summed up as Confucianism. This secular political subordination did not change with reactive modernization. East Asia today seems to be relatively secular by Euro-American standards of religious belief and practice, but it is hardly secularized.

Its world is by no means 'disenchanted' in the Weberian sense, but full of magical forces to be managed, like in the ex-colonial zone. When I visited a Buddhist temple in Tokyo, a Japanese colleague made an offering for his daughter's success in her upcoming exam.

In East Asian reactive modernization, religion was never challenged. Regional religiosity was actually more strengthened than weakened. The Japanese modernizers pushed state Shintoism, the Simaese monarchy guarded its Hindu-Buddhist rituals of legitimacy, and foreign missionaries implanted a minoritarian Christianity, even in Japan and in China, but most successfully in Korea (Protestant) and Vietnam (Catholic).

In the Ottoman empire, by contrast, Muslim clergy formed a bastion of reaction, overcome only by the shattering of the empire and the assertion of Mustafa Kemal Pàsha, later calling himself Father Turk, Atatürk, creating a secular Turkish state from above, with a subdued but pervasive religiosity below. While the Siamese and Abyssinian monarchies successfully managed to enlist Buddhism and Christianity, respectively, as royal supports, the post-Second World War modernizing Shah of Iran was finally felled by an Islamic revolution.

Under widely variable contemporary conditions, religions are still massive forms of modern life. But they are no longer overwhelming. There are more Chinese citizens in China, 1,320 million, than there are Muslims, of all varieties, in the world – around 1,270 million – and only slightly more Catholics in the world than Indians in India – 1,130 million and 1,123 million, respectively (Vatican figures on religion from *International Herald Tribune* 31/3/2009, p. 3 populations from World Bank 2009: table 1). Christianity, of all denominations, is adhered to by a third of humankind, Islam by a fifth, Hinduism by 14–15 per cent. The bulk of the remaining third of humanity is made up of the secularized-cum-pluri-religious Chinese and Japanese, followed by Southeast Asian Buddhism (about 6 per cent), African religions, and small minority beliefs, like Sikhism, Jainism and Judaism.

Windows of Opportunity

The open futures of modernity challenged hereditary inequalities, but in what direction and to what extent were very variable. In Europe, the modern thrust focused on the hereditary privileges of the aristocracy and the high clergy, and on the estates society in general.

The latter was gradually and unevenly followed by an industrial class society. The French Revolution replaced the rights and privileges of estates with a common national citizenship, and its land redistribution changed the distribution of income and wealth. 'Class', succeeding cultural/ceremonial 'rank', emerged as a central concept of European social analysis in the aftermath of the French Revolution, referring to the economically based new internal inequality of national societies (Wallech 1992). On the whole, West European income distribution seems to have been relatively stable for centuries up until the First World War, after which a significant economic levelling took place until the last decades of the twentieth century. Industrial capitalism did increase economic inequality though, as Marx had claimed – in Britain in the second half of the eighteenth century, in Prussia and Germany in the second half of the nineteenth century and in France from the July monarchy to the Third Republic (Lindert 2000; Morrisson 2000).

But from the dialectics of industrial capitalism came also, later, the force of equality – if not of socialism as Marx had envisaged. Europe is the least unequal region of the world, in particular Europe east of the British Isles, west of Poland, and north of the Alps (according to the Luxemburg Income Study, www.lisproject.org/key-figures).

In the Americas, human equality was held to be 'self-evident', as the American Declaration of Independence put it. The key question then became, 'Who are the equals?' – And the answer was also self-evident: white men. White North America in the eighteenth and nineteenth centuries was clearly less unequal than comparable European countries, not only lacking an aristocracy but also having a less skewed distribution of income and wealth than Britain. The liberal French aristocrat Alexis de Tocqueville was so overwhelmed by it in the 1830s that he came to see the 'gradual development' of equality as 'a providential fact', reading it back into French history from the eleventh century on (Tocqueville 1835/1961: 41). But white equality coexisted with black slavery, and the racial divide is still visible today in the urban ghettoes. Moreover, the white equality which mattered to the Founding Fathers of USA referred to 'life, liberty, and the pursuit of happiness', and did not include economics. It was existential and social. 'Class' – except for 'middle class', supposedly including everybody except the ethnic poor and the elite – has always had difficulties in coagulating in a society of settler individualism, ethnic immigration and race.

Hispanic American independence also included lofty declarations of civic equality, and was also rarely respected. Latin America was always more hierarchical than Anglo-America, and racially hierarchical, from Québec to La Plata, rather than dichotomized. The great German scholar Alexander von Humboldt was struck in 1811 by the enormous income inequality in New Spain (soon to become Mexico), but contrasted it with much less inegalitarian Lima (Humboldt 1822/1966: 83ff). Ibero-America was primarily a land of *conquistadores* (conquerors), rather than of settlers and immigrants. It is now one of the most unequal parts of the planet, combining Latin social hierarchies with legacies of extensive Indian servitude and of black slavery, recently augmented by massive 'informalization' of post-industrial, neoliberal labour markets. But at least until the full onslaught of neoliberalism in the late twentieth century, the two Latin countries most shaped by nineteenth-century mass immigration, Argentina and Uruguay, were markedly less unequal than the rest of the region.

In the colonial zone, the demand for equality was above all for equality with the colonizers. This set the stage for a postcolonial social division between the majority of the population, the poor, and the new political elite. Class organization has been confined to small modern enclaves, of dockers, railwaymen, miners, plantation workers, but few industrial workers. Many countries of sub-Saharan Africa are now similar to the Latin American ones in inequality, driven by postcolonial oil and other mineral rent and with even larger, marginalized urban slum populations. Corresponding to the racial divides of the Americas are ethnic ones in Africa, following locations in the colonial structure and/or the ethnic composition of the rulers.

While a sociocultural bifurcation of elite-population is a common feature of postcoloniality, national politics can, of course, make a major difference. In India, important equalizing steps were taken after independence, most importantly land reform and a vast programme of affirmative action for the lower, 'scheduled' castes, providing special access to education and public employment. An organized industrial working class began to develop, centred in the textile industries of Bombay, although it was always a small minority in the overwhelming non-industrial postcolonial economy, and in the 1980s was largely eradicated.

To the ruling elites of reactive modernization, equality was above all equality among modern nations. This was directed against the humiliating unequal treaties which China, Japan, the Ottoman empire and other pre-modern states had had forced upon them by the imperial powers of Europe and North America, providing special trade and port concessions and extra-territorial jurisdiction to those powers.

At the Versailles Peace Conference in 1919 Japan proposed a clause of 'racial equality' in the covenant of the League of Nations, of equality among nations regardless of race. The white settler dominions, Australia shrillest of all, opposed it, and US President Wilson had it thrown out of the preparing commission (Shimazu 1998).

However, the fact that today Japan and the two other Northeast Asian national development states most inspired by it, South Korea and Taiwan, constitute the economically least unequal region of the world, after Europe, also follows from the concerns of national cohesion and the notion of *noblesse oblige* characteristic of reactive modernization. Early on, the Meiji Restoration abolished the hereditary privileges of the samurai warrior estate, not upon popular demand but as part of a comprehensive programme of modern efficiency and cohesion. After the Second World War, fear of communism was conducive to land reform. Although South Korea, after its belated democratization, has some rather strong trade unions, Northeast Asian income equality is hardly able to be explained by internal class relations of force.

Existential status is another matter, the basically conservative reactive modernization wanted to preserve pre-modern hierarchy, etiquette and deference, and has largely managed to do so. While class organization and class conflict have had limited importance in both regions, the current Northeast Asian pattern of inequality is the opposite of the North American, more status and less income inequality.

Patriarchy and the rights of women could not break through as issues in the first decisive openings of political modernity, and gender equalization has its own trajectories, which can also be connected to the main historical pathways to modernity (Therborn 2004). But that is another story. Women played a significant part in the early period of the French Revolution, especially in Paris, and some courageous female revolutionaries tried to push human rights beyond the 'Rights of Man'. But they never managed to get a fair hearing in the male sites of power. The Revolution ended with an affirmation of a secularized patriarchy in the Napoleonic Civil Code of 1804, with its notorious clause of the husband being the '*chef de famille*', kept in France until 1970.

Powerful women's movements were pioneered in the USA and in other white settler countries, such as Australia and New Zealand in the nineteenth century, sustained by Protestant Christianity. They benefited from predominant modernist liberalism, and from their capacity to appeal to the ethnic solidarity of old immigrant settlers.

The first breakthrough of women's political rights came along the frontiers of New World settlement, in Oceania and in the USA west of the Missisippi (see further Therborn 1992).

However, the first egalitarian marriage legislation came in Northern Europe, right after the First World War, with broad centre-left reform in Scandinavia, and with a minoritarian radical revolution in Russia (Therborn 2004). The family was never swept away by modernity. In Europe and the Americas it was, in the end, strengthened by the success of the Industrial Revolution. In other parts of the world, there was always much less of a challenge. When sociologists today ask people in the world to describe who they are, from a list of ten possibilities, most people choose 'family or marital status'. Occupation is a clear second, gender and nationality, coming close together, take the third and the fourth rungs. Family status is most frequently invoked as the person's most important identity in the 'individualization' of white Anglophone countries and of Scandinavia ((Müller and Haller 2009: 182). However, family status has different meanings in the different family-sex-gender systems, which are also being reproduced.

— 2 —

WORLD DYNAMICS: HUMAN EVOLUTION AND ITS DRIVERS

The ground we are standing on, the social wombs from which we come, provide us with a background, an identity, a starting-point. But they provide no force of motion, nor, for that matter, any barriers to motion in any direction. Now we have to get at the dynamics of human society. What drives it? How does this 'what' look today?

The least arbitrary and the most promising approach to social change and dynamics seems to be to start from the evolution of living creatures, and from the specificity of humankind in the dynamics of life evolution. This is not sociobiology but a starting-point of social theory (cf. Runciman 2009). Human social evolution shares a basic framework with animal populations – their mode of livelihood and population development – in terms of both interdependence and interaction with a natural environment. With most sexually reproducing animals, and particularly with primates, we also share existential struggles for recognition, status and sexual access. Unique to humans are two other forces, which in interaction with the first three provide humanity with unique temporal and spatial scales, with history and sociology (social variability) – namely, culture and politics. Culture means transmission of learning via language and symbols; politics is the collective organization of power for a goal.

The evolution of humankind is a contingent, open-ended process, driven, primarily, through five fields of forces, of the mode of livelihood, of demographic ecology, of distributions of recognition, rank and respect, of cultures of learning, communication and values, and of politics (violent or non-violent) by collective organization. Though interdependent and interacting, and often in asymmetrical relationships of influence, these fields are, I am arguing, irreducible to each other. They are rooted in different aspects of the human condition, and of that of living organisms and animals more generally. Each field has its historically variable layout of constraints, inertia, new learning and innovation, traversed by the wide range of human capacities.

The dynamic processes of human evolution are of three basic kinds: interactions between humans and nature; within-field competition and imposition or selection (of technologies and modes of production, of fertility/mortality, of rankings and in/exclusion, of political system and power, and of cultures of knowledge and values); and imposition/selection through the interaction of fields, such as, for example, livelihood or culture changes by military political power, an imposition/selection only sustainable through recurrent economic and cultural processes, respectively. The selection of socialist economics, at the height of Soviet power and attraction, by a number of African countries soon turned out to be unsustainable, for example, as did the US project of imposing a liberal capitalist democracy on Iraq with its 2003 invasion.

The dynamic of the mode of livelihood, in Marxian terms the mode of production, has two elementary intrinsic sources. One derives from vital learning experiences in making a living and the cultural capacity to tell children and neighbours what you have learnt. This also includes negative incentives and cultural barriers to new learning or its transmission, visible in the long historical periods with virtually unaltered methods of livelihood and in the uneven distribution of techniques across the world. The other springs from intercultural trade and exchange, an ancient phenomenon operating among almost all modes of production. Adam Smith referred to it as a human 'propensity to truck, trade, and barter' – not the kind of explanation that is appreciated by sociologists, but, to my knowledge, there is, so far, nothing superior to it. The Marxian dynamic of the interrelation of forces and relations of production, driven from equilibrium to disequilibrium by the former, was really worked out only with reference to capitalism, to which we shall return below. Internal forces apart, there is also the natural environment, which may change for causes of its own – like the coming and going of ice ages – or because of human changes, negatively from, e.g., deforestation or gas emissions, or positively from patterns of irrigation or fertilization.

The relationship between population size, in recent times increasingly also the age structure, and a given area of environment is a second basic force of human history. Densely populated areas tend to give rise to different kinds of societies than sparsely populated ones, not seldom in conflict with each other as sedentary and nomadic populations. Good times can produce unsustainable populations, which then may be forced into decline, by famines, by infanticide, by postponed marriages (the favourite West European method) or by migration. Exogenous and drastic population decline, for instance of the Caribbeans in the early sixteenth century or in Hawaii in the early nineteenth century, can cause societies to collapse.

Because of politics and culture, human struggles for recognition and status become much more than fights for the most attractive (fe) males. They build armies, empires, parties, movements and monumental buildings, from the Egyptian pyramids to, for instance, the CCTV in Beijing. They organize societies in symbolically laden hierarchical orders, castes, estates, classes, elites and the rest.

Cultures qua cultures can reproduce themselves over long periods of time and space. As we saw above, two of today's major civilizations, the Sinic and the Indic, have a core of more than 2,500 years old, and a third, the European, has roots that stretch back as far. They can look back and deliberately renew themselves, in 'Renaissances' (Goody 2010). But they have an inherent dynamic potential, in their capacity to accumulate experience and knowledge, in their power of persuasion through communication. W. G. Runciman (2009) has made a useful distinction between modes of persuasion, coercion and production. Besides storing and transmitting knowledge, cultures provide us with an arc of identity wider than that of kin and flock, and with guides to action in the form of values and norms.

Fifthly and finally, there is politics. From the perspective of human social dynamics, the crucial characteristic of politics is a deliberate collective organization of power for attaining a certain goal. This is the force which creates kingdoms, states and churches, and resistance to them. It has its own logic, irreducible to cultural values as well as to class interests; it is an art of its own, of mobilization, strategies, alliances, tactics, compromises, legitimation, implementation, resistance, repression, negotiation and concession. You find this politics almost everywhere, outside very strict and tight hierarchical bureaucracies – such as exemplary armies, judiciaries and corporations – for instance, in sports clubs, in mosque or church communities, in labour movements and in corporate boardrooms, in politburos as well as in parliaments and in extra-parliamentary social forums.

So, I am arguing that there are five main drivers of humankind: the mode of livelihood, population ecology, existential struggles for recognition and respect, the politics of collective power, and cultural learning and orientations. The dynamics specific to human society derive from their combinations, which make social evolution – i.e., history – possible. The human capacity for cultural accumulation and transmission, and for politics of collective organization, enables us to develop our mode of livelihood or production, to overcome many, though by no means all, environmental constraints, and to elaborate a number of forms of recognition and respect, and of their denial.

How the five drivers worked to bring about our geological grounds of layered historical cultures was touched upon above, albeit without finger-pointing. But our main question is, 'How does this fivefold dynamics look today?' The answer will come from two angles. First we shall take an eagle's view at the current state of our five variables, then we shall look into their current mode of operation on a global level. That will take us to the task of breaking 'globalization' up into a set of distinctive global processes, from which we shall have analytically to separate subglobal ones, in order to make it possible to say something meaningful and empirically grounded about the relative weight of global and national (and other subglobal) forces upon human lives today.

Modes of Livelihood : The Ups and Downs of Capitalism, and the Rest

That there was a historical evolution of human modes of livelihood was first theorized by the Scottish Enlightenment, followed up and elaborated by Marx and his concept of modes of production. Marx also theorized the dynamics of these modes, in the interaction between the forces and the relations of production, the former referring to technology and the mode of productivity, the latter to property, ownership and the social relations of producing. He saw a self-destructive dynamic of capitalism, basically through its competitive dynamism bringing forth an increasingly 'social character' of the forces of production, of large-scale enterprise and dependence on large infrastructural investment and scientific research, less and less effectively manageable in private relations of production, and bringing together vast concentrations of workers antagonistic to capitalists.

By Marx himself, as well as in most later Marxists, this dialectical analysis was inserted into an eschatological frame, pointing to the end of capitalism and a communist future, via socialism. But the analysis may also be looked at on its own, outside political expectations and commitments. For a mid-nineteenth-century social analysis, then, it stood up remarkably well in the twentieth century. Capitalist development did tend to substitute public or quasi-public for original private ownership, in telecommunications, urban transport, railways and energy production, largely independent of right- or leftwing governments. Public investments in education and science have become increasingly important to competitive economic productivity. Enterprises and workers did become more concentrated, and the latter better and better organized in trade unions and in parties claiming to represent them. Industries succeeded each other as centres of working-class organization and protest, from textiles to automobiles (Silver 2003: ch. 3). True, for reasons which readers of this book should not be surprised by now, this story unfolded most fully in Europe, along the European road to and through modernity, but it involves something of the rest of the world as well, in particular the settler New World (for evidence and references, see Therborn 1984, and 1995: 68ff).

But then, in the last third of the twentieth century, economic history took a new turn. High economic development came to mean deindustrialization, with accompanying deconcentration of workers, and privatization was the new government policy, for the left as well as the right. No Marxist, so far, has dared to use analytical tools to explain the recent defeats of labour, socialism and communism. But, at least as far as classical social and economic theory go, a Marxian perspective is probably the most promising.

The unprecedented economic growth of industrial capitalism after the Second World War, foreseen by nobody, did bring workers together, in unions, in parties and as voters, but it also came to include an enormous increase of discretionary consumption, a solid material base of individuation, that was not incompatible with Marx's communist utopia, which was basically individualist, 'from everyone according to his ability, to everyone according to his needs', but which undermined mobilizations for socialism.

The social–private dialectic of forces and relations of production changed for at least three reasons in the last third of the twentieth century. First, the new level of industrial productivity required far fewer workers, repeating an earlier agricultural development – which Marxism never grasped – and the rapidly growing service sector tended to operate on a much smaller enterprise scale. Secondly, new electronic technology provided vastly enhanced opportunities for deconcentrated production and service delivery. Train and telephone operators could now be separated from the networks of railways and telephones, facilitating competing private enterprise. The design of products, from cars to clothes, could be tailor-made to masses of consumers. Thirdly, new financial instruments generated enormous pools of capital, normally surpassing public resources, even in rich countries with well-run states.

The Soviet Union was competitive technologically, in its priority areas, up to the 1960s, especially with the Sputnik space triumph of 1957, and there was a great communist buzz in the mid-1960s about a new 'scientific-technological revolution', which was elaborated on especially in a Czechoslovakian report of the late 1960s (Richta et al. 1969) But the 1968 clampdown on heterodoxy started a period of stagnation, which could never be overcome. The actual imploding process of the USSR was politically driven, but the outcome was, of course, a great victory of capitalism. So too was China's taking the capitalist road in the 1980s. Capitalism in Russia, and in many parts of ex-communist Eastern Europe, has so far proved a disaster for millions of people. In the 1990s, the restoration of capitalism in the former USSR brought about 4 million deaths (above what could be expected from the 1970s/80s), through several psychosomatic channels, from unemployment, insecurity, stress, demoralization and impoverishment (Marmot 2004: 196; cf. Cornia and Panicciá 2000; Stuckler et al. 2009). In China, the price of capitalist success included an additional 30 million illiterates, measured between 2000 and 2005, and an increase in the mortality rate of infant girls in the 1990s produced by the collapse of the rural educational and health care system (Huang 2008: 244ff). Despite its dynamism, capitalism always comes with a price to be paid by the weak and the vulnerable.

In sum, the technological forces of production have turned from being increasingly social, or concentrated, to being more deconcentrated and more private, and private relations have greatly extended their range of operations through new developments of the financial markets.

On the horizon of 2010, there is no sign of a reversal of this pro-capitalist turn of the Marxian dialectic, although the financial crisis of 2008–9 has revealed, at least, that we are still in boom and bust cycle, and, perhaps, in the North Atlantic region, in for a prolonged period of relative stagnation. In the system as whole, however, there are no visible signs of a systemic stagnation, or of a 'stable state', envisaged by many economists of the 1930s and 1940s. A continuing capitalist propulsion of new technology is to be expected. The predominance of finance seems largely to have to have survived the crisis, and remains likely to direct the future dynamics of capitalism.

But while the persistent reign of capitalism is most likely to be our fate for the foreseeable future, it is far from being the whole story of the dynamics of human livelihood.

There is more to capitalism than profit-hunting entrepreneurs on markets. Capitalism also means workers, classes and class conflict. That is why 'market economy' is a misleading ideological euphemism for capitalism. Workers and the working-class movement have been seriously weakened by the recent pro-capitalist turn, but they have not vanished. They are still a very significant force in Europe – although a Scandinavian may be appalled by the apparently publicly legitimate strike-breaking labour arrangements of Royal Mail and of British Airways in the autumn and winter of 2009 and 2010 – and non-negligible in the northern United States. Among the so-called BRIC countries, workers have maintained some clout in Brazil and in Russia. Indian unions are politically divided, and have taken a heavy beating industrially in recent decades, while keeping a public presence. China is, in this respect as in so many others, the decisive but unpredictable joker, to which we shall return in the conclusions below. But in the spring of 2010 Chinese workers showed their strength from the very success of capitalism in China, in very successful strikes against Japanese Honda car plants and against the largest electronic components maker of the world, Taiwanese Foxcom.

The predominance of capitalism is most likely to involve the persistence of workplace conflict, which may or may not spread into further social upheaval. Even if socialism has fallen below the horizon, it continues to flicker between La Paz and Havana, and not everyone in the world is earning their livelihood in capitalist systems. As we shall see later, at most only 40 per cent of humans are doing so.

Population Ecology and the Ending of Modern Ecological Emancipation

Over the long run, human evolution has meant an ascending autonomy in relation to the environment. The Industrial Revolution, and its slightly older and less celebrated sister, the Western European Agricultural Revolution, meant a fundamental break in human ecology, radically loosening if not destroying the link between a sustainable population and the more or less unchanging food supply of its habitat. Until then, in spite of its inventive reshaping of its natural habitats, i.e., in spite of human civilization, humanity was subject to basically the same constraints as other animals. Good harvest and good times generated population growth up to the point at which limited resources curbed it, by famine, malnutrition and disease. This basic principle of population ecology was fully theorized, for humans, by the British clergyman of the late eighteenth century, Thomas Malthus. On a large scale, this merciless ecological equilibration still operated in nineteenth-century Asia, in China for instance (Peng and Guo 2000; Pomeranz 2000).

But eighteenth-century changes in agricultural productivity laid the basis for a sustained and unprecedented European population increase in the nineteenth century, not altogether without famines though, as happened in Sweden of the late 1860s. Then trans-ocean shipping of grain and meat from the Americas and Oceania kept Europeans fed. The steamships also made accessible an escape route for the European poor, from the meagre environment of Europe to the rich lands and vast opportunities of the New World. From the 1960s, the so-called Green Revolution that resulted in higher-yielding rice and wheat relieved much ecological pressure on Asian populations. Industry was originally very nature-dependent, on coal seams and tameable water power in particular. The location of much current manufacturing production, from sneakers and shirts to TV sets, computers and mobile phones, is largely nature-independent, and mainly determined by the cost and the skills of human labour.

However, space and distance have by no means become irrelevant to social development. Like Minerva's owl at dusk, the World Bank (2009) has belatedly devoted major efforts to gauge their importance. The current shape of the social geography of Africa, with its weak, fragile and disrupted transport links, for example, is claimed to be a major constraint on possibilities of development.

Reproduction itself is no longer predetermined amongst human populations. Birth control, once practised only by the elite, became a mass phenomenon in early nineteenth-century France and the USA, the countries of the two most socially profound modern revolutions, and towards the end of the century it became a continental European movement. After the Second World War, birth control and family planning were encouraged in Asia, a very specific piece of global action, and gradually became acceptable in Latin America from the 1960s, reaching sub-Saharan Africa by the 1990s. They reached the poorest continent last, and although Africa is territorially not overpopulated – much lower rates of population density than the world average and on a par with the high-income countries – extremely rapid population growth in the 1960s–80s exceeded continental productive and political capacity, adding

91

significantly to post-independence impoverishment. The tropical load of parasites and disease, once a scourge of European colonial invaders, officials and settlers, is still there, also weighing Africa down.

Current ecological concerns should be seen against the modern background of human emancipation from many demographic-ecological constraints. Between 1900 and 2000 the human population increased from 1.6 billion to 6.1 billion, while life expectancy at birth rose from about 32 to 66–67 years (Riley 2005: table 1). But what humankind faces in today's world is a quite different question. Can the rest of the world live as Americans now expect to live? Or will attempts to move in that direction result in the destruction of many human habitats, brought about by climate change?

If the current course of climate development is not changed, informed opinion tends to agree, natural habitat changes will again bring population deaths and/or force populations to move. Drought will hit some areas – particularly northern South Asia and Africa – flooding others, and low-level islands and densely populated delta countries, like Bangladesh, will be submerged under a rising sea level. How far current climate tendencies will go is anybody's guess, but even in more optimistic scenarios we are likely to see ecologically driven waves of migration, on a scale far larger than from the Oklahoma 'dust bowl' in the 1930s or from the Sahel since the 1970s.

It seems that the modernist emancipation from ecology, from the natural constraints of food supply, endemic disease and of productive locations, made possible only by very different roads and paces of travelling to modernity, is now ending. With respect to microbiotica and infectious diseases, a reverse began already in the 1970s, with the return of malaria and tuberculosis (McNeill 2000: 201ff). Where the world will end up under the new environmental constraints is undecided. Optimists may draw some comfort from the fact that the global environment has lately become an urgent worldwide political concern. On another question – whose environmental interests will come first, those of the rich and powerful or those of the most vulnerable? – the Copenhagen Conference of December 2009 clearly pointed in the former direction.

Ecological demography may have another surprise for the successful late twentieth-century missionaries and practitioners of birth control and family planning. Demographers have been proud of a grand theory, combining universal scope with a strong empirical anchorage, a rare combination in the social sciences (see, e.g., Chesnais 1992). It is a theory about humankind moving from one population equilibrium to another, through a valley of 'demographic transition'. Until modern times, high rates of both births and deaths ensured the equilibrium. Then death rates started falling and human populations increased rapidly, backed up by falling birth rates. The time span of the demographic transition is assumed to run between 1750 and 2050. Sociologists and historians tend to argue over what many see as the too-elegant-to be-true universalist theory of the transition (Therborn 2004: Part III).

But a further issue is that there seems to be no necessary new population equilibrium to transit to. Instead, several human populations in times of peace and economic development are on course to decline. Post-Communist Europe and Germany are already shrinking, and Italy and Japan are about to. Extrapolations of their demography of the 2000s point to a decline of the European population by about 10 per cent until 2050, and of the Japanese by 20 per cent (UNFPA 2008: 90ff). Shrinking populations entail ageing, with accompanying problems of care, and of resources for it.

Other countries are facing other effects of different age structures of their population. A rapidly growing employable labour force is a major boon to economic growth, as experienced by Japan and the rest of East Asia after the Second World War, a boon that is beginning to come to an end in China. On the other hand, having a large number of young people before or out of employment, a 'youth bulge', can be the basis for frustrated sociopolitical instability, discernible in the Arab world and in sub-Saharan Africa. Registered youth unemployment is by far the highest in the world in the Middle East and North Africa, running at between 20 and 25 per cent of the workforce, even before the general economic crisis (ILO 2010: Table A3).

The most ancient and most elementary of human social dynamics, the interdependence of population and environment and the dependence of societies upon their populations, have not gone away, in spite of powerful modern mutations. These are now taking on new forms and a new significance.

The Ethnic, Religious, and Sexual Dynamics of Recognition and Respect

There is a game of experimental economics which has fascinated well-bred economists, but which may seem rather trivial to Mr and Mrs Jones. Two people are allocated a sum of money between them, usually $100. One of them is given the power to propose how it should be shared. The other person can accept the proposal or refuse it, but if it is refused, neither of them gets anything. To the surprise of the experimenters, people tend to refuse offers below a 40:60 division as being unfair and humiliating, even though they can be sure of getting, say, $10, $20, or $30.

Recognition, respect and honour operate differently, and with varying strength, in different human cultures. Nevertheless, they constitute a major existential dynamic of human relationships, from urban street encounters to large imaginary communities or between states. On the whole, the importance of recognition and respect tends to grow in size with the decline of pre-modern deference, because it is more contestable and no longer certain.

Currently and globally, this existential dynamic takes two major collective forms, but several others are also up and running. One is ethnic, spearheaded by the ethnicities suppressed or left by the wayside by the different modern nation projects. They are now emerging as indigenous peoples, or as 'First Nations', rather than as marginalized 'tribes', or simply as ethnic 'fringes' or peripheries. This is a particularly explosive issue in settler countries that impose themselves on densely populated territories. South Africa has already had to abdicate from being a settler country to being an ex-colonial one. Bolivia is on the same road, but with the white dethronement still contested. The Zionist settlers of Palestine are still violently fighting off a similar outcome. Where there are relatively few natives, a new accommodation has generally been reached in recent times, most extensively in Canada and New Zealand.

The second major thrust for respect is religious. Islamism has become a major vehicle of resentment against Western arrogance and bleak life-course perspectives. This should be seen as largely a contingent political manifestation, and certainly not as an intrinsic 'clash of civilizations'. It feeds on the Zionist expansion in Palestine, supported and partly financed by the US, on the American support of the leading authoritarian regimes of the Arab world, Mubarrak's Egypt and Saudi Arabia, and on the presence of American troops in the land of the holy cities of Mecca and Medina. The recent American-cum-British wars in Afghanistan and Iraq and their frantic stoking of warfare in Pakistan have resulted in resentment and outrage.

Western writers have competed in stressing that Islamist leaders, cadres and militants tend to originate from educated and economically secure or well-off backgrounds. That should be no surprise: rebellion against humiliation and disrespect requires a sense of worth, which comes more easily to people who have at least some resources than it does to the most downtrodden. Violent religious clashes in Muslim–Christian interfaces in Nigeria, Indonesia, the Philippines and Malaysia, and Hindu–Muslim ones in India have ethno-economic as well as religious drives, but they are part of the contested landscape of religious recognition.

The working-class movement for the respect of workers is currently subdued, although its struggles continue every day. In the rich world, class has been overtaken by sexuality. Public attention has been homing in on sexual harassment, which has become a legally serious form of disrespect. Since the 1970s, feminists have been quite, if far from fully and universally, successful in claiming recognition and respect for women. The limelight is also on homosexuality; in 2004, a conservative Italian Catholic was successfully prevented from becoming a member of the European Commission for failing in this respect (by calling it a sin).

Pre-modern polities and rulers were generally more concerned with protocols of recognition and respect than contemporary ones. But attention to the latter have by no means disappeared. Among the Americanophile political elites of Europe, there was, for instance, a race to have their leader the first European invitee to the White House of Obama (Gordon Brown, who probably coveted it the most, won the prize.) The status of post-Soviet Russia in global politics has been an important concern amongst the elites. Could drastically impoverished Russia, emerging finally from total Soviet defeat in the Cold War, and, in terms of policy, in the hands of a swarm of Western 'advisers' from economists to political spin doctors, remain a respectable power? It was one of the very few wise decisions of the Clinton government to say, 'yes, it could', and in 1997 to invite Russia to turn the G7 group of the world's then leading economies into G8, without asking for any economic qualifications of the Russians. That is the benevolent reading; a more malicious runs like this. Contrary to Western promises to Gorbachev in 1989–90 (Sarotte 2009), the military power of NATO was vigorously pushed eastward, closing in on Russia. G8 membership was a symbolic consolation prize to the Russians. Nevertheless, respect and recognition count.

In the Palestine conflict, respect and recognition are at the very centre. To the Zionists and their friends, the key questions is, 'Do the Palestinians recognize the right of Israel to exist?' To the Palestinians it is, 'Do you recognize the right of all Palestinians to live in Palestine, in a state of their own?' Given the relations of force, the PLO has conceded the first, while Israel and all pro-Zionist powers and forces have denied the second: no normal Palestinian

state controlling its borders and capable of defending itself is acceptable, no right for Palestinian refugees and deportees to live in Palestine can be conceded. The asymmetric power relations have also given
rise to another game of respect. The Israelis and their international
backers are demanding that the Palestinians – without tanks, air force
or missiles, not to speak of nuclear bombs – should 'renounce violence', while, so far, no 'international community' spokesperson has
demanded that the Israelis and their formidable *Tsahal* army or
global assassination agency *Mossad* should do it.

Respect and recognition are almost always unequal, and therefore
almost always susceptible to contestation. They also call for symbolic
expressions. Commemorations, which seem to have increased
in number in recent decades, monuments and monumental architecture – 'iconic buildings' – owe their existence to cravings for them.
What should be commemorated has become competitive politics and
lobbying, internationally as well as nationally.

Politics of Collective Power: State Apotheosis

States are the most powerful organizations of collective power. This
is an era of powerful states. In terms of destructive and coercive
power, we are currently living with the most formidable state in
human history, which has the capacity to destroy all our homes
across the world and to kill us all, several times over – a state whose
military might is larger than that of all other states combined, at least
to judge from the size of its military expenditure. At no time before
has a single state had the unrivalled military power of the USA today,
a product of the resources of the world's largest economy and a
single-minded political top priority of military superiority.

In the longer run, the ongoing gradual challenges to US economic
dominance make this enormous power of destruction dangerous
to the world. We know already that at any time a US President can
point his finger at any point on the globe and demand that it
be destroyed, as Bill Clinton did in 1998 to a village in Afghanistan
and a fertilizer plant in Sudan in response to a hostile act in a third
country (Kenya). True, military power has its limitations, beyond
destruction. Paraphrasing and technologically updating Henry
Kissinger's role model, the mastermind of the European post-
revolutionary Holy Alliance, Prince Metternich, said 'you can do
much with air-strikes, but you cannot sit on them' ('them' originally
referring to bayonets).

Many state borders are now more tightly controlled than ever before. Passports and visas are required to pass – both of which were exceptional before the First World War – and electronic checks, mostly by taking finger prints, have to be delivered; in addition, your name has to be absent from the ever lengthening lists of suspects. Whatever world we are living in, it is not a 'borderless' one, as a guru of globalization claimed in the 1990s.

We noticed above that the dynamics of capitalism took a new turn in the last decades of the previous century, towards a more harmonious relationship between the forces and the private relations of production. However, with peripheral exceptions – most notably, perhaps, Argentina under Carlos Menem – this did not lead to a dismantling of the core capitalist states. The new path of capitalism stopped the state from growing, but the political logic of collective organization had by then already landed nation-states on a high plateau in terms of size and resources, with public revenue and expenditure around 40–50 per cent of rich countries' GDP. In the most recent financial crisis, those resources were put to rescue private capital from itself, in enormous bank bail-outs and unprecedented 'stimulus packages'.

Twentieth-century politics generated two very successful state forms, which emerged in the 1960s: the Western European welfare state, based on generous, publicly financed social entitlements, and the East Asian 'autonomous outward development' state. They have both been successfully deployed and consolidated ever since. If the core region of the first examples of welfare statism has been Western Europe, it has had an impact on all the original OECD countries, including the USA. Although its European roots go back a long way, it was in the years after 1960 that the welfare stage began to soar – the expenditure and revenue of the state suddenly expanded, in about a decade, more than it had done during its entire previous history. Unnoticed by conventional globalization theory, the last four decades of the twentieth century have seen the developed states grow at a far greater rate than international trade. For the old OECD nations as a whole, public expenditure as a proportion of GDP increased by 13 percentage points between 1960 and 1999, while exports grew by 11 per cent (that is, for the OECD countries before the recent inclusion of Mexico, South Korea and post-Communist East Central Europe). For the then 15 members of the European Union, the corresponding figures are 18–19 and 14 per cent (OECD 1999: tables 6.5, 6.12).

Despite the many claims to the contrary, the welfare state still stands tall wherever it was constructed. Whether measured by public expenditure or by revenue, the public sector in the richest countries of the world is, historically, at peak or top-plateau level. For the OECD countries of Western Europe, North America, Japan and Oceania, the national, inter-country average of total government outlays (unweighted by population, but exclusive of Iceland and Luxembourg) in 1960 was 25 per cent of GDP. By 2005 it stood at 44 per cent. For the G7, public outlays increased from 28 per cent of their total combined GDP in 1960 to 44 per cent in 2005 (OECD 2006). True, the expenditure share in both cases was a couple of percentage points higher during the recession years of the early 1990s than in the later boom, but that should be interpreted as a largely conjunctural oscillation. In terms of taxes, in 2006 the OECD beat its own historical record of tax revenue, from 2000, and registered its highest revenue ever, about 37 per cent of GDP flowing into public coffers. (See OECD News Release 17/10/2007: www.oecd.org. The EU15 stayed slightly below its 2000 record, at 39.8 as compared to 40.4, a difference within the margin of statistical error in the national accounts.) This is not to deny that there is a growing need and demand for education, health and social care and retirement income, which will require further growth of the welfare state – a growth which is currently stultified by rightwing forces, in the spring and summer of 2010 on their march forward.

The second new state form – its breakthrough again coming in the 1960s (after the pre-war Japanese take-off) – has been that of the East Asian autonomous outward-development model, very different from the Latin American alternatives of dependent capitalism and import substitution: internally organized, by state planning and control of finance; world market export-oriented, of manufacturing, not of primary commodities, which are largely lacking; and sustained by universal education and national social cohesion. Pioneered by Japan, the development state soon became – with varying combinations of state intervention and capitalist enterprise – a regional model, with South Korea (perhaps now the archetype), Taiwan and the special city-states of Singapore and Hong Kong blazing the trail for Thailand, Malaysia, Indonesia and, less successfully, the Philippines (the latter, culturally and socially, is something of a Latin America in Southeast Asia, still sporting a powerful landowning oligarchy, for instance). These were the examples that China would draw upon from the late 1970s – as, a decade later, would Vietnam.

There is considerable variation between these states and their differing forms of capitalism. But all arose within a common regional context – a Cold War frontier area receiving a great deal of US economic (and military) support. All shared a regional development model, in Japan; a broken, or absent, landed oligarchy; a high rate of literacy; a strong entrepreneurial stratum – outside Japan and Korea, usually a Chinese diaspora. For the most part, they have also had similar political regimes: authoritarian, but not kleptocratic, and strongly committed to national economic development through international competitiveness, with the will to implement decisive state initiatives of various kinds.

The West European welfarist and East Asian development states were rooted in very differently patterned societies, by civilizations but even more by pathways to modernity, and their political priorities have been quite distinct. But qua states, and economies, they have had two important features in common. First, they are both outward looking, dependent on exports to the world market. Contrary to conventional opinion, there has been a significant, and consistent, positive correlation between world-market dependence and social rights munificence among the rich OECD countries: the more dependent a country is on exports, the greater its social generosity. (In the mid-1990s the Pearson correlation measure of exports and social expenditure as a percentage of GDP in the original OECD countries was 0.26. There is probably no direct cause and effect here. Rather, the link should be interpreted as meaning that international competitiveness has contributed, through growth, to the weight of progressive forces, and has not been incompatible with the latter's policies of extending social entitlements. See Therborn 1995.)

Secondly, for all their competitive edge and receptivity to the new, neither the welfarist nor the development states are wide open to the world market's winds. Both models have established, and maintain, systems of domestic protection. Among the welfare states, this takes the form of social security and income redistribution. When Finland, for instance, was hit by recession in the early 1990s, with a 10 per cent decline of GDP and unemployment climbing to nearly 20 per cent, the state stepped in to prevent any increase of poverty, and maintained one of the most egalitarian income distributions in the world (www.lisproject.org/kry-figures). The Finnish economy is now riding high again – Finnish Nokia is the world leader in mobile phones. By European standards, the Canadian welfare state is not particularly developed; nevertheless, despite the country's close ties with its massive neighbour – reinforced now through NAFTA – it has been able to maintain its more egalitarian income distribution over the past 20 years, whereas US inequality has risen sharply.

The politics among states is largely governed by their geological grounding, which defines their 'national interest', their civilizational roots, their relation to the waves of globalization, old and recent, and their path to modernity. But also by their relative size today.

Current global politics also has another dimension. A virtual *ummah* of militant Islamists, culturally uprooted, isolated individuals or tiny groups, connected through militant websites, seems to be the main force and the breeding ground for trying lethal protests or revenge, 'terrorism', against USA and its allies, rather than the shadowy al-Qaeda organization or any territorial jihadist culture (Roy 2010). In what resembles a war of mosquito versus elephant, the most powerful state in human history has been challenged by a loose international Islamist network which managed a spectacular and bloody attack on symbolic targets in New York and Washington, but which were incomparable in destructive scope to the American air wars of the past two decades. Blowing up this tiny, no doubt vicious, band of violent fanatics into a major threat has become a central theme of US imperial policy in the twenty-first century, spanning regime changes in the White House.

Comparing al-Qaeda to Nazi Germany, as Barack Obama did in his acceptance speech on receipt of the Nobel Peace [!] Prize in Oslo in December 2009, in order to justify his escalation of wars in Afghanistan and Pakistan, manifests the continuity of imperial politics, which started with George W. Bush using the Islamist al-Qaeda attack as a motivation for invading the secular regime of Iraq. Obama, who in contrast to his predecessor is neither stupid nor ignorant, knows, of course, that his argument has no substance, that it was no more than cheap rhetoric employed to trick a most gullible audience. By awarding him the Nobel Peace Prize, the committee of politicians had hoisted Norwegian political sycophancy to the vicinity of North Korean altitudes – Nazi Germany was a big, well-organized state, with strong industrial muscles, the world's most formidable landed army, and a very threatening *Luftwaffe* and submarine navy. The al-Qaeda leaders, in whatever cave they are hiding, might command a few hundred men, without a single aircraft, drone or medium-range missile, and with no tanks, not even body armour. But this is the kind of rhetoric out of which politics is made. (For an analytical, instead of political, overview of recent anti-American 'terrorism', see Shane 2010).

Democracy, in the literal sense of rule by the people as a whole, is a rare species, always endangered. But if we take it in a more permissive sense as competitive polyarchy, i.e., of more than one centre of

100

collective organization legitimately competing for governmental power, then 10 of the 11 most populous countries in the world would qualify, with monocentric China being the only exception. This is a world historical record, and the expensive international effort of armed power to stage elections in Congo, Iraq and Afghanistan is a remarkable tribute to virtue from the vice of big power politics. But current democracy had better not be idealized. It includes not only the political working of wealth, but also the dynastic politics of the US and the Japanese congresses, of South Asian premier politics, of heavy-handed central 'management' of elections in Russia, and of massive local intimidation and fraud in Nigeria, Mexico and Iran, not to speak of Egypt and many smaller countries.

Within states, the most noteworthy recent development is that of new forms of political mobilization, by mobile phones – for text messages and images more than conversation – and via the internet and the so-called blogosphere. The new media were crucial to the Obama campaign in the US of 2008 as well as to electoral protests in Teheran in 2009. In neither case were they substitutes for physical volunteering and presence, but they were decisive in bringing people together. In Egypt on 6 April 2008, Facebook provided a means for remarkable class solidarity between factory workers of the Al Mahalla El Kobra town north of Cairo and young middle-class people of the metropolis. On the day that workers went on strike, there were sympathy actions and demonstrations in downtown Cairo, summoned by Facebook. As in Tehran, the authorities cracked down, but the medium was the message (el Magd 2008).

Cyberpolitics is a new dimension of politics, but it remains within the historically handed down geopolitical parameters.

Culture: Modernism Globalized, Accelerated and Chastened

Our basic cultural orientations are wired into us out of the cultural layers, from civilizations to the latest waves of globalization. As such, they constitute an enormously rich variety of human experience and perspectives. Some of that variety has been touched upon above, some more will be looked at below. Here we shall focus on another question: can anything of substance be said about the predominant cultural orientation of all humankind today?

We might start approaching that question by asking another one: is this a modernist or a postmodernist world? In chapter 1, we gave a definition of modernity, a world following an arrow of time, oriented to a new, makeable future, turning its back, not necessarily without respect, on the past. We took note of modernity's different pathways to victory. In the last decades of the twentieth century, that victory was challenged by 'postmodernism'. Much of the challenging discourse had an aesthetic focus, but it did include a fundamental questioning of modernity and modernism: of their linear conception of time, of their 'master narratives' of progress, growth, development, emancipation, etc.

It was not an esoteric cultural studies or social-philosophical current only. It drew strength from a new environmentalism, summed up in *The Limits of Growth* (1972), by the Club of Rome, from the halting of the 'forward march of labour', the collapse of the Soviet Union and the discrediting of its brutal Stalinist modernization, and by the new movements of indigenous peoples. 'People don't want "development". They just want to live', the front stage banner of the World Social Forum in Mumbai in 2004 proclaimed. (To my knowledge, the full blast of postmodernist challenges has never been systematically assessed. Perry Anderson's brilliant analysis in 1998 – *The Origins of Postmodernity* – is limited by its aesthetic focus, originally meant as a foreword to a collection of writings by Fredric Jameson. The simultaneous rise of postmodernism on the left, and the ex-left, and of a militant, neoliberal modernism of the right, exemplarily incarnated by Margaret Thatcher, has never been clearly treated.)

Now, broad cultural orientations have generally, in the whole history of modernity, been flowing in currents and counter-currents. Dominant North Atlantic progressivism of the late nineteenth century, for instance, had its contraflow of aesthetic and agrarian critiques of industry and industrial urbanism and of philosophical critiques of scientific reason, not to speak of the rearguard wholesale rejection of modernity by still significant religious reaction. But the postmodernist stream was much wider and deeper, and, above all, its major source consisted of disappointing historical experiences of modernism, political, economic and ecological. (The aesthetic take on modernism was mainly its exhaustion, that it was becoming boring.)

As a broad sociocultural orientation, modernism was rescued by capitalism during the latter part of the twentieth century. Three new phases of capitalism produced a renewed belief in the future as a horizon to strive towards, leaving the past behind. Neoliberalism was one, emerging as the political-economic victor of the crisis of the 1970s which derailed the Marxian prediction. It provided the Thatcher and Reagan governments, the IMF and the World Bank, and their admirers and imitators all over the world with a radical, futurist agenda. Liberalism had always been modernist, but neoliberalism was liberalism without a human face, with, instead, an iron fist. Millions of people in the UK and the US were pushed down into poverty; the World Bank/IMF 'structural adjustment programs' in the poor world forced children out of schools and sick people out of healthcare, because new imposed fees could not be paid; in the North and the South, labour rights were torn up and millions of workers were shaken out of secure jobs. (See further Przeworski and Vreeland 2000; Chang Ha-Jon 2008.)

A second new capitalist phase was 'globalization', a modernist escape into space. While globalization and neoliberalism often operated in tandem, the two discourses are analytically different. Neoliberalism offered a new kind of society, consisting only of profit-maximizing individuals on markets. Globalization meant the global extension of what already existed, which in the 1990s, of course, was capitalist markets. But while the planetary space odyssey supplied a fascinating future, critics saw it as a threatening dystopia.

The third futurist thrust of late twentieth-century capitalism came with the success of the Chinese taking a (more or less) capitalist road of development, seconded by a revival of Indian capitalism. Even though there are dissenting voices, prominent at the Mumbai Social Forum as we noticed above, 'development', 'growth' and 'progress' have acquired both concrete meanings and an appeal to huge populations. Beliefs in the positive effects of scientific advance tend to be strongest in developing countries, in Nigeria and the rest of Africa, in China and the Middle East, whereas Japanese and Europeans tend to be sceptical. Americans, North and South, and South Asians tend to place themselves in between (Inglehart et al. 2004: question E022).

Once neoliberalism had repeatedly run aground – on the Asian crisis of 1997–8, which broke the 'Washington Consensus' between an unrepentant IMF and an increasingly self-critical World Bank, on the collapse of its Argentine master pupil in 2001, and on the financial crisis of 2008–9 – and at a time when globalization is becoming boringly repetitive, the vigour of East and South Asian capitalism, flanked by a few other recent success stories, most importantly in Brazil, has become the major force of world modernism.

Against the background of Euro-American dominance of modernism, this shift of economic pride and ambition is in itself a kind of globalized modernity. But the cultural arc of identity, of identification and awareness, has also become global. We notice it most clearly, perhaps, in spectator sports. The Olympics in Beijing in August 2008 gathered 4.7 billion people in front of their television sets over the same two weeks (http://blog.nielsen.com/nielsenwire/consumer/game-on-the-world-is-watching-more-than-ever/). Football fans, of clubs and individual players, are all over the planet, even in countries where it is not a very central pursuit, like in Bangladesh or Malaysia.

It can also be claimed that the pace of human modernism has quickened in the recent past. Whether or not it is accelerating into tomorrow, I leave as an open question. The past 25 years have been ones of unprecedented pace in terms of technological change, socially most important in communications and in body treatment: the rapid diffusion of personal computers, the internet, mobile phones, digital and satellite TV; artificial insemination, sex-change, cosmetic surgery, Viagra, the curing of some forms of cancer – breast and prostate in particular. Tropical medicine and treatment of Alzheimer's and AIDS have not made spectacular progress, in spite of all the effort gone into AIDS research.

So far, we have modernism, globalized and accelerated, as a prevailing cultural orientation. It is also a chastened modernism. Politics has lost most of its modernist drive, apart from economic growth in the poor world and global city status by ambitious big city politicians. Neither liberalism, socialism, nor nationalism, the three major modernist political forces of the nineteenth and twentieth centuries, is any longer able to promise credibly '*les lendemains qui chantent*' – a rosy future. Socialists are bewildered and deeply uncertain of their future, and liberalism has also lost its bearings after the crashes of neoliberalism. After its long history of victories, nationalism has become a vulnerable peripheral movement, of Tamils in Sri Lanka, Uighurs in Chinese Xinjiang, Chechens in the Russian Caucasus and Basques in Spain, although 'patriotic' flag-waving is still a very popular sport in USA.

In art, the notion of the avant-garde has fallen into disrepute since Pop Art and the 1960s. 'Iconic architecture' has displaced 'vanguard' as the cutting edge of the architectural profession. Art and architecture of the highest-selling 'stars' or 'icons' have no direction, as implied by the avant-garde. One of the world's most prominent anthropologists has found himself called upon to emphasize that culture is not only about tradition but also ideas of the future, and that 'strengthening the capacity to aspire' is a major cultural task in the contemporary world (Appadurai 2008: 29).

The main common denominator of social modernism – economic growth or development – is persistently questioned by growing environmental concerns, though the modernist infatuation with development remains dominant, manifested recently in the December 2009 Copenhagen Climate Summit. The emergent powers successfully defended their right to development, and the USA its right to further growth. But modernism is no longer unqualified. 'Sustainable development' has become the mainstream conception. It has entered into Chinese planning discourse, and even into experimental urban projects of the oil-rich Gulf states.

Modernism has veered sharply to the liberal right. But it remains in the driver's seat, globalized, accelerated and chastened, though whether the actual course of the world will be sustainable is another matter. Will the politics of collective power be able to adapt to the end of the modern emancipation from the environment? Will it be able to contain the destructive force of capitalism? Will globalized modernism be able to provide worldwide recognition and respect? At the end of the book, we will come back to those, and similar, questions.

Channels of Operation

The dynamics of the world operate through different channels. In a world perspective, we are naturally primarily interested in how our five dynamic field variables work themselves out on the global level. First of all, they are all enacted on the floor of world history, the main layers of which we discussed above. Currently, they operate, in proportions to be empirically ascertained, in global as well as in subglobal, mainly national, processes.

Global processes can be subdivided into flows, institutional entanglements and worldwide action. Pertinent national (or other subglobal) processes are performance (e.g., economic growth, state development, or cultural or existential processes), population/environment trajectory (population growth, age structure, population load on, or mastering of, the environment), and policy – or the deployment of collective power, for instance of distribution.

Global Processes

Flows

Flows refer to motion, and social flows largely run through social networks, which are ancient forms of social interaction across distances. In pre-modern times they mainly linked traders, scholars and monks. Manuel Castells, in a landmark work of social science

(1996–8), has argued that the rise of a network society and its space of flows are characteristic features of the contemporary world. Ironically enough, current flows are less dependent on networks than before. Capital flows are carried by computerized exchange, in so-called fast trading, in fractions of a second; information flows are beamed by satellites, and increasingly important pollutants are transported by atmospheric winds.

Generally speaking, world flows are driven by the dynamics identified above, in particular that of economic and of demographic ecology, and their routes are largely shaped by previous waves of globalization, of civilizational extension and colonial conquest.

New trade patterns

Long-distance, transcultural trade – across seas and oceans, deserts and mountains, surmounting language barriers and different political rulers – is an ancient, impressive achievement of humankind. True, it was usually interstitial to cultures and realms of power, but it connected the world before, during and between the various waves of globalization. Complex trading networks were often stitched together by ethnic family ties, and particular ethnic groups have played a particular part. From a European perspective, Phoenicians, Jews and Armenians are perhaps the most noticed. Post-Eurocentric research is now uncovering other networks (e.g., Curtin 1984; Markovits 2000).

Because of post-First World War economic de-globalization, international trade took a long time to reach its levels of 1913–14, achieving them only in the 1970s (Bairoch 1997: II: 308–9). In 2007 merchandise exports reached a historical peak, achieving 26 per cent of the world product, before going down in the 2008 crisis. The big countries are usually less dependent on exports, and the US least of all. American exports amount to around 7 per cent of gross national income, while in India exports make up 11 per cent, in Brazil 18 per cent, Indonesia 24 per cent, China 29 per cent, and Germany 34 per cent (World Bank 2009: tables 1, 4). The USA is nevertheless the largest exporter – and by far the largest importer – followed by China, overtaking Germany in 2009.

Trade flows no longer follow the classical imperial trade pattern of primary commodities from the periphery and manufactured goods from the centre. Manufactures now make up half of the exports of low-income countries, although three-quarters of these come from the richer countries. High-technology exports are as important to middle- as to high-income countries (UNDP 2007a: table 16).

Agricultural protectionism is an old policy of the continental European powers, now pursued by the European Union and also, for many years, adopted by the United States. US and EU agrarian interests have become major stumbling blocks in global trade negotiations. Manufacturing has now become a major export item of poor countries. It provides 92 per cent of Chinese exports, 70 per cent of Indian, 45 per cent of Indonesian, 76 per cent of Mexican, 51 per cent of Brazilian, and a third of all African exports, but only 2 per cent of Nigerian and 17 per cent of Russian (World Bank 2009: table 4; 2007c: table 5, on Africa and Nigeria).

Contrary to the conventional picture of globalization, international trade has become more regionalized and less globalized in recent decades. This is due not so much to the European Union as to East Asian trade links, with China, Japan and Korea as their core, but also comprising Southeast Asia, and to the North American Free Trade Area. (World Bank 2005: table 6.5).

International trade has both winners and losers, although there is no strong evidence disputing the economists' general claim that it is positively correlated with economic growth. To losers of their traditional, culturally deeply rooted livelihood, like small farmers in parts of Mexico and Africa and craftsmen of everyday utensils, the loss may be traumatic. But most evidence fails to show any systematic distributive effect, positive or negative (Therborn 2006: 48).

Smuggling and contraband are old features of trade flows, often draped in folkloric legend of border regions. Classic contraband consisted of relatively innocuous drugs, by the hardened standards of today, such as cigarettes and alcohol. The US South, the Caribbean and Brazil were built on the slave trade from Africa. The Arab states of North Africa and West Asia also imported slaves, but on a much smaller scale, mainly for household chores. There was a historical trafficking in women as sex objects from the Caucasus, Circassian women, both to the Ottoman court in Istanbul and to the Egyptian court in Cairo.

Nowadays, global flows of narcotic drugs constitute a major component of the flows of trade, with the US and Europe as the main importers, and Latin America, from Mexico to Colombia, and Central Asia, from Afghanistan to northern Myanmar, as the main exporters (see further Glenny 2008). In Europe, the sex trade is driven mainly by East European men pimping Eastern women in the West, but a larger sex trade seems to involve selling women and girls from rural China, Thailand and Vietnam to urban customers and international tourists.

Capital and the global casino

Global capital flows have cascaded, primarily in purely speculative forms. The daily turnover of foreign exchange markets amounted in April 2007 to US$3,200 billion. That is somewhat more than the annual national income of China in that year. By 2007 the annual global market in derivatives, involving only a few thousand bankers, amounted to US$677 trillion (Augar 2009:34), or about 12 times the income of all humankind. The best measure of the risks involved in this form of betting, as we are assured by the International Bank of Settlements, is the 'cost of replacing all open contracts at the prevailing market prices', or 'gross market value', and that was only US$11 trillion, or 79 per cent of the whole GDP of the United States (Bank of International Settlements, Triennial Central Bank Survey of Foreign Exchange and Derivatives Market Activity in 2007: www.bis.org).

Foreign direct investment is still a minor phenomenon on a world scale, net flows amounting to no more than 2.5 per cent of world GDP or about 15 per cent of global investment in 2005 (World Bank 2009: tables 1, 3, 5). Long-term net capital flows from the rich countries (the G10) to 'emerging markets' increased from 0.2 per cent of their GDP in 1970 to 0.9 per cent in 1998 (Dobson and Hufbauer 2001: table 1.1). Generally speaking, foreign investment around the turn of the twenty-first century was comparable to its role at the turn of the previous century, when British, French and German foreign investment provided domestic upper social strata with lavish 'independent means'. But by the end of the twentieth century, the stock of foreign direct investment in developing countries was a long way below the level of 1914, at 22 per cent of GDP as compared to 32 per cent in 1914 (World Bank 2002: 43). The 2008 crisis seems to be drastically cutting down international investment flows, although outcome figures are not yet known.

Wealth under private control is enormous. For example, by the end of 2006 about 300 secretive private hedge funds in London were holding assets of £360 billion (US$590 billion at the mid-2009 exchange rate), half of the national income of Brazil (Augar 2009: 52).

Finance has become the leading sector of contemporary advanced capitalism, driven by new forms of high-stake gambling or 'trading', and fed by private pension funds and other privatizations. Financial services produced 40 per cent of all US corporate profits in 2007, in contrast to about a tenth of total profits in the early 1980s (*The Economist*, 22/3/2008, p. 91). They amounted to a good 9 per cent of UK GDP in 2006, employing 338,000 people in the City of London (Augar 2009: 10).

'Flows' should not be interpreted as free-running streams, and this probably holds more for flows of capital than for others. Capital is distributed through nodes, which was a main point of Saskia Sassen's *The Global City* (2001/1991). London and New York are indisputably the main centres, though their internal ranking remains contested. While both are global, New York, of course, draws a good part of its strength from being the financial centre of the world's largest economy with by far the world's largest stock exchange. London, successfully mutating from an imperial centre to a European go-between in the 1960s and 1970s (Roberts and Kynaston 2001: ch.5), is the leading international centre, largely run by American firms. Like the Wimbledon tennis court, the City of London has become a major international playground, where national players are confined to second or third rank. In terms of foreign market shares of banking (international bank liabilities minus liabilities to native residents), the UK has a major lead, with 22 per cent as against 13 per cent of the US, and 7 per cent of France (*BIS Quarterly Review*, December 2007: 37).

Other things being equal, international capital flows lead to a decrease in international inequality. Chinese economic growth has benefited enormously from the huge inflows of foreign capital, above all from Hong Kong, Taiwan and Japan. On the other hand, capital flows are usually accompanied by mounting national inequality – very much so in China too – following from rules and policy accommodation to demands of capital and from differentiation of sectoral and enterprise productivity (see further Therborn 2006: 47–8). Capital flows also come at a cost, of recurrent banking and currency crises (Dobson and Hufbauer 2001: 43ff, 67ff).

People

The second, third and fourth waves of globalization gave the world map its main population features of today. It was the second wave that first brought Europeans and African slaves to the Americas. The third wave decided the frontiers of the British and the French, and included the peak of the slave trade. By 1800, about 8 million slaves had been shipped from Africa across the Atlantic, with some 7.5 million surviving the journey (Fernández-Armesto 2008: II: 509). The nineteenth-century fourth wave provided the Western hemisphere with a European mass population, and Europeans flowed into Oceania, large numbers of Chinese went to Southeast Asia, and Indians went to today's Malaysia, Fiji and the Caribbean. European out-migration peaked right before the First World War, while Chinese

Table 2.1   The world stock of international migrants, 2005, by continents (millions)

Africa	17
Asia	53
Europe	64
Latin America	7
Northern America	44
Oceania	5

Source: UN Department of Economic and Social Affairs, Population Division, www.esa.un.org/migration (2008)

and Indian migration to Asia reached their peaks in the late 1920s (McKeown 2004: 185–9). Compared to that recent history, the current flow of people is having less impact (so far). Nevertheless, after a strong decline after the First World War and a gradual upturn after the Second World War, accelerating at the end of the twentieth century, recent international migration has quantitatively overtaken the mass migration levels of the late nineteenth and early twentieth centuries. In 2005 the UN Department of Economic and Social Affairs estimated the internationally migrant population of the world, the foreign-born, to be at 191 million, or 2.9 per cent of world population – up from 2.3 per cent in 1980.

The new position of Europe as the largest haven of migrants is noteworthy, as the continent was for almost half a millennium a centre of out-migration, from around 1500 to *c*.1960. A significant part of the increase is due to new creations of 'foreignness'. The break-up of the Soviet Union augmented the world's foreign-born population by 26 million, from 2.5 to 2.9 per cent (Livi-Bacci 2007: table 6.4). The USA remains the major national destination of emigrants, housing a fifth of the world's total in 2005, up from 15 per cent in 1990 (see www.esa.un.org/migration).

Strictly speaking, current migration is not that much of a global flow, but a cross-national move next door. The main migration flows run from Mexico to the USA – 10.3 million by 2005 (stock of foreign born) – followed by the exchanges between Russia and the Ukraine (8.4 million), India and Bangladesh (4.5 million) and Russia and Kazakhstan (4.4 million). The largest transoceanic migrations have occurred from India to the Arab peninsula (3.5 million), from the Philippines to the USA (1.6 million) and from India, China and Vietnam to the USA (1.1 million each) (Ratha and Xu 2008).

Fully comparable data for 100 years ago are difficult to obtain, and also ambiguous under the best of circumstances. What should be counted as foreign borders in the age of empires, before the universality of nation-states? However, starting from the major destinations of migration a century ago – the Americas, Southern Africa, Southeast Asia, continental European countries such as France and Germany – a picture emerges of a migrant world population on the eve of the First World War. My estimate is between 1.5 and 2 per cent of the world population were migrants in 1913 (based on migration figures from Hatton and Williamson 2006: ch. 2 and population figures from Maddison 2007). For the US, the Pew Research Center has predicted that the 1910 proportion of the population that is foreign born, 15 per cent, will be reached soon after 2020 (*International Herald Tribune* 12/2/2008).

For countries and cities, more exact comparisons are possible, although non-documented migration provides a margin of uncertainty. Among the major American and Oceanian destinations of immigration, only Australia has a larger share of foreign-born residents today than it did 100 years ago, while Argentina has far fewer. Documented US immigration is approaching, but has not yet reached, the 14.7 per cent population share of 1890–1911. But Western Europe and West Asia have become new major receivers, although both take fewer than does North America (Hatton and Williamson 2006: table 2.2). In 2007 the foreign born accounted for 14 per cent of the German labour force, 12 per cent each of the French and the British, and 17 per cent of the Spanish, more than the registered foreign born in USA, at 16 per cent (OECD 2009: 30–1).

Recently, Muslim immigration to Western Europe has created quite a stir, in the wake of violent Islamist actions, which resemble similar 'terrorist' attacks by Italian anarchists in the USA and in Argentina 80–100 years ago. The European response has been much more culturalist than the American one was then. This is to be understood against the background of a unique modern monoculturalism of Western Europe. The Westphalian peace and state system was based on the idea of *cuius region, eius religio* – in plain English: the prince decides your religion. While this rule was eroded after the Enlightenment, there was the new monocultural idea of the European nation, of every citizen speaking the same national language. Even in the last third of the twentieth century, when the prosperous industrial economies of Western Europe needed to import factory labour, the Central European interpretation was that this was not immigration. 'Germany is no country of immigration' was a standing policy stance in that country, a stance also followed in Austria and Switzerland. Imported workers only had the status of 'guest workers'. In the end, European social norms could not sustain this idea of temporary guests, so family reunions were allowed and immigrant families settled. Xenophobia notwithstanding, impressive cultural adaptations have also been made. The Italian Metalworkers' Union, for instance, now distributes collective agreements in Arabic and Punjabi (*La Republica*, 18/2/2008).

Migration often creates enduring diasporic communities, sometimes with economic clout as well as of a distinctive culture, such as Jews and Armenians in Europe and the Americas, and Chinese in Southeast Asia. American Jewry has acquired political significance too, as it were a Praetorian Guard of Israeli interests in the US. Several countries, from Greece to the Philippines, have government agencies to deal with emigration and diasporic affairs. In the mid-1990s, the Chinese diaspora was estimated to be approximately 37 million people, while the much smaller Indian one was 9 million (Poston et al. 1994: 635; Brown 2006: 2). In 2005 the number of residents of one country who had migrated to another comprised 11.5 million each of Mexicans and Russians, 10 million Indians and 7 million Chinese. Proportionally, emigration is most frequent from the West Indies (39 per cent of the population of Jamaica, 28 per cent of Trinidad's), and from the new capitalist ex-communist countries (38 per cent from Bosnia, 27 per cent each from Albania and Armenia) (Ratha and Xu 2008).

Cities are magnets of domestic as well as international migration, today as well as earlier in history. About a third of the population of New York City is foreign born, about the same as a century ago. Half the population of Buenos Aires was born outside the country – similar to Miami today – though that figure now stands at only 8 per cent. London has somewhat less than a third foreign-born residents, 29 per cent in 2004. Dubai is an extreme case, with more that 80 per cent of its population born abroad. Canadian cities such as Toronto and Vancouver have around 41 per cent. Several major European cities harbour foreign-born populations of between a quarter and a third of the total, Amsterdam, Brussels, Frankfurt among them, but cosmopolitan Paris less than a fifth (in 1999) (http://gstudynet.org.gum). (Amsterdam is sometimes presented as having a population almost half of whom are foreign born. This is not borne out by official Dutch statistics – see http://www.cbs.nl.)

A new aspect of emigration, made possible by modern communications technology, are large-scale transfers of money to the home country. Counting such transfers through official channels only, Moldova and Tajikistan receive between 30 and 40 per cent of their national income from emigrant workers, Guyana, Haiti, Honduras. Jordan, Kyrgyzstan, and Lebanon between a 20 and 25 per cent (World Bank 2007b). But for the 'developing countries' as a whole, i.e., non-high-income countries, these sums amount to only 2 per cent of their national income (calculated from World Bank 2008 and 2009).

Migration is pushed by poverty, discrimination and/or disadvantage, and pulled by economic opportunity, along routes of contacts, networks and movement. The resurgence of international migration has given rise to a series of inflamed economic, cultural and political issues. Economically, immigrants tend to take jobs which the natives no longer accept. But under laissez-faire conditions, mass immigration tends to create the dualistic labour market characteristic of the US, of California and the Southwest in particular, pressing down wages of lower-skilled workers. For the countries of out-migration there may ensue a drastic brain drain, as when, e.g., a third of Liberian-trained physicians or a quarter of Ethiopian-trained ones have gone abroad (Ratha and Xu 2008). A diasporic cultural maintenance is increasingly seen as a cultural threat, fanned by mass media and spilling into even the government department at Harvard (the late Samuel P Huntington). Politically, most rich countries' multiparty systems have seen the rise of a xenophobic political party. France was the pioneer, whose National Front drew upon colonialist fights for French Algeria, but the latest advances have been in Denmark and the Netherlands, two countries that were, until recently, known for their tolerance of different lifestyles, and for their old and rapid recent secularization, respectively. Their governments and their mainstream media have now suddenly become the most militant anti-Islamic forces of Western Europe, in spite of their small (in Denmark in particular), and mostly poor, Muslim minorities.

Information and cultural flows

As far as people are concerned, the largest manifestation of the recent wave of globalization has been the sudden rise of the internet and the explosive growth of telecommunications. Individuals in, say, Bolivia, Ethiopia, Bangladesh and Indonesia can now easily communicate with each other, and it is no longer necessary to use a private courier to get a letter to, e.g., an Italian colleague. Family members of immigrant workers in Europe can now watch television by satellite from Turkey, Morocco or Pakistan. Leaders and militants of poor people's protest movements, of small Indian tribes of the Americas, of Arctic Sami and Inuit, or of the global Slum Dwellers' Association are now communicating with each other and with allies through their computers. The new electronic media connect people of the world on a scale that is without any precedent. The *oecumene*, the known world, has suddenly expanded exponentially.

Satellite broadcast television began in the 1960s, first more publicly noticed during the 1966 football World Cup, but took off from the 1980s. CNN International was launched in 1985, and had its break-through reporting from the First Gulf War in 1991 (cf. Briggs and Burke 2005: 231ff). Mobile phones went into public use in 1979, beginning to spread throughout the rich world in the 1980s. The World Wide Web went on air in 1991 (see further Berners-Lee 1999). By 2005 a good third of the world's population had a mobile phone, and more than one in eight people were using the internet. Some countries have many more mobile phone subscribers than inhabitants – e.g., Italy, Portugal, Lithuania, Estonia, the Czech Republic, Norway and a few others. The world still differs in this respect, of course, like in all others. However, more than one sub-Saharan African out of eight had a mobile phone in 2005, almost a third of all Chinese, but only eight out of a hundred South Asians. While India houses some of the world's leading software developers, only five out of a hundred Indians had ever used the internet by 2005 (UNDP 2007a: table 13). And the IT workforce is minuscule: 0.2 per cent of Indian employment in the same year (Xiang Biao 2008: 342).

But how much has it changed the world and people's lives? Is the change more significant than the coming of the telephone and tele-graph at the end of the nineteenth century, or of the radio in the 1920s–30s? Not much seems to be known about that yet. A few important effects are discernible though. While the relative qualita-tive importance of the communications innovations then and recently may be debated, there is no question that the recent ones are of much larger magnitude. For a long time, the telephone reached only the upper and middle classes of the rich countries, and the radio added the popular classes of the same countries. In the 2000s, mobile phones were reaching the rural interiors of China, South Asia, and Africa.

Most dramatic, perhaps, has been the move away from rural isola-tion for long-distance migrant kin, and for all other urban contacts, especially in Africa, Asia and Latin America. Satellite TV keeps migrants more effectively linked to their culture of origin than the emigrant language press – a major phenomenon of the US media world until the First World War, and even until the Second World War – ever could. The internet has been a major vehicle of mobilizing decisive political protest in many countries, from the Philippines and Indonesia in the late 1990s to Spain in 2004, and Iran in 2009. Internet communication is also, in the longer run probably most importantly, creating a new kind of social network, a virtual sociability. By May 2009, Facebook had 316 million registered users – distant middle-aged colleagues are asking this writer to look at their pictures in Facebook – four-fifths of whom were outside their original country of origin, while MySpace, doing less well, had 125 million registered users (*International Herald Tribune*, 24/6/2009, p. 16). The kids' network Habbo Hotel claimed 100 million users in September 2008 (*Guardian*, 2/10/2008, p. 4). To what extent this virtual sociability is in addition to or is a substitute for face-to-face contacts is still an open question, although scanty evidence does point in the direction of the former.

The new media are also increasingly global cultural flows, and in the early 2000s cultural goods – recorded sound media, printed media, visual arts, audiovisual media (video and film), heritage goods (antiques, folklore) in order of value – amounted to 1 per cent of all goods traded in the world, and a larger share of trade in services, a good 2 per cent in the dominant American case (UNESCO 2005).

The Anglo-Saxons dominate the book trade. France has lost its top position in the visual arts market (export sales in 2002, $0.5 billion), where China has had a surprising recent success, perhaps because it includes also prints, statuary and ornaments. The British record industry has lost to the Irish, as well as others, and Singapore has emerged

Table 2.2 The world's main cultural exporters, 2002 ($ billion)

Books	Visual arts	Recorded media	Audiovisual media[a]	Audiovisual services[b]
USA 1.9	UK 2.7	USA 3.1	China 2.3	USA 6.7
UK 1.8	China 2.2	Germany 2.3	Japan 1.2	UK 1.6
Germany 1.3	USA 0.9	Ireland 2.1	Mexico 0.8	Canada 1.4
		UK 1.6		France 1.0
		Singapore 1.6		

Notes: [a]Computer and videogames; [b]Feature films and TV programmes. India is not included.
Source: UNESCO 2005, International flows of selected cultural goods and services, 1994–2003, tables V-2-7, and figure 24

as the recording hub of East Asia. The Chinese have beaten the Japanese at computer games production, the only area in which the big Mexican entertainment industry has a presence on the global top. The data on income from film and TV programmes are curtailed by the absence of India, the only serious, though far behind, international competitor to the American film industry. India usually produces the largest number of feature films annually in the world, and has an important share of releases in parts of Africa and the Arab world, as well as in South Asia (though largely underground in Pakistan).

Global news broadcasts are increasing their importance, especially among the politico-economic elites of the world. BBC World and CNN lead the world market, although there are other competitors, the Francophone *TV5-Monde*, the regional Euronews, and the Qatar-based *Al-Jazeera*, which dominates the Arab-speaking world and now has an English edition, and the smaller, multilingual *Deutsche Welle*. Expanded efforts of the English edition of Chinese news are on the way. Educated Europeans are enjoying Euronews, remembered by some of us from the Kosovo war in the same way as *Al-Jazeera* is remembered from the latest wars in Afghanistan and Iraq, as the only window out of the reigning propaganda blackout. In spite of overdoses of the Venezuelan President Hugo Chavez, many Latin Americans follow *Telesur*, the new Third World state channel from Venezuela. The internet makes it possible to get into global news independently of TV channelling and special linguistic skills, including, e.g., since April 2009 the Chinese *Global Times*.

In TV entertainment, US (Viacom)-owned MTV is the most successful, but here there are many heavyweight players, American, Japanese and Mexican *telenovelas* among them. TV entertainment, film and music all have important regional producers. There is an East Asian pop culture scene that runs from Singapore to Korea, an Indian and Bombay-centred one in South Asia, an Arab one, culturally rooted in Egypt but thriving from the cosmopolitanism of Lebanon and the money and relative liberality of the Gulf, a regionally important Nigerian film and video culture, 'Nollywood', and in Latin America the two major centres of Mexico and Brazil. Cultural flows are losing their North Atlantic centredness of the last past couple of centuries.

Global information flows have been important for at least a century, and in particular after the Second World War, in conveying information about disease, hygiene and medical discoveries, contributing decisively to a narrowing of global vital inequality in 1950–90 before the onslaught of AIDS in Africa and capitalism in the former Soviet

Union (Therborn 2006). Following statistical efforts of the League of Nations and the ILO before the Second World War, a number of UN organizations gathered and published a major corpus of global information in the post-war years. In the two last decades of the twentieth century, this global information was given greater coverage in World Bank, UNDP, UNICEF and other development reports. How countries fared in global comparison became common knowledge. Subsequently, there has been a trend towards global ranking, whether of human development, university status or individual tennis players.

The worldwide flow of information is not only a question of media and entertainment, and art. It is also one of models, values, norms and standards, of emulation and of global cultural patterning (Meyer et al. 1997; Grewal 2008). The first wave of globalization spread religious beliefs and rituals across continents and oceans. With the fourth, nineteenth-century wave of globalization, European standards of being 'civilized' were adopted from khedival Egypt to imperial Japan. This standard of 'civilization' was a broad palette, from European dress code (top hat and dark morning coat for high-ranking males), pair dancing and architecture to legal and administrative structures, forms of military training and political organization (cf. Baily 2004). Historically, the most radical standardizers from above were the Japanese Meiji oligarchs of the last third of the nineteenth century, and between the two world wars, Kemal Atatürk, his follower Reza Shah I of Iran and the more anonymous Central Asian Bolsheviks.

After the Second World War the word 'civilized' fell into disrepute, as racist and imperialist. It was succeeded by 'modern'. During the fifth, political, wave of globalization, the 'modern' could take socialist as well as capitalist characteristics. In the end, it was non-standardized East Asian variants of the latter that won out. World standards returned with a vengeance during the militant rightwing turn of modernism as 'neoliberalism', and in the personae of the 'structural adjusters'. Among the citizenry, these have become horror figurers, best remembered as infamous in Latin America, from Salinas in Mexico to Menem in Argentina.

In recent decades, the EU has been an important standard-setter, above all to Eastern Europe. Usually coming in legal garb, and argued diplomatically, this is a much more subtle flow of standards than the impositions of Atatürk or the IMF.

Flows of matter

Flows of matter have a wide range, covering living matter from viruses to animals and dead matter from water, soil and sand to carbon dioxide and other gases. They are a crucial part of the environment–population interaction. Sometimes they seem to be driven mainly by nature's own forces, such as the changing direction of shoals of herring in the Sound and the North Sea of the late middle–early modern ages, bringing either prosperity and urban growth, or regression and depopulation. The silting of rivers and their demise in terms of transport is another such flow of matter, bringing decline to medieval Bruges, for instance. Other flows run along human tracks – the pestilent rats from Central Asia that travelled under the Pax Mongolica to Europe, bringing the Black Death which killed off about a third of the European population. The conquerors of the Americas carried bacteria and viruses, to which Europeans had adapted, but which proved to be disastrous to the inhabitants of the time, who were almost exterminated in the second wave of globalization (McNeill 1979: ch. 5). At the end of the First World War, the so-called Spanish influenza killed off millions. More recent epidemics have been less virulent, but they remain a recurrent global feature – for example, AIDS, SARS, swine flu, etc.

In this century, the atmospheric diffusion of carbon dioxide and other pollutants is on its way to resulting in a global flow of disasters, through climate change: flooding from higher sea levels, storm destruction, drought and subsequent food shortages. The velocity and the proximity of this latter catastrophic flow are uncertain and under expert debate. Their source in the flow of pollutants has become common sense, and one of the few things that everybody could agree on at the UN Copenhagen Climate Conference in December 2009. How to cope with the despair, anger and rivalry that are likely to follow from this is already the subject of imperial war games at the Pentagon and the US National Defence University (*International Herald Tribune* 10/2009, pp. 1, 4).

The USA and China are the world's biggest polluters, together ejaculating a good 40 per cent of all energy-related carbon-dioxide emitted by humankind, the USA a little more than China, at least in 2005. But China delivers more than double the American dose of methane and nitrous oxide. Historically, the USA is the main culprit, responsible for a third of all cumulated emissions since 1850. Germany is next in line, but with only 10 per cent of the historical total. The argument, from many countries, that the USA should take some financial responsibility for its enormous polluting record is understandable against this background, but is vehemently rejected by the whole spectrum of the US political elite. After the USA and China, Russia, Brazil, Indonesia, Japan and India are also large sources of carbon dioxide, Brazil and Indonesia mainly through deforestation.

Among the rich countries, there has been a noteworthy difference in emission behaviour since 1990. The USA and Japan have increased theirs, by 20 and 15 per cent respectively, whereas Germany has decreased its by 15 per cent, no doubt helped by the deindustrialization of East Germany; the UK, Sweden and Denmark have reduced theirs by around 5 per cent each. One positive effect of the fall of East European communism has been that ensuing deindustrialization, pauperization and, probably, less energy inefficiency have brought about a very significant decline of carbon dioxide emissions since 1990, most notable from Ukraine, Belarus and Russia. (World Bank 2010: tables A1, A2, A2b).

Global-national entanglements

An overlap of global organizations and national states, of global opinion or decision-makers with national ones became a significant feature of the last third or quarter of the twentieth century. It constitutes a particular form of global politics. It has taken two major forms, with very different, almost opposite, social implications, roughly simultaneously but without contact. One developed through UN machinery, originally pushed by the communist Women's International Democratic Federation, and manifested in the UN International Women's Year and its hugely successful Conference on Women in Mexico City in 1975, followed by a UN Decade of Women and Development. This global initiative generated a lot of national legislation countering patriarchal systems, including in Western Europe, and of gender issues in national institutions, as well as providing funds and foci for global feminist networking (see further Therborn 2004: 102ff). The thrust of this global–national entanglement was equality, and global support for the disadvantaged.

The other kind of global–national entanglement had a different direction. It developed out of conditional IMF credits. It was already present in entangled relations with the British Labour government in the mid-1960s, and came of age embodied in the 'structural adjustment programmes' enforced in Africa and parts of Latin America in the 1980s and '90s. The normal social effect was strengthening the strong – capital and the wealthy – and weakening the weak – labour and the poor. Public expenditure and public employment had to be cut, formal sector labour rights were 'flexibilized', the poor found themselves paying towards public education and healthcare, and their food was not longer to be subsidized. These measures were supposed to lift countries out of deep crises, because of which they had solicited IMF loans. In other words, the IMF was only called in after the national government had messed things up. Was the social disaster mainly an effect of the crisis, or of the IMF? Sophisticated econometric analysis has shown up the systematic anti-egalitarian impact of the IMF interventions (Przeworski and Vreeland 2000).

Global action

The meaning of global action is seemingly simple and straightforward: of worldwide action by an identifiable actor or set of actors. Its history goes back to the empires of the second wave of globalization. It remains first of all a manifestation of big state power, to wage war or make credible threats across the world, occasionally to help. The USA is currently the only fully global superpower, but neither Britain nor France has giving up its ambition to remain a big power. China has become a major global player, but its action is so far almost exclusively economic. A large number of minor powers are offered a piece of the global action by their 'Big Brother', so for the first time in their history countries like Albania, Estonia and Honduras are engaged in putting uppity Asian natives in their proper place in Afghanistan as American auxiliaries. Denmark, by the twentieth century almost a symbol of pacifism in spite of its ancient Viking past and once having been a minor colonial and slaving power, has been turned into an aggressive crusader nation, insulting and harassing Muslims at home and enthusiastically participating in the American wars in Iraq and Afghanistan.

Increasingly frequent summits, of G7, G8, G20, and many other combinations of states, are trying to create some peaceful concerted global action – so far with little success. The G20 consultations of 2008–9 were significant, not because they achieved any concerted action, but because the G20 overshadowed the G8. The UN peacekeeping missions have had very little success, being under-funded, under-staffed, under-equipped and over-awed, as the big powers of the organization usually prefer to keep their hands free by staying in the wings. Natural disasters, most recently in Haiti in early 2010, are nowadays regularly met by a competing swarm of state and non-state organizations. For all their inefficiencies, all these actions, and attempts at action, do underline two important things: the strong pan-humanity extension of the cultural arc of identity in times of crisis, and the respect and status of global action.

The United Nations has become something more than an interstate organization controlled by the five veto powers of its Security Council. It functions best as a kind of global 'civil society' of opinion formation, which has gradually generated important instances of global action, on birth control, gender relations, public health and other social issues. Its Human Development Index, developed by Amartya Sen, is setting an important world standard.

Economic global action is more complex. Trans-polity, intercontinental trading networks, usually by diasporic ethnicities, are ancient phenomena. This was not just about flows of exchange, but also included the strategic placement of sons or other relatives in target areas. The Hindu *Sindiworkie* merchants of Hyderabad in today's Pakistan provide one of the most fascinating examples. In the first half of the twentieth century those merchant firms had branches all over the world, from today's Karlovy Vary in the Czech Republic to Punta Arenas in southern Chile, from Yokohama to Cape Town, to Freetown, and to Colón in Panama (Markovits 2000: 112–13; cf. Curtin 1984).

Big corporations have also for long deployed global strategies, and have in recent decades been able to establish complex supply and production chains worldwide, for the production of cars, electronic gadgets and branded consumer items such as sports shoes, as well as huge retail chains. Examples include an American manufacturer, like Apple, a brand, such as Nike, or a huge retailer, such as Wal-mart, and there are also subcontractors, for instance in Taiwan, which then organize production in Mainland China, in Lesotho or in Guatemala. This kind of global action is known as 'global commodity chains' (Gereffi et al. 2005). Corporate global action may be more or less globally uniform or market differentiated. Toyota and the Japanese have led the global car pack, which Ford is now trying to emulate (*International Herald Tribune* 11/1/ 2010. pp. 1, 16).

We shall look further into global action in the next chapter, when taking note of the big actors of the current world stage.

National Processes

National processes still matter. Economic growth rates show no trend of global convergence. Between 1975 and 2005, GDP per capita grew annually by 8.4 per cent in China, 3.4 in India, 2.0 per cent in USA, 2.2 per cent in Japan, 2.0 in Germany – which we will sometimes use

Table 2.3 National population growth
2000–8 (annual %)

China	0.6
India	1.4
Germany	0.0
USA	0.9
Indonesia	1.3
Brazil	1.2
Nigeria	2.4
Russia	−0.4
Japan	0.1

Source: World Bank: table 1

as a proxy for the EU – 3.9 in Indonesia and 0.7 per cent in Brazil, while declining by 0.7 per cent in Russia and by 0.1 per cent in Nigeria (UNDP 2007a: table 14). The current crisis, although global, has underlined that nations matter in the world economy. Between the (northern) spring of 2008 and 2009, GDP declined in the USA by 2.5 per cent, in Japan by 8.8 per cent, in Russia by 9.5 per cent, in Brazil by 1.8 per cent and in Euroland by 4.8 per cent, while growing in China by 6.1 per cent, in India by 5.8 per cent and in Indonesia by 4.4. per cent (*The Economist* 27/6–3/7/2009, p. 105). National populations are also on different trajectories (see table 2.3).

World population growth has slowed down, from a historical maximum in the 1960s of 2 per cent a year (Livi-Bacci 2007: table 5.1) to, currently, 1.1 per cent. But birth rates are not converging globally. Indeed, between 1900 and 2000 they tended to diverge (Therborn 2004: 293–4). In northern Nigeria, women's ideal number of children is still eight, although their practice is about seven (Nigerian National Bureau of Statistics 2006: table 80). The population throughout post-communist Europe is declining, due to plummeting birth rates, a drastic increase of mortality in Russia and other countries of the former Soviet Union and out-migration. The decline stopped (temporarily?) in Russia in 2009, mainly due to immigration. The population of the European Union is being sustained chiefly by immigration. Japan, which is largely closed to immigration, will start to show a strong demographic decline in the next few years. Among the rich countries, only the USA maintains a natural reproduction of its population, a result of high fertility among the large Hispanic immigrant communities.

Distributions: global, national and subnational

European colonialism and industrialism – in still unsettled, controversial proportions – meant an enormous increase of economic inequality in the world. Analytically, it is a question of the relative importance of mechanisms of inequality, above all between distanciation (running ahead) by North Atlantic industrial capitalism and colonial exploitation and exclusion (see further Therborn 2006). Whatever the mechanisms, one good answer to questions of poverty and affluence is that you are poor/affluent because your country was poor/affluent 150–200 years ago. (Maddison 2007: table A7).

Decolonization after the Second World War changed the parameters of the world economy. More than a century of stagnation of China and India changed for economic growth. But there was a big gap to be closed. The urban real wage in India by 1961 seems to have been lower than the one in Agra in 1595 (Allen 2005: 121). On a global scale, economic inequality flattened out in the 1950s–60s (Bourguignon and Morrison 2002). From about 1980, rapid economic growth of huge and poor China has meant global equalization, from c. 1990 supported by reinvigorated growth in India.

But the world polarized in the last quarter of the twentieth century, as most of Africa was falling behind. GDP per capita actually fell in sub-Saharan Africa between 1975 and 2005, by 0.5 per cent on annual average, while high-income countries grew by 2.1 per cent (UNDP 2007a : table 14). Africa was not the only victim of the 'globalization' decades. By 2000, the poorest fifth of the population of South and Central America had only 84 per cent of their average income in 1980. The poorest quintile of Eastern Europe and Central Asia were left with only 70 per cent of the 1980 income. Their loss came after 1990, with the fall of communism, whereas in the Americas the poor had to pay their extra dues to capital in the 1980s. The 1980s were also the years in which the poorest fifth of North Americans had their incomes cut (Berry and Serieux 2006: table 10).

Overall global inequality derives first of all from global history. To what extent current economic inequality in the world is due to recent globalization is another topic for inconclusive debate. Clear, however, are two things. Income inequality is distributed very unequally across the world. Secondly, size and distance matter little with respect to resource inequality among contemporary humans. The inhabitants of a city, or the citizens of a country, may be as unequal as the inhabitants of the planet. In other words, subglobal processes dominate the current (re-)production of income inequality. The Gini coeffient

Table 2.4 Income inequality on the planet, in nations and in cities, mid-2000s (Gini coefficients)

The Planet	70
Nations	
Brazil	57
China	47
Germany	30
India	37[a]
Indonesia	34[a]
Japan	32
Mexico	47
Nigeria	44[a]
Russia	40[a]
South Africa	58[a]
Denmark & Sweden	23
United States	38
Cities	
Brasilia	64
Johannesburg	75[a]
Mexico City	56
New York	>50
São Paolo	61
Washington D.C.	>50

Note: [a]Figure refers to the distribution of household expenditure, which is less uneven than income. For India, comparative measurement research has found income coefficients 8–10 points above expenditure ones.
Sources: The planet: B. Milanovic 2008: table 3; OECD countries: OECD 2007a: table 1.A2.3; other countries: UNDP 2008: table 15; cities: UN Habitat 2008, pp. 63, 69, 75

is the most common summary measure of inequality, running from zero and full equality to 100 and total inequality, where one unit takes everything (see table 2.4).

In spite of heroic collecting and analysing efforts, the figures shown in table 2.4 have to be read with caution, allowing for margins of error. Even within Europe, different statistical centres give slightly varying figures for the same country. However, with this caveat, inequality among the residents of Johannesburg is at least on a par with, possibly even above, that among the inhabitants of the earth, measured by adding national household surveys and making monetary purchasing power comparable. Countries in development vary considerably in their inequality, but Latin America and southern Africa top the list of national inequality – a reproduced historical legacy from European settler subjugation and exploitation of indigenous peoples and, in Brazil, of imported slaves. The fact that the Indian figure refers to expenditure and the Chinese to income means that actual economic inequality in the two countries is roughly similar. (The urban Chinese figures seriously underestimate actual inequality, among other things by excluding urban migrants, and therefore are not used here.)

Comparing nations and their GDP per capita gives a ratio between the richest and the poorest tenths of the world of 39:1 (Milanovic 2008: 425). That global ratio is surpassed by the national ratio of top to bottom in nine Latin American countries and in five African countries. Among the households of the world, Milanovic has found a top-bottom decile ratio of 98:1. Among the citizens of Bolivia the same decile ratio was 168 in 2002. Singular surveys of Lesotho and Namibia in the mid-1990s showed ratios of 105 and 130, respectively (UNDP 2008: table 15). In other words, whatever the force of global history and current global processes, much human inequality is being produced and preserved within national borders and city boundaries. The Scandinavian and the US data show the range of national inequality in the rich OECD world.

National history and national politics appear more important as forces of income distribution than do the flows of global capitalism.

— 3 —

THE CURRENT WORLD STAGE

In an epochal work of the 1970s, Immanuel Wallerstein taught us that there is a modern capitalist world system, governing states, nations and classes. But how much of a system this either is or has been has not been settled conclusively. For my part, I have always thought that the different parts of the world are very significantly autonomous, and therefore never to be neglected in explanations of the world. In the previous chapter we tried to unpack the world system and current globalization into global and subglobal processes, and to weigh them in relation to each other. Less controversial, though less explored, is the existence of a world stage, a global scene on which a number of actors, from states, state alliances and corporations to individual politicians, footballers and pop singers, perform. Actors who, in spite of, by definition, being up to world standards, may not necessarily have been less shaped by their particular subglobal background.

The world stage is actually a vast theatre house, showing many plays at the same time to audiences worldwide. A large part of it is a multicultural repertoire theatre: a political repertoire of UN Security Councils, General Assemblies, of big power summits and theatres of war; an economic one most ostensibly showing up at the annual Economic Forums at Davos, but also visible every day on business news screens; a cultural repertoire with the Stockholm Nobel prizes and the Los Angeles Oscars as the highlights of the year; a huge sports repertoire, with the Olympics and football world cups as recurrent peaks; irregular but frequently recurring and always popular celebrity parades, etc. Irregular but frequent are the horror stories of disasters and catastrophes. Then there are sideshows and special performances of all kinds.

No theatre critic could do justice to this rich supply. Here we shall concentrate on the big political, economic and social players. But let us first take a quick look at the scenography and its history.

Scenography: World Space

The social world stage has a pertinent scenic historical background of planetary geography, of connectors and divides. Plains and rivers are connectors. The early high civilizations developed along major rivers and their surrounding plains, narrow around the Euphrates and Tigris and broader along the Yang-tse and Ganges. The vast Eurasian plain connected the European peninsula with the nomad warriors of Huns and Mongols, as well as with the silk of China. Mountains and deserts are divides. The Himalayas cut Central Asia off from South Asia – although a western detour allowed warriors an access route through Afghanistan and the Khyber Pass – the Andes divided South America, and in the North first the Appalachians, then the Rocky Mountains put up (temporary) barriers to US expansion. The Alps have always divided Europe, if not separated north and south. The Sahara, the Gobi, the Takla Makan and the deserts enclosing the 'Fertile Crescent' of the Middle East have divided Africa, Northeast and West Asia. Seas and oceans both divide and connect. The Mediterranean and the South China Sea are ancient connectors, with the latter more clearly a border as well. The Arab/Persian Gulf and the Baltic, later also the Caribbean, are examples of regional maritime connectors-cum-dividers. The Indian Ocean connected pre-modern South and West Asia, and East Africa, while also separating them. It's annual cycle of monsoon winds governed trade and voyages for long into the era of European imperialism (Chaudhuri 1985; 1990).

The North Atlantic provided the same functions, its main early crossings shaped by the ellipse of winds and currents discovered between Sevilla, the Cape Verde Islands, Havana and the Azores back to Iberia (Benjamin 2009: maps 2.6 and 5.1). The Pacific made the Polynesian peopling of the Easter Island, Hawaii and, with a little help from the Indian Ocean, Madagascar possible, but it was an Asian barrier beyond the Philippines, until the route was opened from the west by Americans. Then the connection soon materialized, in the large Chinatowns of San Francisco and Vancouver, and in the Japanese presence in Lima.

The discontinuous navigability of the great African rivers, like the Congo, the Niger and the Zambezi, has separated parts of Africa, as has the tropical central rain forest and the vast Saharan desert, though traversed by caravans bringing slaves and gold to the north and Islamic culture to the south. The fact that the Siberian rivers, the Lena, the Ob and others, run northwards into nowhere has hampered socioeconomic development.

But while the scenography of the world stage is almost entirely nature-made; the layout of airspace is wholly man-made. And long before that became possible, the ancient Chinese Grand Canal and the more adolescent Suez and Panama Canals connected humankind in new important ways. Currently, with man-made global warming and the accompanying melting of ice-caps, the long dreamt-of North-eastern, north of Russia, and Northwestern, north of Canada, passages are beginning to open up.

The layout of the world as continents, separated and connected by vast expanses of water, oceans and seas, is Eurocentric, in the sense that it is a European invention and discovery. Only Europeans could have hit upon the idea of the western promontory of Asia being a continent. The western part of the great Eurasian landmass has no significant eastern boundary – the Ural mountains are a low, late invention – which is haunting the current political debate about the European Union. Where does Europe end?

But Europeans have a legitimate claim to curiosity, Europe is the curious continent, like Arab West Asia once was.

The Big Players

The uneven field of nation-states

Nation-states come out of unions of states and nations. They were a proclamation of the American and the French Revolutions, which sent shock waves across the globe, arriving in Africa by the late 1950s, fatally hitting the Soviet Union and Yugoslavia in the 1990s. At times, nation-states evolved gradually out of dynastic or oligarchic polities, like Britain in the course of the seventeenth and eighteenth centuries, rarely without some violent conflict though.

In 2010 the world is made up of around 6.8 billion people, internally divided into almost 200 states, 192 of which are members of the United Nations – up from 60 in 1950, of hugely varying size. Since the early 1990s the organization has included some statelets of dubious sovereignty, like the tiny relics of pre-national Europe, Andorra, Liechtenstein, Monaco and San Marino, whose foreign affairs have for long been conducted by their nation-state neighbours, and ex-colonial islets in the Pacific such as Kiribati, Nauru and Palau. Outside are only a few territories of de facto statehood but with little recognized international legitimacy as such: Abkhazia, Kosovo, North Cyprus, South Ossetia, Taiwan and Transnistria. Significant movements demanding new nation-states exist on all continents, except

128

Table 3.1   The most populous states of the world, 2008 (millions)

China	1,326
India	1,140
USA	304
Indonesia	228
Brazil	192
Pakistan	166
Bangladesh	160
Nigeria	151
Russia	142
Japan	128
Mexico	106

Source: World Bank 2010: table 1

Australia. Whatever they are, nation-states have certainly not become obsolete.

In this short tour of the world we have to focus on the big battalions, and we should start by emphasizing that the human world is first of all Asian in population and habitat, East Asian and South Asian, headed by the two state population billionaires, China and India (see table 3.1).

Two countries, China and India, harbour almost two humans out of five (37 per cent). Half of humankind is concentrated in just six countries. A good 60 per cent live in the 11 countries with more than 100 million inhabitants. Any serious social analysis of the world will have to pay special attention to them. A clear majority of the human population (56 per cent) is concentrated in three regions, East, South and Southeast Asia. Together, the European Union and North America, the world centre of the nineteenth and twentieth centuries, house only one human among eight. Europeans should also note that there are, apart from the US, 13 non-European countries more populous than Germany, the giant of the EU, apart from the above, also the Philippines, Vietnam, Egypt and, just recently, Ethiopia. The big countries tend to be large too, of continental size more or less. But like everything else in this world, space is very unevenly distributed among states.

It may give you some sense of world space to think of Russia as only a little smaller than China and USA put together, or of Australia (population 21 million) as more than twice the size of India. And in Greece, 11 million people have almost as much space as 160 million

Table 3.2   The largest countries, in 1,000 km^2

Russia	17,098
Canada	9,985
USA	9,632
China	9,598
Brazil	8,515
Australia	7,741
India	3,287
Argentina	2,780
Kazakhstan	2,725
Sudan	2,505
Algeria	2,381
Congo (Kinshasa)	2,344
Saudi Arabia	2,000
Mexico	1,964
Indonesia	1,904

Source: World Bank 2009: table A1

Bangladeshis. Whereas the largest country of Western Europe, France, has only 552,000 square kilometres, there are 6 Latin American countries and 11 African ones, including South Africa, larger than one million square kilometres.

Countries divide and relate also by the size of national economies, and by their prosperity. The international weight of national economies had better be expressed in US dollars at current exchange rates (see table 3.3).

The economic order among the big countries is almost the opposite of the demographic one. The USA, with less than 5 per cent of the world population, appropriates a quarter of world income. The European Union is no state but a major economic player in the world, housing 30 per cent of world income among 7 per cent of the world population. China and India comprise 37 per cent of the human population and share 9 per cent of the income. The so-called BRICS (Brazil, Russia, India, China) do show up in table 3.3, but together with no fewer than five Western European countries and Canada. The two largest African economies, the South African at 283 billion and the Nigerian at 176, are smaller than that of Denmark and Portugal, respectively.

We are witnessing the start of a return to economic eminence of the central polities of the two richest Asian civilizations on the eve of the dawn of the Eurocentric modern world. They have returned

Table 3.3   The world's largest economies: gross national income, 2008

	$ billions	Percentage of World Total
USA	14,466	25
Japan	4,879	8
China	3,899	7
Germany	3,486	6
UK	2,787	5
France	2,702	5
Italy	2,109	4
Spain	1,457	2.5
Brazil	1,411	2.5
Canada	1,390	2
Russia	1,365	2
India	1,216	2

Note: In spring 2010 China overtook Japan
Source: World Bank 2010: table 1

as nation-states, China's reproducing basically the same extension as the most powerful dynastic empires, India an unprecedented postcolonial unification of the subcontinent. Thanks to its supranational integration, Europe is still a major economic area of the world. But the leadership role and the missionary mantle of European civilization have for more than half a century passed to the greatest success of European settler modernity, the USA. According to the book which more than any other put civilizations into recent limelight (Huntington 1996), a European civilization did not even exist, supposedly succeeded by a 'Western' one, centred on the western shores of the North Atlantic.

While the list in table 3.3 includes two other European off-shoots of settler modernity, Brazil and Canada, West Asian civilization remains splintered and economically weak, in spite of its huge oil revenue, with the Egyptian economy smaller than the Romanian, and the Saudi Arabian similar to that of Austria. Africa has so far never been an intercontinental economic centre, and remains rather marginal, although the twenty-first century has started rather well for it, with GDP outgrowing population increase.

If we want to gauge global standards of living, we should turn to another measure, national income per capita expressed in dollar-translated purchasing power parities; (PPPs). PPPs are estimated from the price of a large basket of goods in the different countries – how

Table 3.4   The most prosperous countries and the income of big countries. Gross national income per capita in purchasing power parities, 2008 ($)

	GNI per capita	Multiple of World Average
Norway	58,500	5.6
Singapore	47,940	4.6
USA	46,970	4.5
Switzerland	46,460	4.5
Hong Kong	43,960	4.2
Netherlands	41,670	4.0
China	6,020	0.6
India	2,960	0.3
Indonesia	3,830	0.4
Brazil	10,070	1
Pakistan	2,700	0.3
Bangladesh	1,440	0.1
Nigeria	1, 940	0.2
Russia	15,630	1.5
Japan	35,220	3.5
Mexico	14,270	1.4
Germany	35,940	3.5
Sub-Saharan Africa	1,991	0.2

Source: World Bank 2010: table 1

much you can buy for x dollars. Getting these price levels right is a difficult process, and particularly in large countries with considerable internal variation. In 2005, the World Bank undertook a major revision of its procedures, finding serious errors in previous estimates, for instance that Chinese income in PPPs was 40 per cent lower than found by the earlier method, whereas the Nigerian was higher than thought (Chen and Ravaillon 2008). It would be rash to conclude that now at last the correct figures have been found. Caution is advisable, but the new set contains the best data available on comparative income in the world (see table 3.4).

Perhaps the most remarkable result is the great prosperity of Singapore and Hong Kong, surpassing almost all Western Europe, the only ex-colonies at the top of the prosperity list. Visitors who witness their continuous shopping sprees and well-managed workaholism are less astonished, though. The world average of per capita national income, taking purchasing power into account, is held in Brazil and in Latin America as a whole, with South Africa just below. The very poorest countries of Europe, Moldova, Bosnia-Hercegovina and Albania, are well below world average, Macedonia just.

Of the world's 11 most populous countries, each with more than 100 million inhabitants, 6 have a per capita national income of purchasing power below the world average, and only 4 are above. The ratio of top to bottom, USA to Bangladesh, is 33:1.

Nation-states are not just big or small, rich or poor. They also group themselves in geopolitical constellations, often overlapping and of widely varying meanings. In recent years there has developed a remarkable global swarm of nation-state leaders flying around from one summit to another.

One aspect of this are efforts at interstate global governance. The UN is here the most central, the most universal, but therefore also the most unwieldy. The World Trade Organization is a wide but non-universal organization of binding statutes, and therefore a stage of serious but peaceful conflict, the only stage where the EU dares to stand tall against the US. A third example of this type is a set of informal summits among countries that consider themselves called upon to govern the world. It began, late last century, as the G7, of the seven biggest economies, to which Russia was politely invited in the 1990s as a costless gesture to an ex-superpower now embracing capitalism. But with the geoeconomic shifts visible in the 2000s, that formula is no longer working. In the 2008–9 financial crisis the G8 has already been surpassed by a broader grouping – the G20 – which besides the rich and the biggest, with a vote extra for the EU, includes a set of emergent state actors of significance: Saudi Arabia and Turkey in the Middle East, Indonesia and South Korea alongside China and India in more eastern Asia, Argentina, Brazil and Mexico from Latin America, as well as Australia and South Africa. Further jockeying for invitations is to be expected.

Secondly, there are territorial groupings of states. By far the most successful is the European Union, currently of 27 members, and with strong supra-state institutions. Similar more or less continental organizations include the American OAS, older than the EU, but hampered by the unbalance between the US and the rest; the African Union, explicitly modelled after the EU, from an early postcolonial base (the Organization of African Unity), although much weaker; and, thirdly, ASEAN of Southeast Asia, much more respectful of national sovereignty than the EU. The OAU/AU has had at least one very important impact, the recognition and thereby pacification of the arbitrary colonial frontiers, sparing Africa the interstate wars which repeatedly devastated the Balkans in the first half of the twentieth century.

All over the world there are also smaller territorial groups of states. Most advanced was probably the Nordic one – grouping Denmark, Finland, Iceland, Norway and Sweden – before the EU division of it, creating already in the 1950s a passport union and a common labour market. In 2008 Brazil successfully launched UNASUR, comprising the 12 states of South America, thus keeping US influence at bay, although Colombia, to the intense irritation of the Brazilian government, has opened up a set of military bases to the US. Little has come out of the post-Soviet Commonwealth of Independent States, largely because Russia has not been generous and subtle enough to provide any consistent leadership. The Arab League goes back to the time of the Palestine crisis after the Second World War, but has always been fractured and ineffective.

Thirdly, there are ideological interstate movements and alliances. Bilateral patron–client relations apart, the only one of any power is NATO, the remaining core of a set of worldwide military anti-communist alliances set up by the US at the beginning of the Cold War. After the implosion of its rationale, the Soviet Union, NATO did not fold up. Instead it expanded, recruiting the former satellites of the USSR, and extending its military ambition far beyond the North Atlantic. It seems to have two major functions today. One is to cement a pro-American political alignment of almost all Europe, continuing its Cold War goal of 'keeping the Russians out and the Americans in'. The other function is more recent, to provide auxiliaries and a symbolic 'international community' to American wars in various parts of the world, occasionally, as in the current war in Afghanistan, of more substantial, if always secondary, help.

Against the very material missiles, bombs and the 'special forces' of NATO, the other ideological state organizations of the world appear rather toothless talkshops, like the vast Non-Aligned Movement of the anticolonial Bandung (1955) generation, the Conference of Islamic States and, most recently, the ALBA group for a 'Bolivarian Alternative' in Latin America, initiated by Hugo Chavez, whose Venezuelan oil revenue gives it some materiality.

While the economic and the ideological interstate organizations mainly reflect interests and concerns of recent decades, most of the territorial ones have deeper roots. The EU comprises the centres of European civilization and the main lanes to modernity in Europe. The OAS got off early as the association of New World states. The

Arab League and the African Union have civilizational roots as well as common semi-colonial and colonial, respectively, experiences of modernity. The ASEAN corresponds roughly to the extension of the Southeast Asian family system and to the meeting place of Sinic and Indic civilizations. But the politics, if not the economics, of the former Sinosphere seems to have been irretrievably ruptured by aggressive Japanese reactive modernization, as was the common civilization history of South Asia by the 1947 Partition.

The collective actors dominating the current world stage are nation-states. Alongside the big state powers, others are 'supporting actors'. But seen as sets, the latter are also very significant players. We shall glance at two such sets below: corporations, including corporate cities, and social movements.

Corporations

Globally operating capitalist corporations are obviously a major feature of the contemporary economy. There are two different lists of the biggest, based on different criteria and not quite overlapping in time. One is the American *Fortune* Global 500 ranked by revenue, and the other is the British *Financial Times* 500, which goes for shareholder value, or market capitalization. Both of them concur that US corporations dominate the world. On the *FT* 2009 list, American corporations made up 6 of the top 10 (including the number 1, Exxon), 23 of the top 50 and 181 of the global 500. That is nevertheless a decline, though, from 57 per cent of the *FT*500 in the late 1990s to 36 per cent (*Financial Times*, 25/7/2008). On the *Fortune* list for 2009, Shell is the largest of all, but 4 out of the top 10 are American, 16 of the top 50, and 140 of the global 500.

Oil profits dominate the revenue list, to seven among ten, while the market value list has only three oil companies (see table 3.5). Instead, the latter has four manufacturers, against one on the *Fortune* list. There is one bank and one retail chain on each, plus a mobile phone company on the *FT* list.

The total market value of the *FT*500 corporations is about 10 per cent larger than the GDP of the USA. US corporations have a somewhat larger share of the value than of the number, but the second place of China is underlined. It holds even if Hong Kong companies are counted separately, which does not seem to be warranted any longer.

China is stronger on the *FT* list, clearly the second location in terms of market capitalization, harbouring 3 of the first 10 (including

Table 3.5   The world's ten largest corporations, 2009 ($bn)

By market value		By revenue	
Exxon Mobil, US	337	Royal Dutch Shell, Netherlands	458
PetroChina, China	287	Exxon Mobil, US	443
Wal-Mart, US	204	Wal-Mart, US	406
Ind. & Com. Bank of China	188	BP, UK	307
China Mobile, Hong Kong	175	Chevron, US	263
Microsoft, US	163	Total, France	235
AT&T, US	149	ConocoPhilips, US	231
Johnson & Johnson, US	145	ING, Netherlands	227
Royal Dutch Shell, UK	139	Sinopec, China	208
Procter & Gamble, US	138	Toyota, Japan	204

Note: The old Anglo-Dutch oil company Shell is located differently by the two sources, presumably because its main stock exchange listing is in London but its headquarters is in The Hague.
Sources: Market value: *Financial Times*, 30–31/05/2009, www.ft.com/Ft500; Revenue: *Fortune*, http://money.cnn.com/magazines/fortune/global500/2009/full_list

Table 3.6   Market capitalization shares among major countries, 2009 (% of the total market value of the *FT*500 companies)

USA	40
China (incl Hong Kong)	12
Japan	7
EU	24
UK	7.5
France	5
Germany	4
Brazil	2
Russia	1
India	1
South Africa	0.6

Source: Calculations from www.ft.com/Ft500

PetroChina as number 2), 7 out of the top 50, and 41 among the top 500 (Hong Kong companies included). According to *Fortune*, Chinese corporations had one among the top 10, 3 among the top 50, and 37 (fewer than France at 40, and Germany at 39) among the top 500. The Japanese are faring much better on the American list, 1 of the first 10, 3 among the top 50, and the second largest number, 68, among the top 500. On the *FT* list there was only one Japanese company among the most capitalized 50, Toyota, at number 22.

In comparison with the big states, corporations are rather dwarfish. In their peak year of profits, in 2006, the *Fortune* US 500 made a total profit together amounting to 16 per cent of the tax revenue of the US government. The gross revenue of the world's 10 biggest corporations together corresponds to little more than a tenth of US taxes (taxes taken from OECD, http//: stats. oecd.org).

The world's largest private employer by far is the anti-union US retailer Wal-Mart, with about two million employees worldwide. That is less than a tenth of US civilian public employment, at 22.6 million in 2009 (www.bls.gov/news.release) and little more than half the size of German public employment (OECD 2009: 30). Corporations are big, resourceful and powerful, but once you stop leaving states out of the picture, they no longer look so dominant.

In the latest wave of globalization, many scholars and consultants tried to catch cities in corporate nets, as 'global cities' or as part of 'world city networks' (Sassen 2001/1991; Taylor 2004, respectively). While this perspective throws little light on cities as built environments of urban human life, it does highlight important and interesting aspects of the corporate world.

First of all, Sassen's work demonstrates that globalized corporate capitalism is firmly grounded, and not just floating about on the flows of capital, with 'command centres' in a small number of places. Two cities stand out as centres of capitalist finance and business services: London and New York (in an outsider's cautious alphabetical order). Sassen included Tokyo as a top trio of 'global cities', but the decline of Japanese capitalism generally and of Japanese banking in particular has made that categorization obsolete. In a recent (2009) piece of extensive ranking commissioned by the City of London, the most noteworthy thing is perhaps not that London comes on top, closely followed by New York. It is the fall of Tokyo to rung 15. Frankfurt is put in eighth position, after Singapore, Hong Kong, Zürich, Geneva and Chicago (www.cityof London.gov.uk).

At the University of Loughborough, Peter J. Taylor has developed extensive research and databases on the spread and linking of firms and their subsidiaries across cities of the world. They provide another very interesting picture of the spatial hierarchy of global capital (see table 3.7). The two leading centres of finance and business services are still on the two shores of the North Atlantic, but in the second tier, six of the seven nodes are on the western side of the Pacific.

Table 3.7 A global urban hierarchy of business services, 2000, 2008

Alpha ++ cities	2000	2008
	London	London
	New York	New York
Alpha + cities	Hong Kong	Hong Kong
	Paris	Paris
	Tokyo	Singapore
	Singapore	Sydney
		Tokyo
		Shanghai
		Beijing

Source: Taylor 2009

Hong Kong seems to be benefiting from the Atlantic financial crisis of 2008–9 (*Time*, 1/02/2010, 'Big City Shake-Out', pp. 38ff). It should be added that, among the total of 17 companies making up the only partly overlapping lists of the world's 10 largest corporations by the *Financial Times* and by *Fortune* (table 3.5 above), only one is headquartered in London (BP) and none in New York.

Missions and movements

The world stage has, of course, many more actors beyond states and corporations, and there even exists, from the mid-2000s a Yearbook of 'Global Civil Society', defined as 'the sphere of ideas, values, institutions, organizations, networks and individuals located between the family, the state and the market and operating beyond the confines of national societies' (Kaldor et al. 2009: 2). The Union of International Associations has registered 36,000 active international organizations (in 2005/6), 5,000 intergovernmental organizations and 31,000 non-governmental organizations (www.uia.org/statistics), for which there is also a yearbook, prohibitively expensive to those who are not registered.

While there is in some sense a mediated world society through which rather small, professional organizations can raise important global issues, of human rights and environmental threats e.g., most international organizations are minor players, with small, specialized roles and a limited impact. Four exceptions stand out.

One is the Christian Catholic Church, which, with 1.13 billion adherents, is by far the largest non-state organization on the planet. It is probably the most ancient non-state organization, and it is older than any existing state, with the arguable exception of the Chinese with its discontinuous regimes. Catholicism is not only a religion, but a worldwide organization with a universally accepted leadership, of the Pope and the Collegium of Cardinals. The Pope is widely respected and popular, but his authority is very limited. Christian state leaders ignored his appeals for peace in the run-ups to the Kosovo and Iraq wars, and even in Italy the church's view of abortion and divorce is largely ignored. Nevertheless, the Catholic Church remains an impressive world actor.

Missionary activity, pursued by many religious organizations, has picked up enormously in the past two decades, including into the reopened fields of post-communism. Here, the Catholic Church is a major loser, as the largest and most successful missionary drive has been conducted by Pentecostal and similar 'Evangelical' Protestant organizations, largely if by no means exclusively at the expense of the church. Spectacular inroads have been made in Latin America, under Catholic rule for 400–500 years, since the second wave of globalization. By the late 1990s, Protestants numbered around 30 pert cent of the population in Guatemala, 20 per cent in Chile, 13 per cent in Brazil and 6–7 per cent in Mexico (Martin 1997: 6). The thrust has come from Protestant organizations in the USA and is very much linked to an American 'spirit of capitalism' (Micklethwait and Wooldridge 2009: 216ff), but it very rapidly mutates into local off-shoots. The latter may go global too. South Korean Protestant denominations – going back to nineteenth-century missions, which until the Second World War had their regional centre in Pyongyang – have about 16,000 missionaries abroad. A Nigerian church has recently successfully produced a branch in the Ukraine (Roy 2008: 214–15). The Mormons, another American religion, have also been very successful missionaries, now with about as many adherents as Judaism (Roy 2008: 213).

The other world religions have been much less active missionaries. Islam has not been passive, but it has operated internationally in different ways. One is major state input, by Saudi Arabia and the other Gulf states, in financing mosque construction, from West Africa to Central Asia to Europe, including the Swedish university town of Uppsala, my former base. Korans and other religious material are supplied in profusion. State input also includes provision of *imams*, to Central Asia, the Caucasus and to Europe, a supply mainly coming from Turkey and the North African countries. Support for *haj* to Mecca and for Islamic studies, at al-Azhar in Cairo and other places, are also part of the picture. Missionary activity proper appears secondary to these state contributions, but it is also important. The Egyptian-based, only semi-legal, Muslim Brotherhood provides teachers and preachers. The fundamentalist South Asian *Tablighi* currently pursues mission very actively, as do many of the more mystic Sufi Brotherhoods, both African and West Asian. In the West the most important Islamic inroads have been made among African Americans. But Islam's most remarkable successes have been among Indians of Chiapas in southern Mexico, brought about by converted Spanish missionaries (Roy 2004: ch.3 and passim; Roy 2008: 213f).

Buddhism has staged a strong comeback in China, where about 10,000 temples and monasteries have been (re)built since the early 1980s (Croll 2006: 290). It seems to have been mainly generated internally, though, without much missionary activity. The latter, from Taiwan, has been more focused on the Chinese diaspora (Poceski 2009: 265ff). Amorphous pluralistic Hinduism, too, has formed organizations to reaffirm a straightened-up faith and moral worldviews in the Western diaspora, and several Indian gurus have proved themselves successful competitors in the rather small world of a Western 'New Age' movement (Roy 2008: 230ff).

'God is back' in the modern world, chastened by postmodernist challenge, as the *Economist* journalists Micklethwait and Wooldridge (2009) argue.

The Catholic Church and the missions are two of the main non-state, non-corporate actors on the world stage. Two others are forces of opposition to globalized capitalism. One, according to its 2002 Charter of Principles, is a global meeting-place of movements 'opposed to neoliberalism and to domination of the world by capital and any form of imperialism', the World Social Forum (www.forumsocial-mundial.org.br). The other is the main organization of labour, the International Trade Union Confederation.

The World Social Forum (WSF) was launched in 2001, as a direct alternative to the capitalist World Economic Forum in Davos, by a confluence of Brazilian trade unions and radical social movements with entrepreneurial leftwing intellectuals of the Parisian monthly *Le Monde Diplomatique* (Cassen 2003). It began in the (then) left-governed Brazilian city of Porto Alegre in January 2001. It was an instant success, and generated an international council, a long line of regional and national social forums and a recurrent global rallying point of the radical *oecumene* in the 2000s. Its first venture outside

Latin America, in Mumbai in 2004, was a great event, and its global regionalization in 2006, in Bamako, Caracas and Karachi, went rather well. After a not very successful, weakly organized forum in Nairobi in 2007 and a certain European fatigue – with an internal split within the French Attac current (an important international component of the WSF, the Association for the Taxation of Financial Transactions for the Aid of Citizens, founded in France in 1998) – the WSF bounced back very vigorously in Belêm, Brazil, in 2009, with 113,000 participants, including the left-of-centre presidents of the Southern Hemisphere. Except for Nairobi, its central forums have attracted 100,000 participants or more; in 2005 in Porto Alegre there were estimated to have been double this number (Glasius and Timms 2005: 200). The WSF International Council has decided to convene the World Forum again in 2011, somewhere in Africa.

The International Trade Union Confederation (ITUC) was consti-tuted in 2006 as a historical reunion of secular and Christian trade unions, a process under way on a national level since the 1960s. Claiming 166 million members in 156 countries and territories (www. icftu.org), ITUC is a major global player, though more as a movement of solidarity and support than as a worldwide organization. Most union practice is local or national, and so is its politics of decision-making. The secular–religious merger did not fully overcome the Cold War division , which, in the form of the World Federation of Labour continues to live a shadowy existence even after the implosion of East European communism. A third of worldwide union member-ship is in Europe (Waterman and Timms 2004: 183), with about a tenth of the world population.

Membership is a slippery cross-national indicator of union strength, however, because inflated by the number of heteronomous unions and deflated by the significance of non-member followers, which is an important feature of French industrial action, for instance. Therefore, trade union weight is probably best captured by the extension of collective wage agreements.

Trade union collective bargaining is a lasting achievement mainly of European trade unions, although there is an impressive coverage in part of South America too. Argentina and Uruguay have a strong trade union culture, including not only the classical meat-packing industry, the car assembly workers of Argentina and the public sector, but also private white-collar employees, such as in banks. The orga-nized tin miners were a pace-setting social force in post-Second World War Bolivia, and when the mines closed they brought their organi-zational skills to other areas, above all to the coca growers, the core

Table 3.8 Collective bargaining coverage, 2007 (% of employment)

Less than 15%	15–50%	51–70%	More than 70%
Turkey	Poland, UK	Germany	France & most of the EU Russia, Ukraine
USA	Canada		
Korea			
China			
SE Asia			
Brazil, Chile			Argentina, Bolivia, Uruguay
	South Africa		

Source: ILO 2008b: table 3 and 39ff.

base of current President Evo Morales. In India, by contrast, a mere single per cent of employees are covered by collective agreements (Venkata Ratnam 1994: 6). (Below we shall return to issues of work and class in India and China.)

Trade union organization remains a violently contested activity in most of the Americas. Corporate prevention of collective organizing is still standard practice in the US – and a lucrative consultancy business – outside the old industries and skilled building trades of the north, and south of the Rio Grande hundreds of union organizers are killed every year. An international tabulation of labour rights violation, which discreetly leaves out the US, show persistently low rates in Western Europe, and high ones in Latin America and the Middle East (Mosley 2007: figure 5.2).

On the whole, trade unions have been on the defensive in recent decades. Advances have been few and far between, though very significant in themselves. Workers' unions played key roles in the final breakdown of apartheid in South Africa and in the democratization of South Korea, both in the 1980s. A quite special, simultaneous case was *Solidarnosc* in Poland, a remarkable example of the importance of political logic in social dynamics. At its core a genuine working-class movement, *Solidarnosc* became, because of its Polish government adversary, a spearhead of global anti-communism, generously supported by the Vatican and by the anti-union governments of Reagan and Thatcher.

New movements of exploited and/or disadvantaged have hardly been able to compensate for the weakening of unions and workers' rights, especially in China and India, but they have added a positive dimension to the social landscape of the world. Indigenous peoples all over the globe have come together in several forms, with the UN-focused Unrepresented Nations and Peoples Organization as an umbrella. Since 1996 there has been a tricontinental confederation of poor dwellers' associations, claiming 3.5 million members: the Shack/Slum Dwellers International. In Durban in 2002 StreetNet International was founded, a confederation of 300,000 street vendors (Scholte and Timms 2009). These and similar organizations, like the Latin Amerian peasant movement Via Campesina, are strengthened by their participation in the social forums.

Above, we have surveyed the big elephants on the world field, the nation-states, the capitalist corporations, the religious denominations and their missions, the world social forums and the international trade unions. Some are very powerful and aggressive, others have to manoeuvre and to accommodate, still others are steeled by the belief in their ideas. Some make up the politico-economic world power system, others its main resistance and challenge. The big corporations and the social movements are products of recent capitalism and politics, while their locations have visible historical roots, corporations in North America, Northeast Asia and Northwestern Europe, and international social movements in Europe and the Americas.

The main nation-states of today, on the other hand, have a long gestation – China has been going for more than two millennia, with the Indian flag with the wheel of Ashoka claiming a similar ancestry for India, both modern states of ancient civilizations. Japan looks back at least a millennium and a half. By comparison with Asia, European and American big powers both look pretty juvenile on an eonic time-scale, but no one should ignore their prolonged historical formation. The realm of the Franks, today's France, has at least more than one millennium on its shoulders, and Russia and Britain more than half a millennium. Modern Germany may be only little more than a century old, but before that there were 844 years of the Holy Roman Empire of German Nation (962–1806). The European settler states of the Americas constituted a 'New World', and the USA and Brazil are slightly more and slightly less, respectively, than two centuries old, still far beyond a human lifespan. Colonial Indonesia and settler South Africa, by contrast, were born in living memory, although both are claiming the importance of events and achievements far beyond that.

Contemporary world religions and the equivalent comprehensive moral philosophy of Confucianism have an age of 1,400 years (Islam) to about 3,000 (Hinduism). They have mutated, branched out, divided, but their foundational texts, the Confucian Analects, the Bible and the Koran, or its Hindu equivalent the *Ramayana* epic, and others, are still eagerly studied – and their interpretations disputed with fervour. To capture this amazing historical depth of the current world stage and of its largest actors, an approach of sociocultural geology is imperative.

An individual lifespan is much shorter, even in the best of circumstances. But we individuals also carry world history, global geology within us. We were all born located in them, which have largely determined our life-chances, and we have all been educated in selective scraps from them.

— 4 —

OUR TIME ON EARTH: COURSES OF LIFE

What all of them – the history, the dynamics, and the stage of the world – lead up to are outcomes of human lives and deaths. Wherever and however we live, we all have a life-course, running, if complete, from birth and childhood to adolescence and youth, to adulthood, and finally to old age and death. For many, the course is severely truncated, quite often in the first year of life. In standardized studies, life-courses are usually analysed probabilistically with respect to certain key passages of life, such as leaving school, entering the labour market, marriage or cohabitation, having a first child, etc. Comparisons are usually confined to a few birth cohorts and a few, mostly similar, countries (see further Mayer 1990; Blossfeld et al. 2005). The method is time-, energy- and money-demanding, but in its carefully sanitized way, shed of the rich textuality of autobiographies and *Bildungsromanen*, it does show that social structures and the formations of cultural geology are lived life-paths.

Here, we cannot follow individuals along their itineraries, but we can try to map the paths they find before them, in the world of the early twenty-first century. People do have choices, and they will meet luck, good or bad, so the map is likely to reflect the streams of their individual life-courses, like a situated road map is likely to capture the distribution of traffic.

Our global life-map may be seen as a projection from three sources. First, our map follows from the genetically programmed, socially mutated, human life-course. It begins with our birth and is followed by a long, vulnerable, sometimes exploited, childhood, and by sexual maturity which may or may not be part of a transitional period of adolescence or youth, into adulthood, with its expectations of reproduction, livelihood and, often but not always, a new habitat. After adulthood, there comes a period that moves at a slower pace, of retirement, paid or unpaid, a time of mostly gradual decline and increasing dependence, and finally death, a major cultural event as well as a biological terminus.

Secondly, from what we know about the geological formation of the social world, its topography, its divisions and its connectors. The major civilizations and their derived or related family systems impact the current gendering of childhood and adolescence, adult choices and elderly alternatives, providing modal life-courses, always differentiated by gender, often by ethnicity, usually by class. The waves of globalization and the pathways to modernity shape our religious beliefs, our linguistic competence and our adult citizenship. The history of modernity has provided us with different adult opportunities and perspectives. Its mid-nineteenth-century division of the world into what is now euphemistically called developed and developing countries is still governing human chances of survival, from birth to old age.

Finally, our life-courses derive from the current world dynamic, its fundamental drives, and its larger-than-life major *dramatis personae*, directing our youthful aspirations, openings or closures, our adult motivations, and a large part of our adult and post-adult possibilities.

Life is a journey from birth to death. Our task here is to outline the most important, most frequent itineraries of that travel.

Birth and Survival

There are about 128–9 million human births a year, around 350,000 a day. A small number, three million since 1978, have been produced 'artificially', mainly in Western Europe and the USA, with the aid of 'assisted reproductive technologies' (www.eshre.com). The average fertility rate for women of the early twenty-first century world is 2.5, a remarkable historical decline over a century before, when Asian, African, Latin American and most European women tended to bear five or six children in their lifetime, in North America almost four and in Russia seven (Therborn 2004: table 8.7). Today's fertility poles include, on one side, sub-Saharan Africa – with an average of around five children per woman, as in Nigeria and Ethiopia, in some even six, in Uganda and Congo, or more – and, on the other, developed Northeast Asia and Eastern and Southern Europe with little more than one. The population of Eastern Europe is declining, stagnating in Europe as a whole, while most of Africa is growing at a pace of 2.5–2.6 per cent a year. Japan is bound for decline very soon, but total Asian as well as American populations keep growing, a little more than 1 per cent a year, the world total (UNFPA 2009: 86ff).

A subterranean, illegal birth control movement spread across the European continent and overseas settlements from the last quarter of the nineteenth century. A hundred years later, state-sponsored, rich-country-financed birth control conquered the world, a global process of information flow, gradually winning over Third World leaders, and resulting in global/national institutional entanglement. Birth control reached Africa in the 1990s, but the high fertility values of the African civilization remain resilient, in force even in urban middle-class milieus. Given the mortality rate and the lack of any extra-familiar support in case of need, a high fertility rate is also a rational insurance policy.

Human births are naturally gendered systematically. Given male biological weakness, human populations naturally give birth to 105–6 boys per 100 girls. The two most populous countries of the world, China and India, have both strongly deviant sex ratios at birth, China with 120–1 boys to 100 girls in 2004–8 (*Global Times*, 27/11/2009) and India 112 to 100 in 2004–6. In the most misogynous states or provinces the ratio is higher, reaching 124 and 121 respectively in Indian Punjab and Haryana – with their common modernist capital Chandigarh – and 132 in the central Chinese provinces of Anhui and Shanxi (Guilmoto 2009: 521; cf. Li and Peng 2000: 68–71). Albania in Europe, the three republics of the Caucasus, Pakistan and Vietnam also have misogynous sex ratios of births, between 112:100 (Georgia, Pakistan and Vietnam) and 121–2:100 (Armenia, Azerbaijan). This may be a transitional surge, of modern birth control plus traditional preferences for sons; the sex ratio of South Korea was back to the norm of around 107:100 in 2007 (Guilmoto 2009). The jury is still out.

Traditionally, in both China and India infanticide and gendered postnatal neglect have been practised. Nowadays selective abortions are more important, illegal in India but nevertheless rather inexpensively available, as is the neglect of vaccinations and healthcare. Official birth control policy, a one-child policy in China so far heavily implemented and new family norms of having fewer children have seriously aggravated the female deficit in both India and China. The current sex bias is a modern phenomenon, which has grown in recent times, more urban than rural, more widespread in rich provinces than poor ones, and in India spreading south from the traditional patriarchal belt in the north (Srinivasan and Bedi 2009).

In spite of its relative decline in comparison with selective abortion, postnatal neglect of girls when food, and time and money for medical treatment are scarce is a significant feature of five countries in the world. In Afghanistan, China, India, Nepal and Pakistan, more girls than boys die before the age of 5. Everywhere else, the mortality rate is mostly significantly higher among boys, or at least about the same (UNFPA 2008: 90ff).

Children are born into this world under different conditions and with very different auspices. In the least developed countries every eleventh child will not make it to his or her first birthday. In the worst cases, in Sierra Leone, Afghanistan and Angola, about one in four will die before the age of 5. In Congo, a big country of about 60 million, one in five will never celebrate a fifth birthday, and the same is the case in Nigeria. In India death before the age of 5 will hit seven or eight in every hundred children, in China two or three, and in the rich countries four to nine in every thousand (UNICEF 2008).

However, overall, children's chances of survival are definitely getting better, largely due to the post-Second World War wave of globalization, involving not only the Cold War but also the UN population machinery, the WHO and even significant imperial investments in tropical medicine, like spraying against malaria mosquitoes, and vaccination. Between 1970 and 2005 the global under-5 mortality rate was halved, from 148 to 76 per 1,000. But in proportional terms, there was more progress in the richer countries. In high-income countries mortality rates went down from 32 to 7 per 1,000, in middle-income countries from 127 to 35, and in low-income countries from 209 to 113. Relative female survival chances have also bettered. Now male:female life expectancy at birth is about equal in Afghanistan and Pakistan, and slightly higher, though abnormally little, for Indian females (UNFPA 2008: 87).

Class, and often ethnic belonging, weigh heavily upon childhood, upon chances of surviving – very class-differentiated in Latin America, economically the most inegalitarian part of the world – upon the likelihood of emerging unscathed by malnutrition and, of course, by educational opportunities. Even those who survive entry into the world may be stunted in their development and left with a proneness to illness and weakness in adulthood as a result of being undernourished as a child. Significant underweight, by normal human standards, befalls about one child in four worldwide, in South Asia two out of five, worse than in Africa which more or less follows the world average (UNICEF 2008: table 2). Subglobal sociocultural configurations cast their long shadows on human childhood. A cruel divine, or this-worldly irony, has also placed a large number of the most vulnerable children, born to poor, young, and little educated mothers, in the most dangerous tropical habitat.

Your chances of survival do not depend only upon the country where you happen to be born. They are also much affected by the class of your parents and by the subnational area of your birth. This is true of all countries, including the least unequal rich ones, like Sweden, where infant mortality according to Statistics Sweden currently ranges from 7.3 per cent in middle-sized towns to 1.5 per cent in small municipalities with a population of less than 12,500. But the numbers affected by class differentials of mortality are larger in the poor or developing world. Between the poorest and the richest fifth of parents – a range much narrower than that between the upper middle class and the poor, but rather among better- or worse-off 'ordinary people' – the under-5 mortality ratio is usually around 1:3, which in India means an extra death frequency among the poor quintile of 10 per cent of all children, in Brazil and Indonesia 7–8 per cent. There are variations – for example, in little developed but modestly organized Uganda there is no difference between the quintiles, and in notoriously unequal Peru, where the overall rate is much lower, the death ratio among children with parents in the highest and the lowest fifth of income is 1:6 (UNDP 2007a: table 8).

Subnational regional differences of survival may be as marked as they are among income classes, or even more so. Under-5 mortality varies among Indian states from 19 per 1,000 in the outlier Kerala – socially well organized, politically leftwing, literate, with weak male domination by South Asian standards but not very well off economically – and 138 per 1,000 in patriarchal north-central Madhya Pradesh, with much abject poverty and a notoriously polluted (by Union Carbide) capital Bhopal (Nanda and Ali 2007: table 2.7). The difference in life expectancy at birth between the two states is 18 years, 73 years in Kerala and 55 years in Madhya Pradesh. Provincial differences are less polarized in China, ranging from 64 in Tibet and 65 in Yunnan in the West and the South to 75 in Eastern Zheijiang and Guangdong or to 78 if the metropolitan province of Shanghai is included (www. stats.gov.cn). However, it is mainly Kerala that accounts for the Sino-Indian difference. Excluding Delhi, the second safest life-course state in India is Punjab, providing 12 more years of life than Madhya Pradesh, and 10 more than northern Uttar Pradesh and Orissa.

Brazil is a regionally very polarized country, between a poor, underdeveloped northeast with a huge slavery mortgage, and a prosperous, if also inegalitarian, southeast, dynamized by free labour coffee cultivation and later by industrialization. The ratio of infant mortality between the regions was almost 2.5 : 1 in the 1990s, but this was overshadowed by the education differential of 10 : 1 between illiterate mothers (about 3.5 million of fertile age) and mothers with 12 or more years of schooling (www.ibge.gov.brasil, *Evolocão e Perspectiva da Mortalidade Infantil en Brasil*: tables 1 and 7). Nigeria, like most West African countries, is polarized between north and south, and children in southwestern Yorubaland and in southeastern Iboland have a 2.5 better chance of survival until the age of 5 than the children of northeastern and northwestern Nigeria, where a good quarter of all children born will never reach their fifth birthday (www.nigerianstat.gov.ng).

Life expectancy is, to a large extent, and particularly in poor countries, determined by what happens in the first five years after birth, but adult stress, and ways of coping with it are also important. Also, because of the latter, national borders and national levels of development tend to be overshadowed by class and ethnicity and their entanglement with cultural patterns. Table 4.1 gives some illustrations. It refers to men only, as the length of life usually varies more among men than among women, even if the same pattern of differences is there for women as well.

District class differences in the UK amount to 28 years, wider than between sub-Saharan Africa and high-income countries (26 years; World Bank 2010: 379), or between Australian Aborigines and settlers. From the outside, the Calton eastern inner-city district of Glasgow, with some 20,000 inhabitants, does not look particularly run down, and part of it, with recently built low-rise redbrick buildings, looks rather nice. But about 60 per cent of the working age population are out of employment, and there is much relative poverty, compounded by alcohol and drugs (see further Hanlon et al. 2006). Lenzie is a prosperous villa suburb. Montgomery County is a mainly white, rather dense and urbanized suburban area just north by northwest of the Washington DC boundary. The majority of the residents of the US national capital are African American, many of them relatively poor. The male American racial gap is six years of life expectancy at birth, the same as in 1950. The female gap has been halved since then, but is still four years. The national class differential is smaller, 4.5 years for both genders together, but it has increased since 1980 (Congressional Budget Office, Issue Brief 17/4/2008).

150

Table 4.1 Class, ethnicity/race, and nation in male life expectancy at birth, early/mid-2000s (mean years of life expectancy)

Nigeria	46
Glasgow Calton	54
Aborigines of Australia	56
Russia	59
India	62
African Americans in Washington, DC	63
Brazil	69
US African Americans	70
China	71
US whites	76
Cuba	76
UK	77
Australia	79
Montgomery Co. USA	82
Glasgow Lenzie & London Kensington/Chelsea	82

Sources: Glagow, London, Australian Aborigines, Washington, Montgomery Co.: WHO 2008a: 30, 32; US whites and blacks: US Dept of Health and Human Services 2008: table 26; the rest: World Bank 2009: tables 1 and 5

Childhood

Childhood has a very different place in the social life of various parts of the world. In sub-Saharan Africa as a whole, 43 per cent of the total population are children under 15, in Uganda and Congo almost half. In India they make up a third, in Brazil a quarter, in China and USA a fifth, in Germany and Russia about a seventh, and in Japan an eighth (World Bank 2010: table 1).

Parenting

While it takes a man and a woman to make a child, far from all children are growing up with both their parents. As a large-scale phenomenon, single mothering is a historical product of the plantation slavery of the Americas, where slaves were prohibited from marrying, and where the commerce in slaves paid no attention to couples and parents. After emancipation African Americans were able to marry, but marriage required a certain economic stability to be maintained. The ghettoization of a black underclass in the USA and in the Brazilian *favelas* in recent decades, exacerbated by a culture of drugs, and the almost constant poverty of the Caribbean have spawned a pattern of absent fathers. In Europe, east and west, in the white Americas and in the urban slums of Africa, births out of wedlock and divorce have created a significant minority of children being brought up by a lone parent, usually the mother. It is still rare throughout Asia. The British Isles are moored unsteadily between their overblown North American offspring and their well-kept but ageing and slightly despised or feared European aunt, and generate some dysfunctional social patterns. One is child poverty. Currently, a sixth of all British children are living in a jobless household – worse than anywhere else in Europe (Stewart 2009: figure 13.3).

Death is the greatest disruption of families, not divorce, and it cast its shadow over childhood throughout the world until the twentieth century. Giving birth was a high risk adventure for women everywhere. Now it is a significant risk only in Afghanistan and in Africa. In Nigeria and in several other African countries one mother in 100 dies giving birth; in Sierra Leone one in 50 does not survive childbirth (UNDP 2007a: table 10). AIDS is creating orphans en masse in Africa. Currently, one out of 8 African children has lost his/her mother, or father, or both by the age of 18. One out of 14 of Latin American children and one out of 16 Asian children have the same traumatic experience (UNICEF 2006: fig. 3.2).

African children tend to belong to an extended family. Around 2000, at the age of 10–14 about a fifth of Nigerian and Ethiopian children were living with neither parent, a situation which only about one Brazilian child out of 9 or one US child among 25 is likely to experience. Growing up with both parents is an experience of the minority in southern Africa, ravished by AIDS and separated by long-distance, long-term labour migration. At the other end of the family world, Asian children usually grow up with both parents, as do 80–90 per cent in Indonesia and Turkey, for example, and very often as a single child. Two-thirds of American and of Swedish children grow up with both parents (Therborn 2004: 180).

Grandparents are important everywhere, but the presence and the significance of siblings, cousins, aunts and uncles vary considerably. A good quarter of all 20 million Indian children born in 2000 already had three or more siblings, a rare experience in Europe, North America and China nowadays. Extended kin does have significance in most parts of the world, – not the least in diasporic communities, e.g., of Jews, Armenians, Greeks and Chinese; exceptions to this are Western Europe, North America and the Oceanic offshoots of Europe. Among the popular classes of Chile, for instance, to whom healthcare has been recently extended, when somebody has to go to hospital for a serious investigation or for an operation, a large kin network tends to accompany the patient.

African children seem to have the most authoritarian parents. If we go by values which parents think most important to implant in their children and calculate the percentage of parents stressing obedience minus the proportion valuing independence in their children, we get the picture shown in table 4.2. There are some regional patterns: African obedience, East Asian, North Germanic and North American independence, and at least two in Latin America – an axis of obedience from Mexico to Brazil, and a balanced valuation in the south, from Uruguay to Chile. But Europe is very differentiated, without any east–west fault-line like other family dimensions, but, rather, a north–south one. The Portuguese, scoring +17, have the strongest culture of obedience. In South Asia, much more than geographical distance and the Bengali language seem to separate Bangladeshi, ex-East Pakistan, from Pakistan. Egypt sticks out among the Arab Muslim countries as unexpectedly independent-minded.

Table 4.2 Especially important values in children; % stressing obedience minus % selecting independence

Sub-Saharan Africa[1]	42
Pakistan	31
Brazil, Mexico, Peru (average)	25
Algeria & Morocco	19
Russia, Ukraine	3
Argentina	1
India, Vietnam	0
Great Britain	−4
Egypt	−20
North America	−30
Bangladesh	−57
Germany & Scandinavia[2]	−60
China, Korea, Japan (average)	−64

Notes:
[1]Average of Nigeria, Tanzania, Uganda and Zimbabwe.
[2]Average of Denmark, Norway and Sweden. Finland had −28.
Source: R. Inglehart et al. 2004: tables A029 and A042

Schooling

Almost all children go to some school for some time nowadays. Primary school enrolment in the world is about 87 per cent of the relevant age group, in sub-Saharan Africa 72 per cent. From USA and Western Europe we know that even many years of formal schooling does not result in universal functional literacy, and the problem of effective education in poor countries is, of course, much larger. About half of all children in Nigeria and Pakistan, a third of Indian children, but only 10–15 per cent of Indonesian, Egyptian and Mexican children do not reach grade 5. Recent Chinese data are lacking, but already in 1991, 83 per cent of Chinese youngsters reached that grade (calculated from UNDP 2007b: table 12). In the 1990s, rural education declined in China, humorously and mildly satirically described in the film *The Teacher*, apparently producing significant new cohorts of illiterates (Huang 2008: 238).

In many places in the world, girls are discriminated against in elementary education. Boys' primary school attendance is 11 percentage points higher than that of girls in Pakistan, 8 in Nigeria, 7 in India, while about equal in Egypt, Iran and Turkey. Attendance is gender-equal in Bangladesh, Indonesia, Vietnam and in Eastern and Southern Africa – probably in China too, although attendance data are lacking (enrolment there is gender-equal) (UNICEF 2006: table 5).

Secondary education, on the other hand, is beyond the opportunities of most children in Africa – only 20 per cent of a cohort attended in 1996–2004, in Nigeria a third, in South Asia and West Asia/North Africa two in five were in attendance. Even in Latin America, somewhat less than half of eligible youngsters attended secondary school in the period. There, more girls than boys attended, noticeably so in Brazil, while it was clearly the other way around in South Asia and in West Asia/North Africa. Chinese gross enrolment compares favourably to the situation in Latin America as well as in India – at 70 per cent in all, and also more or less gender equal, in contrast to 58 per cent of boys and 47 cent of girls in India (UNICEF 2005: table 5).

The ways in which inequality is reproduced as a result of unequal access to education are major staples of empirical sociological research, though mainly concentrated on the rich countries (e.g., Shavit and Blossfeld 1993; Müller and Kogan 2010). The global scale is both under-researched and more complex. India, for instance, has a powerful system of positive discrimination into higher education and public employment, favouring 'scheduled', 'backward' castes.

Nigeria runs a state quota system, which, given the history of the country, can hardly be expected to avoid class bias, but which may have significant ethnic effects. Brazil is experimenting with racial quotas, so far with controversial and uncertain results. But the elitist Brazilian system of education is clearly a central part of the country's globally notorious inequality. By the end of the twentieth century, almost half of the black or mulatto population of Brazil had fewer than four years of schooling, as compared to a quarter of whites (Chronic Poverty Research Centre 2004: 81). In the first decade of this century, the Lula presidency has meant a massive expansion of poor and low-income children and youth, though.

On a world scale, there are now more women than men in tertiary education, and many more in most high-income countries, in post-Communist Europe and in Latin America. Exceptions are Japan, Germany and Korea. Higher education is undermining conservative Muslim patriarchy in Iran and in North Africa, and even in the Gulf states. As in many other respects, women are also in this respect worst off in sub-Saharan Africa and South Asia (UNDP 2007a: table 30). This trend towards greater involvement in higher education is clearly a global one, and has occasionally proved to be strong enough discreetly to overrun national male conservatism.

The education investment of Korean middle class parents is probably unique. Among my students in Korea, many had been sent abroad in childhood, from the age of 10–11, to study in an English-speaking country, for the less well-off often to Australia or New Zealand, otherwise the USA and Canada. Some were sent out alone, others had a parent or a relative with them. All went in order to learn English properly, and to prepare themselves for applying to an American university. But searching out, and paying for, special private schools, and *Kindergarten* even, for propelling their children into the world is generally a middle-class pursuit in countries with significant private institutions of education. Elite universities, in contrast to elite primary and secondary schools, are state institutions in most countries, with notable exceptions in the USA. In Brazil, where aspiring and middle-class students almost all go to private secondary schools, private universities, apart from a couple of Catholic ones, are generally regarded as second or third class.

Labour

Child labour, a major feature of industrializing Europe, petered out from the late nineteenth century on, as a result of compulsory schooling, industrial technological changes and campaigning by trade unions and social reformers.

But labour is still very much part of Third World child life, whether it is domestic chores, of cleaning, weeding, fetching water, taking care of younger siblings, of market labour, of peddling, serving or, less frequently, hard labour like weaving or bricklaying, or disgusting sexual trafficking. UNICEF (2005: table 9) has estimated that a good third of all children aged 5–14 in sub-Saharan Africa are engaged in labour, either in long domestic chores or at least short spells of extra-domestic work; elsewhere the figures are about one child in seven in South Asia, and one out of ten in East Asia (excluding China), Latin America and the Caribbean. In the poorest African countries (e.g., Burkina Faso, Sierra Leone, Togo) up to 60 per cent of the children had been doing some work in the week preceding the survey. The Indian figures are likely to be underestimates, and so may the others. Around 2000, about a third of children aged 9–11 were working in some form in major Indian states, in the south (Tamil Nadu and Karnataka) as well as in the north (Bihar, Uttar Pradesh, West Bengal) (John and Narayanan 2006: 183).

If you are unlucky in Brazil, in bringing home what is expected, or if you run into an evil stepfather, you may end up as a street child and a legitimate prey to the violent Brazilian police. Even in Accra, of very familial Ghana, street children are appearing. But to indict 'globalization' as the culprit of Latin American street children, as the fine family historian Elizabeth Kuznesof (2005: 866) does, seems unwarranted, again an example of the hyperinflation of 'globalization'. The continued emigration of the impoverished ex-plantation/share-cropping region of the northeast, the neoliberal informal 'flexibilization' of labour, and the local version of the extension-fragilization of sexual relationships, plus the brutalization of the street by the drug trade, all appear more to the point.

The social meaning and consequences of childhood labour differ greatly. At one end it means bonded or forced labour, being trafficked into prostitution or proto-industrial labour, like carpet weaving, football manufacturing, similar to early nineteenth-century Manchester; at another, it is contributions to family subsistence by domestic chores, farm work or hawking. Concerned citizens of child labour countries usually argue a differentiated reform approach, taking the many constraints and the few options of dire poverty into account. A successful social policy has been developed in Mexico and, above all, in Brazil, where a cash subsidy and a free lunch to poor children for attending school have been introduced, thereby considerably reducing the pressure on child labour. The policy has spread to other Latin American and developing countries.

Youth: Sex and Culture

Youth in social history is first of all sexually defined, as the period between the coming of sexual capacity, with its bodily changes of menarche and puberty at one end, and the full legitimacy and the regulation of sexuality in marriage, recently also by cohabitation, at the other. In traditional African societies, in particular, entry into youth is a major *rite de passage*, a secluded, often painful preparation for coming adulthood. Protestant Christianity provides a passage rite into adolescence, which has now lost most of its social significance, but as late as the 1950s in very secularized Sweden the *konfirmation*, normally at the age of 14 and the end of primary school, meant the end of childhood. It was a lightly religious preparation for coming adulthood, ending with a first church communion, an important rite also among Catholics but there occurring earlier in life.

It is a period of freedom and adventure, emancipated from childhood but not yet burdened with full adult responsibility, nor with the full powers of adulthood. It is a period of physical strength, and, according to most human cultures, a period of particular human beauty, male and female, a time of body culture and of erotic self-display, now including on the internet. However, it is also often a period of frustration and anger, over lacking adult recognition and comprehension, accompanied by experiences of exclusion from the amenities of older generations – a job, a dwelling of one's own, power and influence in society. (A recent European overview focuses on current social exclusion and political participation of young people: Tezanos 2009.)

Little wonder, then, that modernist political cultures, about to change the world into something never seen before, exalted youth as their favourite subjects. In the 1830s, Giuseppe Mazzini founded a national republican movement, Young Italy and Young Europe, mutating into many other 'Young' movements, also outside Europe: the Young Ottomans of the 1860s, the Young Tunisians from 1907, the Young Turks of the 1910s, Young Indonesia and its Oath of Youth of 1928. Italian Fascism was, more clearly than Nazism – which also drew upon reactionary German Romanticism – the black dog of modernism, in spite of its pragmatic Concordats with the monarchy and the church. Its battle hymn was *Giovinezza*,

'Youth'. The rebellious American generation of 1968 drew a moral line of demarcation between the young and the rest: 'Don't trust anyone above 30!' In the anti-communist upheavals of Eastern Europe in 1989, the most militant and the most rightwing force in Hungary called themselves *Fidesz*, 'Young Democrats', the same party that won a parliamentary majority in 2010, under the same leader, though now more middle aged than young. The party's most successful poster in 1989 showed the gerontic Communist leaders, Brezhnev and Honecker, kissing each other on the cheeks in the Russian way with the text 'Their love – and ours'. Communism was dismissed as aged homosexuality.

Historically, modern youth politics was, above all, student politics. In spite of their then small number, students played a prominent role in the European revolutions of 1848. In the twentieth century they often constituted the vanguard of anticolonial movements. As a much larger force, they were at the forefront of the rebellions of 1968, an almost worldwide movement of the second half of the 1960s, and they carried the Chinese protest movement of 1989.

Today's political picture is more varied. Few universities are as radically politicized as that of Buenos Aires. Students play a big role in contemporary middle-class revolts, from Caracas to Bangkok. But the image of young protest is also that of rioting unemployed second-generation immigrant youth in the low-class suburbs of, say, France or Sweden.

At the same time, continuing education has become a major feature of contemporary youth. In the rich countries now, on average about two-thirds of a generation continue to tertiary education, whether university or vocational. The USA and South Korea have enrolments above 80 per cent. In India and China, by contrast, only 11 and 13 per cent, respectively, were enrolled by 2003, and in Nigeria 8 per cent. There is more higher education in Latin America: 18 per cent in Brazil and 21 in Mexico in the same year. But this is well behind Southeast Asia, with corresponding figures of 27 per cent for Malaysia, 31 per cent for the Philippines, and 37 per cent for Thailand (World Bank 2005: table 2.11). Expansive post-primary education has been a central part of the successful East and Southeast Asian development strategies.

In African politics today, governing the most youthful societies of the world, the minister of youth and/or the leader of the youth organization of the ruling party is a powerful man (so far, never – or hardly ever – a woman), although always of second rank. But, on the whole, youth is no longer a major political subject. Youth culture has lost its political connotations to the world of leisure. However, youth has become something of a threat to political leaders in Washington, DC: the 'youth bulge' is one of the nightmares of the Washington planners of US world rule or 'national security', having an academic echo in the work of Gunnar Heinsohn (2003), who is also a NATO consultant.

What is being referred to is a surge in population rates of youth, and of young men in particular aged 15–25/30, and their probable questioning of and rebelling against the existing social order. This is not pure paranoia. After all, the post-Second World War baby boom became, 20 years later, the base of the radical youth and student movement of the 1960s. In Africa, and in West and South Asia, new large cohorts of young people demanding jobs and rights to participate in the politics of the world are likely to shake regimes as well as national border poles, and they may also turn violently against each other. A 'youth bulge' is most evident in sub-Saharan Africa, where 15–24-year-olds make up a good third of the total post-childhood (15 and above) population. In the early 1990s that proportion was almost reached throughout the Third World, from China to Latin America, including the prime NATO targets of West Asia and North Africa, but outside Africa it is on its way down (ILO 2008a: fig. 7).

However, in the world outside the bunkers of the Pentagon and NATO, youth culture has acquired a very different, hedonistic, leisure meaning, only occasionally political. A leisure involving pranks, adventures and show-offs, of erotically charged, if usually not sexually discharged, gender encounters, has a long history in youth culture, particularly among large-scale societies of relatively lightly chaperoned Northwestern Europe. A dance-hall culture among the youth of Northwestern European and North American popular classes is more than a century old. The mass practice of sport surged in the second half of the nineteenth century, also enlisting mass audiences, both young and not so young. But I don't think it is generational bias to say that youth culture rose to a new stage in the 1960s, sustained by the affluent cohort of the 1940s. Pop music was the centre of it, pushed forward by a mighty confluence of media, a very professional recording industry, moving fast from EPs and LPs to cassettes, spectacular concert *mises en scène*, radio, film, TV, CDs and video. This became, in the 1970s and 1980s, a youth cultural wave of globalization, which has continued to develop ever since.

New to the 2000s is an electronically supplied music culture, through MP3, iPod and other devices, and, more importantly socially, an intense virtual intercourse, of chatting and image-sharing, meeting across the world in Facebook, MySpace and other electronic clubs. The attraction of this feverish self-exposing culture is not that easy to understand for an older generation, although it has an intensity similar to previous best-friends relations among teenage girls. Judging from invitations I have received from generational colleagues, something of this ethereal intimacy seems to have attracted some adults as well, but, above all, it is a generational youth experience of the 2000s.

It is a global youth world, but a culture of planetary variation as well of connection. It has a hegemonic centre, in Western Europe and North America, the US and the UK in particular, where the main TV, film and recording studios are, where most successful ideas originate, where most stars are made. Then there are regions and regional centres, Latin America with Brazil and Mexico, East Asia with a contested Japanese centrality, South Asia directed from Mumbai, the Arab world with Cairo as the prime centre challenged by the money of the Gulf. And sub-Saharan Africa, particularly vibrant in terms of music, where any centre is fragile but where Congo-Kinshasa and Nigeria have been important.

In other words, global cultural history is still impinging heavily upon contemporary youth culture and its new forms. Something similar holds for the sexual revolution, another youthful achievement of the 1960s.

A sexual geography of the young world

The 'sexual revolution' of the 1960s and 1970s was not universal, but largely 'Western'. With some delay, changes have got under way in the big cities of East Asia, Tokyo, Taipei, Shanghai and others, but they take quite specific forms. The economic crisis of Africa from the late 1970s undermined family control, changing African sexual mores and practices in distinctive ways. Latin America and the Caribbean have all the time had a more positive and informal approach to sex than the North Atlantic Puritans, but, because of that, and also because of the remaining effects of formalization and stabilization following upon mid-twentieth-century economic development, dramatic changes are hard to detect. The extreme rigidity and control in South Asia and in West Asia/North Africa seem, on the whole, to have loosened somewhat, but only within its own walls of discretion.

The vast expanse of African sexuality

African customs predated the Western sexual revolution by a long time; sex there was regarded as a legitimate human pleasure. The intricate marriage rules often included a considerable flexibility for pre- and extra-marital sex, provided discretion and particular taboos were respected. Biological paternity has always been strongly subordinate to social father's rights, located in the lineage. The value of pre-marital chastity is part of most African culture too, but as a rule placed well below values of fertility and working capacity.

Africa shows no very clear trend to earlier sexual debuts, no 'revolution' in that sense, although there has been an increase in adolescent pre-marital sex in southern Africa and on the West Coast. Because of early marriage customs, the large majority of African women born around 1950 were sexually experienced by the age of 18, with Ethiopia, Rwanda and Zimbabwe being the only known exceptions. The cohort born around 1980 is rather similar, but the marriage age has gone up. The African age of marriage is still low in a global context, with a majority married by the age of 20, in the Sahel and in Uganda before 18, which is the median marriage age in Ethiopia.

By Northwest European standards, young non-married sex starts rather late for most African girls. Of Nigerian girls born around 1980 only one in five had pre-marital sex before 18, in South Africa half of the cohort. Only in the Muslim Sahel, with some leeway in Burkina Faso and Mali, and in Christian Ethiopia and Rwanda is there a strong coincidence of first sex and of marriage. Many more African than Asian teenage girls are sexually experienced, and, above all, many more have pre-marital sex. African girls do have a youth of their own, in contrast to most South Asian girls, and their mobility and their sexuality are clearly less circumscribed than they are to their West Asian or North African sisters.

The devastating economic crisis of the 1980s, was the background to a remarkable, though minoritarian, African phenomenon of female sexual autonomy-cum-dependence, resulting in sexual liaisons between secondary school girls and much older and prosperous 'sugar daddies'.

An odd national case is Catholic Rwanda (most likely to be joined by Catholic Burundi for which I have no data), with rare cases of teenage sex, birth and marriage. At the other end are Botswana and Namibia, where teenage sex and births are common, but where teenage marriage is rare. . Under the local viral conditions of the age

161

of AIDS, this has been a lethal mix. Marriage before 20 is a norm for women in the Muslim Sahel, and to be expected also in Mozambique and Uganda. Many African teenagers become mothers, about a fifth of all, in some countries, including South Africa (in 1998), up to a third.

Grooms and fathers are regularly considerably older, both in Asia and in Africa. In other words, there is almost always a period of youth for young men.

Asian ways: control and/or discretion

Sexuality and marriage in Asia (and North Africa) are still basically channelled within a clearly defined framework. But we may distinguish two major variants on the threshold of the twenty-first century. One involves strict controls on female sexuality, in poor South Asia still largely by moving girls directly from childhood to marriage, in West and Central Asia and North Africa with tight controls on youth cultures. This control has meant that most comparative surveys of West and South Asia have refrained from asking explicit questions about sexual experience.

In Turkey in the late 1990s, school authorities sent suspect girls for virginity tests, and if found non-virginal the girls, including young student nurses, were expelled from school. Only in 2002 did the Turkish Ministry of Education delete lack of chastity as a reason for expulsion from the educational system. Most girls do not experience a period of youth in South Asia, and the same is true in Indonesia, Central and West Asia/North Africa, although a few young women smoking water pipes may be seen in gender-mixed upper-class cafés in Cairo .

But in East and large parts of Southeast Asia there is now a second Asian variant with considerable sexual freedom and youth autonomy, coupled with a widespread practice of decorum and discretion, as well as traditional normative inhibitions – of course outside the commercial sex circuits. The latter is a very important part of domestic male culture – not only for sex tourists – especially in Thailand. East and Southeast Asia are still largely governed by youth self-discipline, without the severe surveillance of South and West Asia, but nevertheless, and by relatively late, mostly post-teen sexual debuts, and marginal, though discreetly growing, cohabitation; cases of extra-marital births are rare. Japan, with its historical socioeconomic edge, is the pace-setter, and China, because of its weight, is the paradigm. South Korea has the strongest traditional institutions. For instance, in the autumn of 2008, the Korean Constitutional Court declared for the fourth time that the criminalization of adultery was still valid law (news.bbc.co.uk: 26/11/2008).

China had a median female marriage age of just over 22 in 1990 (the official minimum age), with the first quartile having married just before 21. Until recently, premarital sex was penally repressed, including college cohabitation (in 1987) and a sexual commune in Shanghai (in 1988). Since then, China, and its pre-communist capital of sex Shanghai, in particular, has 'opened up', with a wide repertoire of possible sexual encounters on offer. But for the overwhelming majority of young Chinese women, born around 1980, sex starts with marriage, or just before, with her fiancé. A quarter of males reported other sexual experiences.

Creole inequalities

Latin America is the world's most unequal region economically. The inequality of the sexual order has been institutionalized there from early colonial times. Widespread sexual enjoyment outside marriage and frequent informal unions still coexist with official Catholic conservatism, manifested in the extremely restricted abortion rights across the region (including a recent total ban in Nicaragua, as part of a murky deal of the Sandinista leader, Daniel Ortega, with the right). But within this distinctive Creole dualism, much stronger than the US one, there is also a centre–periphery division, of an ethno-territorial, not only class, character. The free-wheeling Caribbean and, at least outwardly, buttoned-up Chile make up the two current poles of national socio-sexual orders, with a complex quilt in between, checkered by subnational regions, ethnicities/races and classes.

Sex began, for the median Latin American girl born in the 1970s, around the age of 19, similar to Southern Europe and later than in the North Atlantic region. Except for Brazil, there has been no lowering trend from the cohorts of the 1940s. The median age of a first sexual union is two years later, between 21 and 22. Around 2000 the median age of first intercourse in Mexico City and Buenos Aires was 18 for girls and 17 among boys. In Buenos Aires half of the boys still start with a prostitute, a classic Latin initiation, in Europe as well as in America. Within the hemisphere, the earliest transitions to sexual intercourse, sexual union and birth, with sexual debuts in the early or mid-teens, are to be found in peripheral, largely Indian-populated and/or cultured regions, from Mexico outside the central high plateau down to northern Argentina and to Patagonia.

Four 'Western' variants

Let us end this sexual tour of the world by summing up some aspects of the current socio-sexual order – particularly its youth–adulthood interface – in Europe and North America.

The Northwestern European pattern
of early and informal sex

The average age at which both boys and girls first experience sexual activity is between 16 and 17, but adolescent births are rare, occurring in 1 per cent or less of women aged 15–19. Cohabitation, starting in the early or mid-twenties, tends to be the norm before marriage and is a major form of coupling generally. Single parenting is not at a very high level, and has actually gone down in Sweden in recent decades. The 'ideal typical' populations of this socio-sexual order are the Nordic ones, but what makes it a major European variant, and not just an Arctic outlier, is that, by and large, the same pattern is apparent in France, the Low Countries and, with some qualifications – of more adolescent births, more single parents and less cohabitation – in Britain, and in Germanic Central Europe, also with much less cohabitation.

Scandinavia was probably the only part of the world where sexual issues were not relevant to the student movement of 1968. Universities and colleges there were not *in loco parentis*; students were treated as adults. For instance, when I entered Lund University in 1960, student dorms were self-evidently gender-desegregated, and there were no controls over who visited whom at what time. On the other hand, this did not prevent a strong sexual restraint from reigning. In France and in the US, by contrast, student demands of sexual freedom were explosive.

The Southern European shadow
of the parental household

This variant is rather similar across the southern belt of Europe, from Greece to Portugal. Young people tend to stay with their parents until they marry, which now happens quite late, ranging from an average age of 25 in Portugal to 28 in Italy and Spain. Sex begins later than in the north, at 19–20 for women born in the 1960s, and has a gendered pattern, with boys starting a year or two earlier. Regional intra-south differences are also important. Between Emilia-Toscana, on the one hand, and the Mezzogiorno south of Naples, there is, on average, a two-year difference in the average starting age, with the more chaperoned southern women, of course, being later.

The brief sexual freedom of Eastern Europe

Here, sex starts relatively late and marriage earlier than west of the Trieste–Saint Petersburg line, so the period of premarital sex is the shortest in Europe. To move directly from one's parental home to marriage is normal, and marriage, at least in Russia, has very often entailed living with parents or parents-in-law – as was the custom in pre-communist times.

American dualism of marriage and non-marriage

Characteristic of the USA is a dualism of sexuality and its opposites, of marital virginity and adolescent fertility, of early youth independence and early marriage. The median age of sexual debut was probably somewhat higher in the USA in the 1990s than it was in parts of Northwestern Europe, and the marriage age was lower. The space of pre-marital sex was thus smaller. More noteworthy, however, is the finding that about a fifth of American 18–24 year-olds and about one in seven of those aged 25–34 were virgins upon marriage, a condition nearly extinct Britain and the rest of Northwestern Europe. The USA has the highest rate of teenage births of all Western countries. These are most frequent among African Americans, but white Americans also have a rate much higher than in Western Europe (Therborn 2004: 211ff; Haavio-Mannila and Rotkirch 2010).

Marriage and the End of Youth

Youth, in the sense of non-married individuality, is a period of very varying length. Not everybody marries, but in Asia, the largest part of the world, almost everybody does. The profound and protracted socioeconomic crisis of Africa since the mid-1970s has eroded the universality of marriage, but has not done away with its centrality in the mainstream life-course. Eastern Europeans and North Americans have historically been strongly committed to marriage. The post-communist socioeconomic crisis of the former and, less so, the 1960s sexual revolution among the latter have significantly devalued the institution of marriage, but it has nevertheless survived, particularly in USA. In Western Europe and in African Creole and Indian Creole America, singlehood and (in Creole America and Northwestern Europe) informal cohabitation have for a long time been established options, historically overtaking marriage only in some ex-slavery and ex-peonage areas. In short, among a majority of humankind, marriage constitutes the end of youth and the entrance into adulthood.

All over Asia, weddings are extravagant and extraordinarily expensive *rites de passage*. A friend and academic colleague of mine in Baku gave a wedding for one of his daughters a few years ago, with 500 guests. A Korean friend, a young university administrator of middle-class background, married two years ago in the company of 900 guests. A vast country like India has, of course, its internal geographical, as well as class, variations. A student of mine from northern India had a full-scale wedding in her home city, but in her husband's West Bengal they had only 'a small reception', with 200 guests. Conspicuous high society weddings can certainly be found in Africa, but in the main traditions of sub-Saharan Africa weddings are not that important, and are generally of secondary importance compared to funerals in terms of expenditure as well as significance (Goody 1976: 10). Bride-wealth, to be paid by the groom to the family of the bride, on the other hand, is a very serious and costly business in Africa, but is often a drawn-out process. In Europe – apart from royals, aristocrats and celebrities – weddings are usually rather ordinary festive occasions. In Sweden, the biggest party in a person's life is likely to be the 50th birthday party.

Marriage age and marriage conditions constitute a major landmark in any comparison of human life-courses. In the countryside of South Asia and of sub-Saharan Africa, where two-thirds of the population of the two continents live, half of all girls see their youth end in marriage before they reach 18 (UNICEF 2006: fig. 3.3). Among the urban population youth lasts longer, but a quarter are married before 18. According to the Nigerian Demographic and Health Survey of 2003, women's median age of marriage is 17 nationwide and 15 in the north.

In the strict Chinese birth control order, young people are officially prohibited from marrying before the age of 22, but by the early 1990s a quarter of Chinese women had married by the age of 21 (Zeng 2000: 94). The female median age of marriage in Latin America is in the early or mid-20s, similar to that of Eastern Europe and the USA. But in many rural areas of Latin America, unmarried youth ends early, before 18, particularly in the Indo-American countryside, as we noticed above (UNICEF 2005: table 9).

Western Europeans have always married late by world standards, and still do – in the major countries women marry on average at the age of 28 and men at 31, in the Nordic countries 1–2 years later. In Africa, North America and Asia, marriage usually required the fulfilment of two criteria only: age, which could vary, and the consent of the parents, who then settled the economic transactions involved. In Europe, west of the Trieste–St Petersburg/Leningrad line, that was not enough. A new couple had to have the means to set up their own new household, apart from their parents. It seem that this was a medieval custom, following the line of Germanic settlements in Eastern Europe. Neolocality, as anthropologists would call it, was a Germanic norm, not observed by the Slavs (Kaser 2000). The norm of neolocality meant late marriages – the couple, whether poor farmers, maids or labourers, had to save before being able to set up their own household – and a significant minority of people never actually married.

This East and West European pattern of millennial provenience spanned the coming and going of communism. The East European tradition of early and almost universal marriages survived the Bolshevik revolution, the Stalinist terror and industrialization, the post-Stalinist social development and its implosion. Whether it will survive the reintroduction of capitalism and the concurrent upheavals is uncertain. But the marriage-dominated order is still there in most countries, including the biggest, such as Russia, Ukraine and Poland.

Northern Europeans tend to leave their parental home soon after the age of 20–21, seldom earlier, having finished secondary school at 18. Independent living in your twenties is considered normal and important to your human development, and is facilitated by student grants, social assistance and a rental housing market. Non-married cohabitation is a fully legitimate form of coupling, and in Scandinavia as many first children are born to such couples as to married couples. Southern Europeans, on the other hand, tend to live with their parents for a decade longer. In Southern Europe and in Japan unmarried young people usually stay with their parents until well into their thirties.

West Asian/North Africans, South Asians, most Africans and, still, a significant proportion of East Asians tend to move in with the husband's parents upon marriage. East Asian men and (especially) women tend also to live with their parents before marrying.

North America, perhaps due to its early historical prosperity, has had an earlier marriage age than Western Europe, while largely following the neolocality norm. African Creole and Indian Creole American adulthood was always sexually early and informal, governed neither by Native Indian nor by African *rites de passage*, nor by a European savings account or accomplished apprenticeship, but basically by your body features of sexual maturity. The US marriage pattern, like that of its youth, is remarkable dualistic, consisting of strongly promoted and flaunted married family values together with massive rates of single parenting, of ostentatious public display of the nuclear family and of the extended sexuality of matrifocal ghetto 'random families', of high marriage rates as well one of the world's highest divorce rates.

In many parts of the world, early married life, as well as marriage itself, is dependent on parental arrangements. In the big northern Indian state of Bihar (with a population of more than 80 million, the same size as Germany) there are many more married couples than there are households and only half of the couples have a separate bedroom (Census of India 2001: table H7).

Parents exercise a strong influence over the selection of a marriage partner among 40 per cent of the human population, in South Asia, the rural interior of China and Vietnam, most of Sub-Saharan Africa except the south and the west coast, large parts of Central Asia and most of West Asia (save urban Turkey) and North Africa (Therborn 2004: 129–30).

Girls' or women's choice, in particular, is restricted. Parental marriage wisdom still carries widespread legitimacy even among educated urban women of South and West Asia. My female students in Tehran in the early 1990s were overwhelmingly in favour of parents having a decisive, or at least a very important, say over marriage choice. The strong-willed, British-educated late prime minister of Pakistan, Benazir Bhutto, had a parentally arranged, lasting marriage.

Youth experience worldwide is on a spectrum between rural Africa and South Asia, on the one hand, and Northwestern Europe on the other. In the former areas, girls go from childhood, with often more work than play, to marriage in their mid- or late teens to a husband in his twenties living with his parents, and more often than not into the household of his parental family. At the other end is a prolonged youth of independent living, of unmarried sex and of money to move around, even if employment prospects tend to be less bright for the current generation than they were for the baby-boomers.

Adulthood

Adulthood always most clearly means a right to start a new family, which is why, above, we put marriage as the end of youth, although marriage in Northwestern Europe was never obligatory and the recent sexual revolution has reduced its significance.

But once the threshold into adulthood has been climbed, one way or the other, what lies in front of the human adult? Family apart, there are two basic tasks of adulthood. Finding or making an abode and making a living, which a sociologist may divide into two further parts: finding an occupation and getting a remuneration. In other words, this will take us to housing and habitat, to work and to income. Now, even if we leave 'adult entertainment' to one side, adult life is clearly more than a house/apartment, a job, and an income. There exists nowadays, for masses of people, not just for the (rich, non-working) 'leisure class' of Thorstein Veblen a century ago, leisure: paid vacations, week-ends off and discretionary consumption.

Where to live: The urbanization of the world

When this book was being written, slightly more than half of human adults were living what in their country goes for an urban life, and many more will be going to do so. The human habitat is currently roughly half rural and half urban, but the definitions of and the boundaries between the two kinds vary a lot. They are no more than rough indicators. The World Bank (2009: 55) has recently developed a more uniform measure, which it calls the 'agglomeration index', which is the proportion of a country's population in settlements with a minimum of 50,000 inhabitants above a certain threshold of density. For the world as a whole, the differences between the UN database on urbanization and the new index is not that great. In 2000, 47 per cent of the human population was urban, according to UN data, and 52 per cent, according to the World Bank index, but for some countries, mainly small ones but also including India, the discrepancy is large, due to different national definitions of urbanity. Both calculations are important – the agglomeration index as a worldwide standardization and the urbanization ratio as pertaining to national meanings of urbanity, which are important to people's rights and opportunities, particularly in China.

The poor world is still largely rural, in spite of the extremely rapid growth of Kinshasa and other African cities, of Dhaka and other megacities of Asia. The still mainly rural character of sub-Saharan Africa is rather well, even if slightly exaggeratedly, represented by Ethiopia and Congo, its second and third most populous country, while Nigeria, with its already big pre-colonial cities Kano and Ibadan, remains an urban outlier in the region. The largest differences between the administrative and the agglomeration density definitions

Table 4.3 Urbanization of major countries in the 2000s (% of urban among total population)

	National Urbanization 2007	Agglomeration Index 2000
Bangladesh	26	48
Brazil	81	64
China	42	37
Congo (Kinshasa)	33	26
Egypt	43	90
Ethiopia	16	12
Germany	75	80
India	29	52
Indonesia	50	55
Japan	66	91
Mexico	77	68
Nigeria	50	41
Pakistan	36	54
Russia	73	65
UK	90	84
USA	81	72
Vietnam	27	47

Sources: Urbanization in 2007: UNFPA 2007: 90–3; Agglomeration index: World Bank 2009: table A2

in a more agglomerated direction show up in densely populated countries, delta Bangladesh, Nile valley Egypt, Japan and in countries with high regional centre concentrations, in India, Pakistan and Vietnam. The differential runs the opposite direction in Brazil and USA, Mexico and the UK, which may be due to small country towns in the large countries and to low-density suburbia.

Urbanization has been a major change of the global human habitat in the past half-century. In 1950 a quarter of the human population lived in cities. The world is living something comparable to the nineteenth/early twentieth-century urban trek of Euro-America, or the Japanese in the first half of the twentieth century, a similar attraction of the opportunities of modernity. The world rate of urbanization doubled between 1950 and 2010, as it did in Britain in the first half of the nineteenth century and in continental Europe in the second half. Between 1800 and 1900 the British rate of urbanization increased from 19 to 68 per cent. The North American rate rose from 13 per cent in 1850 to 35 per cent 50 years later, and to 54 per cent in 1950. Between 1950 and 2007 Chinese urbanization increased by about the same percentage points as the UK in the second half of the nineteenth century, from a low base of 12 per cent to 42 per cent, i.e., at a much faster speed, and in Africa the figure went from 12 to 39 per cent (data for 1800–1950 are from Bairoch 1988: tables 18.1, 19.1, 31.1; for 2007, see UNFPA 2007: 90ff. The urban definitions of the two datasets may not be identical, but there is at least a clear, approximate comparability).

We know, from Friedrich Engels on Manchester and Upton Sinclair on Chicago and from other sources, that for all their industrial development and capital accumulation, the rapidly expanding Euro-American cities historically offered their new residents a life that very frequently was nasty, brutish and short. The pressure on the new African and Asian metropolises, with their much faster flood of immigrants and, in the African cases, much slower economic development, is enormous. It is true, as the World Bank (2009) economic geographers are eager to point out, that historical urbanization was also a time of slum growth. But the current scale of slumming is unprecedented. Housing below rudimentary standards, such as durable building material, access to safe water and to sanitation, and to electricity, and/or overcrowded conditions are categorized as slum dwellings by the UN Habitat organization – conveniently located in a plush, secluded garden colony of Nairobi, with easy access to two of the largest slums in Africa (UN Habitat 2007, 2008).

Access to safe drinking water and to sanitation are elementary requirements of a decent human habitat. As these are far from universal, they form one of the Millennium Goals set by world leaders in 2000. While there has been sizeable progress since 1990, there is still a long way to go. By the mid-2000s only a minority (37 per cent in 2004) of the people in sub-Saharan Africa and in South Asia – where a special caste of 'untouchables' had to dispose of human waste – had access to any toilet facilities, whereas little more than half and the great majority of South Asians were using 'an improved water source' (UNDP 2007a: table 7).

However, in spite of the pressure, today's poor urban dwellers tend to fare better than their rural compatriots. The hardest evidence comes in death rates. Throughout most of the nineteenth century, European cities, for which good historical data exist, had higher death rates and lower life expectancy than the countryside. Many growing cities were in fact incapable of reproducing themselves naturally, with death rates exceeding birth rates (Clark 2009: 160f, 282).

This is no longer the case. All available evidence indicates that, at least for the population as whole of the African megacities, urban life, for all its squalor for the large majority, keeps an edge of real advantage, not just a hope of a big win. Professional help with birth delivery, vaccination, elementary clinics, public health surveillance and primary education (not to speak of higher) are much more accessible in cities, also to the poor, than in the countryside, 'in the bush' (UN Habitat 2007). This development should be put onto the credit account of recent waves of globalization, in the form of diffusion of health knowledge and prophylactic practices, and put into urban–rural relief by the capital and big city-centred focus of Third World independence.

The urban–rural income and consumption gaps are huge. In India the urban:rural consumption ratio was 1.9:1 in the early 2000s. In China the income ratio in the mid-2000s was 3.1:1 (for India, see National Sample Survey Organization 2003: 7; for China, see China Statistical Yearbook 2008: main statistical data, www.stats.gov.cn/english).

Poor housing – i.e. slums – has historically accompanied rapid urban development. The mismatch between rapid urbanization and slow or absent industrialization creates a new social situation, in Africa especially; it is more volatile, more violent, more magical than the historical jungles of Manchester and Chicago and their contemporaries. How far this will go is anybody's guess, but the thoughtful, dark picture painted by Mike Davis in his deserved bestseller *Planet of Slums* (2006) should be noticed.

However, slumming is not a constant feature of big cities. Scales of privileged and disadvantaged neighbourhoods tend to persist, but few people would see any slums in contemporary Europe. In Santiago de Chile urban planners claim with some plausibility to have achieved a city without slums (information gleaned from oral presentations at an inter-American workshop on 'Justice and the City' at the Faculty of Architecture of the Catholic University, in March 2008), and the last remaining slum I saw in Seoul in 2007 was a small neighbourhood on the southeastern outskirts of the city.

The adult habitat is changing, with rural locations shaken and dislocated, and urban glitter shining. The latest message from the powerful World Bank (2009) is for more urban concentration. All over the rich world – including the Arab/Persian Gulf and appropriate parts of China – there is currently a major interest in urban, opposed to suburban, development, of waterfront developments, solvent condominium density, recycling ex-industrial brown sites, in ecologically sustainable cities. Iconic architecture is more in demand than ever, but mainly as city branding, not as urban design of social change in the twentieth-century modernist lineage. It is noteworthy that the high-rise apartment block has been established and accepted as the natural habitat of the modern East Asian middle class.

Making a living. I: Classes of work

Entry into the labour force by people of the popular classes in Africa, most of Asia and Latin America tends to be gradual and irregular, very often starting before puberty, as we noticed above when looking at childhood. A large part is governed not by a labour market, but by family relations, helping in family subsistence on a plot of land or in some craft – like pottery or weaving – in hawking small things, as a domestic help, or in some more factory-like establishment, like carpet-weaving. Access to industrial labour, like garment work or subcontracted electronic assembly, is also often shaped by kin and caste, or by neighbourhood connections. An interesting ongoing comparison between Paris, São Paolo and Tokyo has found that entry to a job in São Paolo is largely governed by personal contacts through family and friends, whereas in Tokyo and Île-de-France (the metropolitan region of Paris) you tend to get your job through a labour market, either through direct contact with an employer or through ads and labour exchanges. (Guimarães 2009: 69ff). Tongue in cheek, one might perhaps venture the loose generalization that, in terms of getting a job, the Third World begins in São Paolo, the economic capital of Latin America. Under the institutional uncertainty of the current Chinese labour market, the role of *guanxi* personal relationships and networks has become increasingly important for getting a job (Janjie Bian, 'The increasing role of *guanxi* in China's transitional economy', guest lecture at the Cambridge Sociology Department, 26/2/2010, drawing upon labour force surveys).

In countries where two-thirds of the population is rural, as in Bangladesh, India and Pakistan, or at least more than half, as in China, Indonesia and Nigeria, landownership and land inheritance govern a major part of the world of work. While in China peasants have use-rights to land – now being marginally encroached upon by capitalist industrial development schemes – in South Asia there are still classes of dominant landowners and money-lenders and dominated ones of landless labourers and indebted poor peasants, although substantial classes of propertied farmers and more resourceful subsistence peasants have emerged since independence.

The relative importance of these agrarian relations is still a matter of scholarly controversy (Jodhka 2006). Inheritance rules vary, but in spite of central state legislation of equality, practice tends to discriminate against daughters and widows, in Africa as well as in South Asia and in China (Therborn 2004: 111–23).

In most countries of the world participation in the paid labour force is considerably lower among women than among men, with women doing most unpaid domestic labour. In the rich OECD countries, the gendered labour force participation rates differ by 20 percentage points, the female rate being only three-quarters that of the male. The differential owes a great deal to Japan, to recent OECD members like Korea and Mexico, and, in Europe, to Germany, Italy and Spain. In the USA, the difference is 10 percentage points, in Scandinavia only it is even smaller. China and Russia, with their communist legacy, are rather similar to Scandinavia in the gendering of employment. Brazil resembles Italy more than Mexico in this respect, but still has a differential of about 25 percentage points. In India, urban female employment is little more than a quarter of that of the male. The starkest gender differences of paid labour are in West Asia/North Africa, followed by Pakistan and India, whereas they are considerably less prominent in Bangladesh (with its important garment industry largely employing young women) and in less patriarchal Indonesia. (See OECD 2007a: table 1.A1; World Bank 2005: table 2.2. The figures of these two sources are not directly comparable to each other.)

Total world employment in 2009 was about three billion people, roughly the same size as the urban or rural population. Registered unemployment amounted to 200–220 million, i.e., more than all the inhabitants of Brazil. The International Labour Organization estimates that the financial crisis of 2008 will push up the number of unemployed worldwide by about 50 million – equal to the population of Argentina (ILO 2010: figs 3 and 4), i.e. by more than the populations of South Africa, South Korea or Spain, a chilling illustration of the enormous power of a handful of reckless gamblers at the helm of a few US and British banks.

The ILO figures for the world and its regions, shown in table 4.4, are estimates and should be read with a margin of uncertainty as indicating an overall pattern. Regions also differ internally. The Nigerian census of 1991, for instance, registered a 45 per cent agricultural share of the economically active population (Nigerian National Bureau of Statistics 2006: table 208), much lower than the current African average. Nevertheless, the pattern may be summed up in,

Table 4.4   Work in regions of the world, 2008

	Agriculture (%)	Industry (%)	Services (%)
World	34	23	43
Developed economies & EU	4	25	71
Sub-S. Africa	62	10	28
North Africa	32	24	44
Middle East	17	25	58
Latin America	16	23	61
East Asia excl. Japan	37	28	35
South Asia	47	22	30
Southeast Asia	44	19	36
CIS, non-EU Balkans, Turkey	19	25	56

Note: CIS here refers to all the former republics of the Soviet Union except the Baltics. For statistical purposes the EU, including its poor Eastern members, is treated as one part of the developed world.
Source: ILO 2009: table A6

first, there being two work-poles in the world, an agrarian pole in Africa and in South and Southeast Asia, and a services pole in the rich OECD economies, and, secondly, a major industrial shift, from the North Atlantic to the China Sea.

In the nineteenth and twentieth centuries, the rich world was 'industrial', made up of 'industrialized' countries. Even countries whose labour force was never industrial even as a tri-sectoral (of agriculture, industry and services) plurality, like USA and Japan, were frequently summed up as industrial, and they did derive their prosperity from their industrial dynamics.

Now, Europe is losing its world centrality. After the eastern enlargement not all EU members would globally qualify as 'developed', but as it is practical to treat the EU as one statistical unit, the ILO has created a new category, 'Developed economies and EU'. (The International Labour Organization is a member of the UN family, from the post-First World War League of Nations generation.) The social structure of world capitalism has changed profoundly. Industrialization in the OECD peaked, in labour force terms, in the mid-1960s, and has been followed since the 1970s by a process of deindustrialization. No country will ever again be dominated by industrial employment, as Europe once was. Even in China, the service sector is already larger than the industrial sector.

Currently, only 17 per cent of world industrial (manufacturing, mining, construction, energy) employment is located in 'Developed economies and EU', less than in South Asia (19 per cent) and in East Asia (a third of all) (Calculation from ILO 2008). China dwarfs everywhere else in manufacturing employment. Official Chinese statistics put it at 83 million in 2002, when the big rich countries together, the G7, had 53 million employed in manufacturing. Including rural pre-industrial self- and household employment and workshops, American labour statisticians put the Chinese figure up to 109 million in 2002 and to 112 million in 2006 (Banister 2005; Lett and Banister 2009). A very large part, according to one estimate two-thirds, of Chinese manufacturing work is done by immigrant labour, i.e., by rural migrants without full urban resident rights (Cooke 2005: 197).

Manufacturing output is still centred in the (global) North, although, with Western Europe (EU15) producing a good quarter and the USA a fifth of that output. In national terms, 2006 China was the second largest producer in the world, making 12 per cent of global output in 2007, in front of Japan with 10 per cent and Germany with 7 per cent (US Department of Labor 2008: charts 3.7 and 5.9).

The world of work is, then, very varied and, on the whole, on the move from agriculture to services. In 2002, agricultural employment in the world was overtaken by services (ILO 2008a: figure 3). The historical European trajectory, from agriculture to industry and then to services, is not followed. The exit from agriculture is currently rapid, on a world scale down by seven percentage points since 1997, and fastest in East Asia, South Asia and sub-Saharan Africa, by eleven, ten and ten percentage points, respectively. Other strongly agrarian regions, such as Southeast Asia – with Indonesia as the largest labour market – and North Africa are moving much more slowly (ILO 2008a: table 4). Farm work is more important to women than to men in the developing world, mostly involving working for husbands and fathers. In Latin America, the gender balance is the other way around, though, and in Southeast Asia sectoral economic gendering is about equal (ILO 2007: Box 4b).

The relative importance of the social structure of work depends on the economic sector in which it operates. Here again, your prospects depend very much on the part of the world you are living in.

For all the success of capitalism, it is notable that only half of the world's working population is in an employer–employee relationship. Subsistence household economics still constitutes a major phenomenon. Furthermore, far from all wage–salary relations are capitalist.

Table 4.5 Status at work in the regions of the world, 2006. % of total employment

	Waged/ salaried	Employer	Self-employed	Contributing family member
World	47	3	33	17
Developed economies & EU	84	6	8	2
Non-EU Balkans, CIS, Turkey	77	4	16	4
East Asia	43	1	38	18
Southeast Asia	39	2	35	24
South Asia	21	1	47	31
Latin America	63	5	27	6
North Africa	58	10	16	16
Sub-Saharan Africa	23	3	49	25
Middle East	62	5	23	11

Source: ILO 2008b: table 1

There is also public service, of many kinds, from repression via administration to teaching and caring. The global size of the phenomenon is difficult to estimate with any exactitude. But piecing together various bits of evidence, from China, India, Russia, the USA and the rich OECD world as a whole, plus some World Bank Third World data from the 1980s, which, in a few control cases checked still seem to be indicative, we arrive at an estimate of 285–360 million government employees, including public utilities and similar undertakings, but (mostly) not public industries or banks. That is 10–12 per cent of world employment.

The China Statistical Yearbook of 2008 (www.stats.gov.cn) lists 43.9 million employed in public services in 2002 and another 73 million in public utilities – water, energy etc. – together, 14 per cent of total employment. The 2001 Census of India (www.censusindia. gov.in) registered 34 million in public administration and related services, which probably include private but mainly non-capitalist providers. An industrial relations website (industrialrelations.nuakri-hub.com/employment-in-India) gives a public sector employment of 18 million in 2004. The US Bureau of the Census (www2.census.gov) gives a total of US public employment, federal, state and local, of 23 million in 2008. For the rich countries as a whole, the OECD (www.oecd.org) gives a 2005 total of 14 per cent public employment, including the USA, which amounts to 75 million people. Official Russian statistics yield 14 million people, 21 per cent of Russian total employment, working in public administration and defence, education, health and social work (www.gks.ru/bgd/reg1/b209). Using a World Bank labour market database on the 1980s, Dani Rodrik (1997: table 2) found that government employment in Africa, East Asia and Latin America ranged between 5 and 10 per cent of total employment. The OECD source found similar 2005 figures for Korea and Mexico. If we take that as a basis for an estimate of public employment outside China, India, Russia and the OECD, we arrive at 5–10 per cent of 1,260 million people, i.e., 63–126 million.)

In other words, disregarding state capitalism, a major phenomenon in China – and very significant also in India, Russia and Brazil and several small countries – no more than 40 per cent of the global labour force work directly in a capital–labour nexus. Bad enough, a socialist would say, but far more complex than Marx could have foreseen.

From 1996 to 2007 the share of employees went up by four percentage points, in spite of falling two points in Latin America, due to neoliberal 'flexibilization' and its crises. The overwhelming majority of self-employed, or 'own account workers', as the ILO calls them, are peasants, small farmers, street vendors and small shop-owners. The ILO groups them with non-waged family members into a category of 'vulnerable employment', which makes sense for the majority. But in medium and high-income countries the self-employed are often rather well off. In Latin America the probability line in that respect runs between Argentina – or rather Greater Buenos Aires, which in much Latin American statistics stands in for the whole country – and Chile, on one hand, and the rest (CEPAL/ECLA 2008: table 24).

When looked at more closely from a Northern world vantage point, the ILO work status figures may give too bland a picture. In a book that I initiated on different dimensions of inequality in the world (Therborn 2006), a Norwegian-American colleague, Arne Kalleberg, contributed a very good chapter on 'non-conventional', precarious forms of work, like part-time, short-term contracts, etc. He was writing about the rich OECD world. In the poor parts of the planet there is precious little 'conventional work' in the American sense.

Most labour there is either subsistence or 'informal'. In India in the mid-2000s, for instance, 14 per cent of the working population were in regular waged/salaried employment, but only 6 per cent in the formal sector of labour rights, i.e., the public sector and in registered private enterprises with 10 or more employees. Indian formal sector employment has moved slightly downwards in the past two decades of high economic growth (Oommen 2009). Among urban Brazilian wage workers, about a third are in informal employment, outside the social protection system. This hadn't changed over the previous 15 years, although compared with 1990 it was up (OECD 2007a: table 1.6). For the world as a whole, the ILO (2010: table A11) found a small decline in what it calls 'vulnerable employment' from 1998 to 2007. There is no formal record of informal employment in China, but it is clearly pervasive. A survey of 2005 found that almost half of all urban employees have no written labour contract, and in the private sector a third of employees do not even have a clear verbal agreement or contract. Non-payment of wages is a constant grievance (OECD 2010: 169–70); Lee 2007a: 164). A comparison between Taiwanese firms in China and in Vietnam found a much more brutal labour regime in China (Taylor 2008: 22).

The overwhelming majority of us work within the country in which we were born, although labour migration picked up towards the end of the twentieth century, returning to and surpassing the proportions of a century earlier. By the mid-2000s the ILO estimated the number of economically active transnational migrants in the world to be about 86 million, not quite 3 per cent of the global workforce. Of these, 54 millions were estimated to be in the rich world (ILO 2008b: 5).

Class formations of twenty-first-century capitalism

There are three main meanings and usages of the concept of class, academic technicalities and competition aside. One focuses on culture, on 'U[pper class] and non-U' in a British public discussion of the 1950s (Mitford 1955) on style, accent, education – on *habitus*, as Pierre Bourdieu would say. Max Weber would have talked about *Ehre* ('honour'), and latterday Weberian American sociologists about 'status'. Without the code of pollution and divine sanction, it is similar to the Brahmanic conception of caste – the lower classes are simply less cultured, less respectable, in the caste conception not (quite) culturally clean. This is class as a 'put-down', mainly concerned with distinguishing people of 'good' families from others.

Secondly, there is class as victimization. Here, class is more a 'stand-up' perspective, highlighting unequal life-chances. The children of poor and little educated parents have less chance of going to Eton and of landing a juicy job in the city of London or on Wall Street. Manual workers are less likely to go abroad on holiday and much more likely to die before they can enjoy their pension. Class here is a way of criticizing the privileged and their unfair appropriation of the goodies of life, not a means of pushing nosey non-belongers down the ladder.

The third perspective has become rarefied recently, but it was once quite powerful, and I think it is still the most interesting. This is class as a social force, of certain values, practices and/or interests. It is a 'come-together' conception.

Historically, class in this third sense has asserted itself, and been resisted or admired, in two manifestations above all. One has been as 'middle class', once, in the French Revolution, as the Third Estate, in Germanic lands often as *Bürgertum*, rarely as the 'bourgeoisie'. Middle-class affirmation and pride have travelled widely and for a long time, from early nineteenth-century Britain to mid-/late-nineteenth-century colonial Lucknow in India (Joshi 2001) to post-Communist Bulgaria (Tilkidjiev 1998). The other has been as 'working class', heralded by the labour movement from the second quarter of the nineteenth century, theorized by Karl Marx and the official protagonist or director of the twentieth-century revolutions in Russia, China and Eastern Europe, not to speak of its socially more hollow invocations in the final third of the century, from Cuba to Ethiopia.

The peasantry, or the class of farmers, has also had its time in the limelight. After the First World War it was a very significant, but seldom dominant, social and political force throughout most of East-Central Europe, from Bulgaria to Finland, and in the north bending west to include all of Scandinavia, and Iceland. In the East Asian revolutions, peasants may have been objects of political manipulation as well as social subjects, but their support was decisive to the victories both of Mao Zedong and Ho Chi Minh.

From the *plebs* of the French Revolution and on, there is a more amorphous social force, which in times of social upheaval may be identified as the 'popular classes'. Normally this will include workers and peasants, but the label adds a sometimes important contingent – the urban poor and informal hawkers and workers. The latter groups were quite prominent in the anti-IMF riots of Africa and Asia in the 1990s. They may also be mobilized for sectarian or communal purposes, frequently in South Asia ever since the time of Partition, also in Muslim–Christian clashes in Indonesia and Nigeria, or Sunni–Shia petty wars in Pakistan and in Iraq.

While class in the forms of cultural snobbism and of socioeconomic disadvantage are obviously continuing, it is an open, and because of that interesting and important, question whether class as a social force will still be important in the twenty-first century. The only thing a serious scholar may say with some certainty is that it cannot be excluded, and that if mobilized it has a forceful potential. The middle class is perhaps the safest bet, recently visible, in streets and public squares of Eastern Europe, West, Central, South and Southeast Asia, and in South America. But the capacity of the popular classes, in the broad sense, has also been proved again, for instance in social upheavals after the crash of Argentine neoliberalism in 2001, and in the social struggles, 'wars' in local parlance, which brought Evo Morales to the Bolivian presidency, and kept him there in the new elections of 2009. Their potential for angry, powerful protest, hinted at in many moments of limited crises recently, is haunting regimes across the world, from France to South Africa, from Nigeria to China, from India to the Philippines.

Against this background, it makes some sense to try to draw a class map of the two major countries of the planet. Its fault-lines may provide some indications of forces of possible social change and of preserved paths of growth. The lines of class, and of potential class organization and class conflict are drawn differently from the European industrial society analysed by the Marxian tradition.

The peasantry is still the largest class in both countries, about three times as large as the industrial classes, of workers, managers and owners, together. Its internal differentiation cannot be dealt with here, but especially in India there has developed a significant stratum of capitalist farmers cultivating their land with hired, casual labour. On the whole, the farms are very small, by northern European standards the size of a potato plot. In the early 1990s, the average peasant plot in China was half a hectare. At the same time, the average cultivated farm area in India was 0.3 hectares, according to an Indian scholar. A World Bank report gives a higher figure, referring to landholding – but still modest, 1.4 hectares. In Bangladesh average landholding was 0.6 hectares. In Brazil, by contrast, the corresponding size was 73 hectares. (For China, see Summerfield 2006: 189, citing a Chinese scholar, Zhou Jian-ming; For India, see Mukherjee 2002: 260. Cf. World Bank 2007c: 87.)

In another major Asian example, only a quarter of the economically active population of Indonesia are waged or salaried, and the industrial working class comprises at most 8 per cent of the total (Sugyarto et al. 2006: tables 6.8 and 6.11; industrial employees with senior secondary or higher education are here assumed to be managers).

Table 4.6 Popular classes in China and India in the mid-2000s (% of total economic activity)

	China	India
Self- and family employment	45	57
Of whom peasants	39	47
Informal, casual wage-workers	14	29
Of whom rural labourers	(0)	25
Regular employees	41	14
Of whom urban	19	9
Of whom in the public sector	14	4–6
Industrial classes	24	18

Note: In line with the methodology of the OECD but in contrast to most Indian scholarship, regular employees in the table may be in the informal, no-protected rights sector as well as in the formal, rights-providing one. The lower Indian public sector figure is from the OECD source cited below, the higher refers to Indian sources, discussed in the note after table 4.5 above. The industrial classes cut through the other categories, and should not be added to them. They refer to all those working in manufacturing, mining, construction, and energy and water supply. *Sources*: Employment classes calculated from OECD 2007a: table 1.Al.3. Industrial classes from two papers presented at a seminar in 2007, in connection with the launch of the first-mentioned source, Nagaraj (2007) on India, and Liu Yanbin (2007)

The Sino-Indian differences derive mainly from two sources: from the enduring communist legacy of China, and the different levels of industrial development of the two countries. The communist legacy in this case is primarily the agrarian class structure, the abolition both of feudal or capitalist landownership and of a landless proletariat. Agricultural land has not (yet) been privatized, despite insistent Western neoliberal urging, but is leased to households by the village. Households of urban migrants may let their land to a local household. The Chinese revolution did away with the 'cultures of servitude', produced and maintained by landlessness, caste and debt bondage still alive in India, not only among rural labourers but also among urban domestic servants (Ray and Qayum 2009). Domestic servants have, though, returned in post-Mao China, kept by about a tenth of households in Shanghai (Yan Hairong 2007: 156). Unsurprisingly, public sector employment is larger in China, but by how much is not a robust datum.

China's much larger class of regular wage and salary workers has a background in the socialist economy and in communist urban controls, but now it is mainly based on a much higher level of factory employment.

The gap between the subsistence peasantry and the urban wage-workers is huge in both China and India. Because of more rapid urbanization and industrialization, and an extensive pattern of young urban immigrants maintaining ties to parents and grandparents in the countryside, there may be less of a social chasm between the popular classes in China. Even so, the urban–rural contrast is stark. 'We observed unimaginable poverty and unthinkable evil, we saw unimaginable suffering and unthinkable helplessness, unimagined resistance with incomprehensible silence', a massive 2004 *Survey of Chinese Peasants* concluded (quoted in Croll 2006: 161). At the bottom of the Indian pile, there is a village-based migrant landless proletariat, which moves back and forth between low-paid casual urban and rural jobs, shepherded by a recruiter (Breman 2007).

The popular classes of China and India are more internally divided than their counterparts in modern European class history, who also had their divisions between the skilled and the unskilled, the 'respectable' and the 'rough'. In China the *hukou* registration system separates workers with full rights of urban residence from 'floating' migrant workers from the countryside, who are viewed as guest workers in the cities of their own country, with, at most, precarious possibilities of family life and proper housing, and tenuous workplace positions. In the early 2000s these workers amounted to about a fifth of the urban labour force (Hertel and Fan Zhai 2004: 1).

The formal–informal divide, less widespread and clear-cut in China than in India and other Third World countries – dividing urban Latin America roughly half and half, with informality ascending in the 1990s (Tokman 2004: 186ff) – is sharp. It divides workers with rights, of whom there are more men than women, with rights recognized by the state and backed up by trade unions, from workers without. Formal workers and their unions may, as often in India, see informal workers as competitors and as potential threats, useable by capitalists as strike-breakers, for example (cf. Breman 2004: 416ff; Breman 2003: chs. 9–10). But they may also make big efforts to organize them, offering their resources as a national organization, like the National Labour Congress of Nigeria (Gunilla Andrae, oral presentation at the World Congress of Sociology, 16/7/2010).

True, in some times and places informal sector workers have movements of their own, like the famous Indian Self-Employed Women's

Association, a combination of trade union and cooperative, claiming 700,000 members in the mid-2000s (Bhatt 2006: 16), or the South Africa-based international of street vendors, StreetNet. In the industrial cities of southern China there are special magazines for migrant workers, usually individualist in their message, but also critical of existing conditions (Chang 2008: 59ff).

The formal–informal divide might be overcome in three ways. First, by extending labour rights, fought for in Euro-American class struggles until the trend-break of the 1980s. Secondly, through some broad existential issue that transcends the fragmented mode of livelihood while requiring workers' support, such as national dignity and respect, for example, the anticolonial path from the Chinese May Fourth (1919) movement to the anti-apartheid struggle in South Africa. Neither is very much on the current horizon, but neither is to be excluded. There is a third possibility, perhaps closer and already on some economists' agenda, a generalization of 'informality', marginalizing labour rights under the slogan of 'flexibilization'.

Indian classes are further significantly divided by caste and by religion, mainly between a Muslim sixth of the population and a Hindu majority. The so-called (for promotion) 'Scheduled Castes' make up another good sixth of the population, 16 per cent according to the Census of 2001. They are strongly overrepresented, without being overwhelming, among agricultural labourers and casual urban labourers, but draw regular wages as often as other caste Hindus. They are underrepresented among the self-employed, particular in agriculture. Muslims, on the other hand, are heavily overrepresented among the urban self-employed, and correspondingly under par with respect to both regular and casual wage employment. The complexity of the social set-up of the popular forces in India is further illustrated by the fact that, in spite of their different occupational locations, Scheduled Castes and Muslims have about the same poverty rate, almost twice that of other caste Hindus, somewhat more than double the incidence in the cities, somewhat less in the countryside (Das 2010: 356ff). Indian hierarchy and struggles against it have generated another caste category, 'Other Backward Castes', OBC, who are also claiming compensatory rights. They amount to about 40 per cent of the rural and a third of the urban population. There are also recognized tribal peoples, making up about a tenth of the rural population of the country (National Sample Survey Organization 2003: Statement 2.18), many of whom have been mobilized by 'Maoist' insurgency.

The world has about 1.4 billion wage- and salary-earners, of whom one billion are outside the rich, most developed world (ILO 2008a).

The new (2006) merged International Trade Union Confederation claims about 166 million members, one third of whom are in Europe, as we noted above. Significant, autonomous trade unions do exist in Africa, Asia and Latin America, but outside the latter they are few and far between. In Brazil almost half of employees in paid manufacturing employment were unionized in 2002, in Canada not quite a third are unionized, and in Mexico a good fifth. In Africa, trade unions, though small, are an organized urban force to be reckoned with, today particularly, but not exclusively, in southern and western Africa. In Asia, their importance is largely confined to Taiwan, Japan and Korea, where their influence is not as great as that of Western European unions, and to small countries like Sri Lanka and Singapore, where their autonomy is questionable (Lawrence & Ishikawa 2005; cf. Felipe and Hasan 2006: table 3.5). Indian trade unions are incredibly fragmented, with 12 different national federations, but if a recent (2007) 'verification' is to be believed, they cover a good tenth of the proletariat, or 25 million people, including organizations of the self-employed, a figure much higher than in 1987 (Oommen 2009: 88). While the small Indian formal sector labour force – 6 per cent of the total – seems to have more employee rights than most European workers, not to speak of American, to the dismay of OECD (2007b: ch. 4), India has acquired what is probably a unique pattern of industrial relations. For two decades, since 1987, lockouts in India have cost more in terms of work days lost than have strikes (Datt 2002: 182–3; Nagaraj 2007: fig. 4).

The Chinese have forced American Wal-Mart, for the first time, to recognize the trade unions, but they are not an autonomous class force, and in the Special Economic Zone of Guangdong they are mostly run by enterprise managers. In the indigenous private sector they are almost totally absent, covering no more than 4 per cent of the workforce (Lee 2007a: 58–9). There is more industrial relations space in Russia, but the post-communist industrial implosion there keeps workers down (Clarke 2008). Indonesian trade union organization, emerging from the long military dictatorship of Suharto, is embryonic and fragmented (Hadiz 2001).

The labour movement, once a proud, major force of the Eurocentric twentieth century, is now quite weak. Deindustrialization, or industrial restructuring, and occasional defeated grand stands against capital and/or state challenges, have hit the most organized working classes hardest, from American auto and steel workers, to coal miners in Britain, Poland and the Ukraine, steel and engineering workers in the Ruhr and all over ex-communist Europe. Further afield, too, to the textile workers of Mumbai and Ahmedabad, and to the heavy manufacturing workers of Northeast China (Sherlock 2001; Breman 2003: ch. 10; Lee 2007a).

But in an empathetic book of impressive global historical sweep, Paul Mason (2007) has argued that we are standing on the eve of militant workers' struggles and union organization similar to the heroic trans-continental labour struggles in the decades preceding the Second World War. That is perhaps more hope than prediction, but it is certainly true that the new global industrialization and out-sourcing has generated a wave of strikes, demonstrations and riots among the new industrial working class and the out-sourcees, from post-communist Eastern Europe to China, with 87,000 officially reg-istered 'mass incidents' of popular protests in 2005 (Lam, 2009: 20; see further Lee 2007a, 2007b). The collective voice option coexists, though, with individual exits, and massive turnover from one employer to another in the hot labour markets of eastern China (Chang 2008: 25ff). In the 1990s there developed, with the help of human rights lawyers, the significant Bangladesh Independent Gar-ment-Workers' Union (Rock 2001). In the 2000s, the heavily guarded South Asian workers in the Gulf staged mass strikes and riots in the autumn of 2007 and again in the spring of 2008. Many of these protests have had some success, expressing a market strengthening of labour. In response, the religious authorities of Abu Dhabi instructed all imams to devote their Friday sermons on 25 April 2008 to the rights of (foreign) labour. In Africa the trade union movement is playing a very important role much larger than its size, in struggles for democracy, from Zimbabwe to Guinea-Conakry and Nigeria and as a leader of wider popular protest movements, for instance in Nigeria in the 2000s (Okafor 2009).

These struggles may very well generate figures of the stature of Big Bill Haywood, Tom Mann, and other Paul Mason early twentieth-century heroes. But there is no vision of radical social transformation in sight today, as there was in anarcho-syndicalism and Marxist socialism a century ago. They might also yield a quite different type of popular leader, like Lula, the moderate, laid-back, but very decent current President of Brazil, emerging from the metal workers of São Paolo fights against both employers and military dictatorship in the 1970s. And the movement may become embedded, without much strategic vision, in a democratic but cautious political regime like the COSATU in the ANC regime of South Africa.

So far, this century has been much more conducive to middle-class revolutions than to popular uprisings, not to speak of working-class revolutions. It started in Belgrade in 2000, moved on to Kyiv in 2002, to Tbilisi in 2004 and to Bangkok in 2008. It has been visible in the streets, if not revolutionarily successful, from Beirut, Tehran and Chisinau to Caracas and Buenos Aires. Karachi, Lahore and other Pakistani cities witnessed something similar, though more of a professional – lawyers' – pressure movement, rather successful in its limited demands for an independent judiciary. University students, now allied with their parents – rather than, as in the 1960s, with the workers of their parents – urban professionals, urban entrepreneurs, in person as well as with their pocket-books, have rallied against authoritarian or democratically dubious populist governments, sometimes in favour of parties with even more dubious democratic credentials, like the losers of elections in Thailand and Moldova. There is nothing inherently democratic in these middle-class protests, and in 1973 they paved the way for the military coup in Chile. Anyway, the middle-class street has become a noteworthy feature of the new century.

The big city middle class is a globalized class of consumption ideals and of electronic information, to whom authoritarian populism is both a barrier or threat to their aspired lifestyle and an affront to their knowledge and view of the world. There is no agreed definition and counting of a national middle class, and, of course, even less so on a global scale. But the topic is getting hot, both among liberal political writers looking for allies, and among businesses and consultancies eager to supply consumer demand. One of the most promising serious definitions in terms of global consumption has been argued by the World Bank economists Milanovic and Yitzhaki (2002), defining it as people with incomes between the averages of Brazil and Italy. Outside the rich world, 'in the emerging markets', this grouping comprised about 400 million people in 2005, 7 per cent of the population of those countries, 5 per cent of India (*The Economist*, 'Burgeoning Bourgeoisie', 12/2/2009, special report, p. 4).

At the high end of the class structure a transnational capitalist class is emerging. The transnational operation of corporations is a manifestation of global capitalism, but not necessarily of a global capitalist class. For the latter, a global integration or unification of the executive corporate actors has to have happened. The pioneering work by Leslie Sklair (2001) is not always clear on this point, and his inclusion in the class of 'globalizing bureaucrats and politicians', 'globalizing professionals' and 'media' (p. 17) is perhaps not fully focused. But the tendency is undisputable. At least since the mid-1990s there has been a global labour market for business executives, and on the stock exchanges foreign investors are major players alongside national ones, even in smaller places like Stockholm. International business schools are forming the managers of tomorrow, and an international business press is setting the standards of today – sometimes high, it should be noted. The *Financial Times* is the mouthpiece of an enlightened bourgeoisie in the best nineteenth-century European tradition.

London is the hub of this new transnational capitalist class, a favourite base of business operations and a very attractive major residence, after national bases and tax havens. The big players in the City are all non-British, mainly American investment banks. One third of the largest corporations, according to the FT (London) Stock Exchange Index, are non-British. Among the top ten richest persons in the UK listed by the *Sunday Times* in 2008, only the Duke of Westminster – a recycled feudal landowner, owning, good chunks of prime London land and coming third on the list – is in all respects British. Also British in most senses is Sir Philip Green, of British birth and retail business, although he resides in Monaco. The steel tycoon Lakshmi Mittal, number one, has an Indian passport, and the Hinduja brothers of various international investments, fourth on the list, are also Indian. Three are Russians of Yeltsin-era wealth, one is an Italian-born Swiss pharmaceutical billionaire, one is Swedish of Tetrapak invention wealth and eighth on the list is a Norwegian ship-owner.

On the other hand, on the somewhat differently structured *Forbes* list of the world's billionaires, among the 53 richest of 2008 (the odd number is due to tied rankings), only Lakshmi Mittal and two of the three Swedish families on the list have another country of (prime) residence other than where they are registered citizens (www.forbes.com/lists/2008). (In contrast to the *Sunday Times*, *Forbes* counts the Russian oligarch and Chelsea football club owner Roman Abramovich as residing in Russia.)

Major transnational corporations have by now achieved a substantial international recruitment of CEOs and of board members. Among the 100 largest US corporations, 15 had a non-American CEO by the end of 2007, including Indians directing the large Citigroup bank and PepsiCola, and an Irishman at the head of the big oil company Chevron (*International Herald Tribune*, 13/12/2007). The recent privatization rule that the two British aerospace and arms corporations, BAE and Rolls-Royce, should have a British executive is already regarded as an anomaly in UK business circles, and the companies are lobbying against it (*The Economist*, 22/3/2008).

However, national patterns of management and ownership are still predominant, and with a great deal of business rationality, even if it is combined with a global outlook and a spread of English as the boardroom language of big corporations, e.g., in German Siemens. Only in 2008 were the 500 largest US corporations on the Standard & Poor list expected to have more than half their sales outside the USA, up from a third in 2001 (*International Herald Tribune*, 13/12/2007). Among the 32 US companies with revenue exceeding $50 billion on the 2008 *Fortune* 500 list, foreign sales amounted to no more than a third of their revenue (*Fortune*, 5/5/2008, p. 129).

But 'national' has in many cases an ethnic minority aspect. Most well known are the Chinese (people of Chinese descent) of Southeast Asia, who control the overwhelming part of the private economy of the region, from Burma/Myanmar to the Philippines. Nigerians and Lebanese largely control the urban economy of West Africa. The seven Russian 'oligarchs' who in the 1990s appropriated a bulk of the wealth of Russia, with the help of Yeltsin's foreign advisers, counted six Jews and one ethnic Russian (Chua 2003). Carlos Slim, the richest man in Mexico and, indeed, Latin America as a whole, and the second richest in the world, is a second-generation Maronite immigrant from Lebanon. A great deal of the current transnationality of the world's capitalist class derives from earlier waves of globalization.

Making a living. II: The rich and the poor

Hard work is neither necessary nor sufficient for a decent income. Your income depends on where you were born and to whom, on your skills, on the productivity environment of your job and on luck. Working for poverty is the lot of many in this world.

South Asia, India, Pakistan and Bangladesh, above all, and sub-Saharan Africa, including more developed South Africa, are the poor workhouses of the world. Two-fifths of the world are working for $2 a day or less (in 2005 prices), in South Asia and Africa four-fifths. However, changes are going on, both dramatic and gradual. Between 1998 and 2008, the $2 or less workforce in East Asia (read: China) went down from 77 to 29 per cent, while in South Asia it slipped only from 86 to 80 per cent, and in sub-Saharan Africa from 86 to 82 per cent. In 1998, 57 per cent in South Asia worked for $1.25 or less a day, in East Asia 52 per cent. Ten years later, the figures were 46 and 11 per cent, respectively (ILO 2010: table A12). If the ILO is at least approximately correct, for all the ruthlessness of

Table 4.7 Working for poverty in the world, 2008 (% of the poor among all in employment)

	Working for <$1.25 a day	Working for <$2 a day
World	21	40
Non-EU Balkans, Turkey & CIS	4	13
East Asia	11	29
Southeast Asia	23	52
South Asia	46	80
Latin America	7	15
Middle East	8	23
North Africa	14	31
Sub-Saharan Africa	59	82

Source: ILO 2010: table A12

the Chinese accumulation regime, Chinese labour has drawn benefits from it.

At the other end of making a living in today's world, we find the *Forbes* magazine annual list of the world's dollar billionaires. By late March 2009, after a year of financial crisis, there were 793 billionaires owning between them a total of $2.4 trillion. That is equal to the annual national income of France. A year earlier they had numbered 1,125, gobbling up the equivalent of the national income of 128 million Japanese, or about a third of the national income of more than 300 million Americans. True, we are here comparing wealth and income, but these seem to be the best available data on the super-rich of the world.

Americans dominate the scene, as is to be expected, providing 359 of the 793 in 2009 and 473 of the 1,125 in 2008, not quite the half of all. The richest people on earth are Bill Gates of Microsoft and Warren Buffet, a professional corporate investor, but the top ten included (apart from a third American) two Indians, two Germans, one Spaniard and one Swede (Ingvar Kamprad, the founder of IKEA). In 2008 Russia provided the world's second roster of billionaires, 87, and Moscow was the billionaire city of the world. But the current crisis has hit the Russian oligarchy exceptionally hard, carving 55 off the list, and Moscow had to yield to New York as the main site of billionaires. All other countries are far behind the US, but Germany, with its many inherited family enterprises and fortunes, stands out in the third rank, with 54 billionaires in 2009. Chinese citizenship is held by 47 billion fortunes (28 on the mainland and 19 in Hong Kong). In a third tier we find the UK with 25, India with 24, Canada with 20, and, just, Japan with 17.

Sub-Saharan Africa, after South Asia the poorhouse of the world, sports four billionaires: three South Africans and one Nigerian. Among the most populous countries, Bangladesh and Pakistan are absent, and Indonesia has a minor presence only, five super-rich. Brazil has 13 and Mexico 9 (www.forbes.com/2008, www.forbes.com/2009).

How is the gap between the poor and the super-rich filled? By vast distances and by income clusters defined and delimited only with difficulty and uncertainty. But after the super-rich we should look at the top end of the income distribution of the rich countries, which basically means the OECD. As among the super-rich, the top tenth of American income earners then make up a class of their own, and are much more prosperous than other deciles (OECD 2008: 36). If you translate the income of this stratum into the World Bank ways of calculating poverty, this group of US earners and each member of their households were living on $255 a day after tax in around 2005, which, in terms of purchasing power, means 204 times above the global poverty level. In the rich world, the British fall into the second class amongst the rich, if we disregard the Luxemburgers, but only the top 5 per cent of earners in the UK can match the US top ten. Adding these two groups together, we get a population of 33 million, 0.5 per cent of the world population. But these are not the only such earners in the world. It seems reasonable to assume that 1 per cent of the medium well-off world and of the rest of the rich world, and about 0.1 per cent in sub-Saharan Africa and South Asia also enjoy a high income by North Atlantic standards. That amounts to around 75 million people, 1.2 per cent of the global population. Academic caution would interpret this as 1–1.5 per cent.

The prosperous – as opposed to the rich – of this world may be defined as those earning more than the median income of the rich OECD world, the average white-collar employee and skilled worker. However, the OECD has become more unequal by inclusion of less wealthy countries, like Mexico and Turkey. The median income is reached only by the top tenth of Turks and Mexicans. To them we should add the most advantaged tenth of the rest of Latin America, Russia, South Africa and Malaysia, and a tiny proportion of the rest of the world. Without counting the rich twice, we would end up with 500–600 million prosperous human beings, generously translated as 8–9 per cent of the world population.

191

Between the prosperous and the relatively poor or marginalized in the rich countries, there is a substantial group whose incomes are below the median of $55 a day and above the relative poverty level of $27. They amount to about 390 million people, lower-skilled workers, most often in the service sector. In terms of living standards, they may be grouped with a middle class of the rest of the world. The boundaries between the latter and what we have above called the prosperous have no accepted statistical definition. But a reasonable estimate according to the criteria used here should yield 500–600 million.

The marginalized people of the rich countries are not poor by global standards, but they are clearly disadvantaged in their own countries, getting less than half the national median disposable income. Single mothers make up a large proportion of this contingent. If we restrict the rich countries to the OECD minus Mexico and Turkey, these relatively poor people of the rich world comprise 129–130 million people – 2 per cent of the world total. There are at least as many marginalized people in the rich world as there are rich. The USA contributes more than half of rich country marginalization – 50 million (calculations from OECD 2008: table 5A.2.1; relating poverty proportions to country population size).

Above the upper Third World poverty line of $2.50 and below the US line of around $13 per day, we find the formal sector working class and the lower-middle class of the poor world. They make up about 2,120 million people, about a third of the world population. Of this income bracket, 40 per cent can be found in China and East Asia, 15 per cent in Latin America and Eastern Europe/Central Asia, 10 per cent in South Asia and West Asia/North Africa and just 6 per cent in sub-Saharan Africa.

Now we come to the poor. Almost half the population of the world, 47 per cent in 2005, is earning less than $2.50 a day: 3.085 billion people. Of these, 40 per cent are in South Asia, almost a third in China and the rest of developing East Asia (such as Indonesia and Vietnam) and a fifth are in Africa.

A summary of what making an income means in today's world can be seen in table 4.8.

The polarization of the world is not only between those on the *Forbes* list and the rest. The extremely poor of the poor world are more numerous than all the inhabitants of the high-income world put together, about 300 million more. But it is also important to notice that discretionary consumption has become a mass possibility, and mass practice. A good half of the world population can now indulge in it, to a widely varying extent, it is true, and this does not include

Table 4.8   Income groups of the world, *c.*2005 (% of world population)

The Super-rich, wealth of >$billion
   793 families in 2009
The rich, income, >$255 a day
   75 m, 1–1.5% of world population
The prosperous, >$55 a day/ <$255 a day
   500–600 m, 8–9% of population
Substantial, below average income earners of the rich world,
   >$27/<$55 a day
   500–600 m, 8–9% of world population
Marginalized in rich countries, <$27 a day
   129 m, 2% of world population
Ordinary, non-poor people in the poor world, >$2.50 a day
   2,124 m, 33% of the world
Poor people of the poor world, <$2.50 a day
   3,085 m, 47% of the world.
The extremely poor, <$1.25 a day
   1,377 m, 21% of word population

Sources: Calculations from *Forbes* magazine 2008 and 2009 (the super-rich); OECD 2008(the rich and the marginalized); Chen and Revaillon 2008 (the rest)

the poor of the poor world. This is changing the social parameters of the world. In the North Atlantic of the twentieth century, mass consumerism made the USA culturally 'an irresistible empire', as a magnificent study has called it (De Grazia 2001; cf. on China, Croll 2006). On the other hand, although a very important social variable, mass discretionary consumption is no more likely to determine the fate of twenty-first century Asia than it shaped the twentieth-century history of the USA and Western Europe.

Adult enjoyment: Leisure and consumption

Adult life outside work for hundreds of millions of people has been transformed by social changes of the past century. After the austerity of industrial capitalism, most people now have more free time. Between 1900 and 1975 a typical French worker gained 40 per cent more annual leisure time (Fourastié 1979: 75). Paid vacations for ordinary workers started in Europe in the mid-1930s, their two weeks a proud achievement of the French Popular Front, and of Swedish social democracy. In Britain, working-class seaside resorts emerged, like Blackpool to the west and Scarborough to the east of the English industrial heartland. The USA still provides no legal vacation entitlement, and a quarter of US businesses do not provide any paid leave at all (Fleck 2009: 21–2). Chinese labour law is more progressive. From 1 January 2008, Chinese employees with more than a year of employment have had a right to five days of paid vacation (ILO, Natlex database, www.ilo.org./dyn/natlex). The South Korean Labor Standards Act of 1997, Article 57, gives employees one day of paid leave per month, but as in Japan most of these are not used for holidays but for sick leave or other uses (Fleck 2009: 22).

Free Saturdays spread across Europe in the 1960s and 1970s, reaching Japan by the 1990s and China – at least officially – by 1995. A Korean decision made in 2004 is still being phased in; Korean enterprises with fewer than 20 employees have until 2011 to implement a five-day week.

Work and leisure are still allocated very differently, even in the rich world. West Europeans have the shortest working year, 1,350 hours on the average in Germany and 1,648 in the UK, while Americans and Japanese work much longer hours: 1,809 in the USA and 1,842 in Japan. But the Koreans are the most workaholic, with a mean working year of 2,302 hours. (The data are far from ideal in that they do not distinguish between what is considered full- and part-time employment. They all refer to 'dependent', i.e., waged, employment only and to 2006. See OECD 2007a: table F). To what extent this expresses different cultural preferences or different constellations of employer–employee power seems to be unknown.

But in the rich world, whatever the division of work and leisure, there is money for consumption above what is needed for food, shelter and basic clothing. In early twentieth century, households of the developed countries spent about half their consumption on food. In the 1950s, almost a third of British private consumption was spent on food, in France more than a third, in Italy 40 per cent and in Spain in the early 1960s food accounted for almost half of all consumption. By 1990 the rich country average had gone down to 18 per cent (Bairoch 1997, III: 387; Deaton 1976: table 4). In 2005, 6–9 per cent of consumer spending was enough for food and non-alcoholic beverages in the USA and the major countries of Western Europe. The Japanese spent an eighth and the Russians a quarter of their money on food. The picture is, of course, different in the poor world, a difference likely to be strongly underestimated by widespread subsistence farming. Nevertheless, in Congo and Nigeria 60 per cent of individual consumption is food, in India a third, in China a quarter, and in Brazil 15 per cent (World Bank 2007a: table 11).

We may add housing and health expenditure to food in order to get an idea of the size of discretionary consumption, although there are choices of cheaper or more expensive food and housing. For the OECD world as whole, it would mean that some 60 per cent of the consumer budget, or a good 40 per cent of national income, can be spent on individual discretion.

Middle-class discretionary consumption developed in the second third of nineteenth-century Europe, with the galleries and the department stores of Paris, Milan and other West European cities, and in New York and other North American cities, before spreading south in the Americas and reaching Tokyo in the last quarter of that century. Mass popular consumption emerged in the United States of the 1910s–1920s, the era of Fordism, the object of an interesting and controversial ILO study of 1929–31 (De Grazia 2005: 78ff). It hit Europe in the late 1950s, Japan somewhat later and then the rest of East Asia. The private car was a major item, perhaps more than anything else defining the 'American century'. In 1938 there were 41 cars per 100 inhabitants in the US, and 3 in the other rich Western countries (Bairoch 1997: 556). In 2009 China became the largest auto market in the world, and the Indian equivalent to the *Volkswagen* (known to the English as the Beetle), the *Nano*, has just taken to the road.

'Lifestyle', a term in Europe going back to post-Detroit reflections of the early 1930s by the French labour economist François Simiand (De Grazia 2005: 93), has typically become much more topical than terms such as 'life-course' or 'mode of living', indicating the new possibilities of choice. Market research and pop sociology are understandably much into uncovering clusters of lifestyles. Consumer style and fashion are firmly established enjoyments, even among the urban poor who cannot afford it, but who have developed an impressive vicarious connoisseurship of it. A spectacular example are the urchins of Kinshasa, inspired by popular band leader Papa Wemba's *Société d'ambianceurs et de personnes élégantes*, arguing the relative merits of Armani, Gucci and other luxury brands for different kinds of clothes (Wrong 2000: 174ff).

The world of movies and also long-distance travelling for pleasure – i.e. tourism – have become major phenomena of adult life outside work. The cinema is a century old, and was once a major feature of urban life. Now there are also TV, video, internet downloads and mobile phone uploads, which above all make the

195

contemporary world one of constant spectacle. The 2008 Olympics became a kind of global communion of simultaneous TV watching.

Tourism is a more exclusively adult enjoyment than watching TV, which, though governed by adult consumption, is also a favourite childhood pastime in many countries. As a popular phenomenon tourism goes back only to the 1930s and the first large-scale vacations, and then, of course, mainly as a trip to the national seaside. Upper-middle-class tourism started a century earlier, aided by the British Thomas Cook agency and by the German Baedeker guidebooks.

By the 2000s, international tourism had become a major industry, in 2003 generating 6 per cent of the total world export of goods and services. In 2008, 924 million international tourist arrivals were recorded, many of the tourists no doubt counted more than once. Since 2003, the world tourism organization, set up in 1970 with a parent from 1947 and a grandparent, the Union of Official International Tourism Propaganda of 1934, has become an official UN organization (ww.unwto.org).

The origins of tourism are largely governed by resources, upper-class Europeans first, now reaching upper-middle-class Chinese. Destinations are more complex. Some are simply geographical: scenic mountains (the Alps early on), the sea, from early promenades to beaches. Others are mainly commercial: Miami for Latin American middle classes, Singapore for Asian ones and, most recently, Dubai for Eurasians, not least for the privileged of Eastern European post-communism. Some locations are attractive for their combined offer of culture and commerce, like Paris, London and New York, others because of their exoticism, of which the offers have been extending feverishly in recent decades.

The ruling and the non-ruling generation

In states and in modern societies, in contrast to the pre-modern societies of elders, adults are the normal rulers. Since there are relatively few of the latter, adulthood is also a division of rulers and non-rulers, and therefore, given a common adulthood, of political conflict. It is among adults that the determinants of the world all come together most clearly, the historical geology of civilizations, waves of globalizations and pathways to modernity, and the current drives of the world dynamic.

Political concern, political interest and political activity are very unevenly distributed in the world, in patterns which seem to have different roots of experience and opportunity. On the whole, East Asia – Vietnam, China, Japan, South Korea – the USA and Central and Northern Europe appear most politically involved, together with a few odd African countries, such as Tanzania, in some respects also Nigeria. At the other end, with the least everyday interest in politics, are most of Latin America, Latin Europe, North Africa and Pakistan, which may surprise visitors of metropolitan café society there, but which probably indicates the isolation of a narrow, male public sphere (Inglehart et al. 2004: A004, A062, A086, E023). Americans are by far the most active in electoral campaigning than other people, but are less likely to vote than people in other rich democracies (Kumar et al. 2009: 335–6).

Old Age

Old age in pre-modern societies was mainly a condition of respect, for wisdom from long experience. It seems to run through all civilizations, although often coexisting with artistic homage to the beauty of youth. It was not only in stateless societies that the formal governing stratum was made up of 'Elders'; sometimes, 'Oldest' was used as a title for the head of a polity, as in the Estonian state between 1920 and 1940, or in religious institutions, such as Orthodox monasteries. The entrepreneurial head of the Lodz ghetto in Nazi Poland signed himself as 'Der Älteste der Juden' (the Oldest of the Jews). True, the medieval Christian pictures of the 'staircase of life', going up to adulthood and then down, also indicated physical decline as a major aspect of old age. In some presentations the curve of life began to bend downwards, or at least to flatten out, by the age of 35, in others at 50–55. In France, by no means uniquely in Europe, old age frailty led to certain rights under the *ancien régime*, e.g., the right not to be tortured under penal law or sent to the *galères* (from the age of 70), and to be admitted to a 'hospital' if without means of support, minimum ages varying between 60 and 80 (Gutton 1988: 12ff, ch. 4).

Contemporary cultures also differ in their respect for old age. There is generally more respect in Africa and Asia than there is in Europe and the Americas, deriving from patriarchy, stronger bonds of kinship and from roads to modernity that preserve much more of pre-modern values, norms and practices. Seniority is still much more of an asset in the labour market in Japanese capitalism than it is in Europe or America, for example. India is currently an interesting example of a competitive electoral democracy with quite gerontic leaders. When this writer was middle aged, his white-blonde hair elevated his status on African visits because of his supposedly advanced age. But the modernist priority for the young, from its adulation of novelty and change, has, of course, its effects also in Africa and Asia.

In 1996, the Chinese government saw reason to promulgate a special law for the Protection of the Rights of the Elderly (cf. Therborn 2004: 310). With an artist's critical foresight the post-war erosion of filial piety in Japan was foretold in 1953 by Yasujiro Ozu's beautiful movie *Tokyo Story* about the sad visit by a provincial old couple to their busy children in Tokyo. In the World Values Survey of the early 2000s a good quarter of Japanese people did not fully agree with the statement that one owes one's parents unconditional love and respect, a proportion that was almost the same in Western Europe, while only 5 per cent of the Chinese deviated from the norm of filial piety (Inglehart et al. 2004).

Modernity, like all history, includes ironic twists. Among the rich countries, the USA, without any powerful domestic traditionalism but drawing upon its anti-bureaucratic and individualist settler tradition, stands out because of its severe restrictions on the idea of a mandatory age for retirement (through the Retirement Act of 1978 – see Graebner 1980). This extension of old age social space is envied by many healthy and active 65+-year-old academics and professionals in Europe.

Retirement and pensions

In today's waged societies, retirement is a major boundary between adulthood and old age. Because of retirement expectations and rights, and with birth rates having fallen well below reproduction, ageing has become a major issue in the rich world, particularly in Europe, Japan, Korea and Singapore. In the OECD as a whole, 14 per cent of the population is 65 or over, in Japan 20 per cent, in Germany and Italy 19 per cent, and in France and the UK 16 per cent (in 2005). Some countries are bound to have significant numbers of old people very soon. By 2015 one Japanese out of four, and more than one among five Germans and Italians will be 65 or older. In China 10 per cent and in India 6 per cent will be of that age.

However, a 'third age' – following childhood/youth and adulthood – is a luxury in some parts of the world. In Zimbabwe, for instance, a country which by early 2010 was still being ruled by an iron-fisted 85-year-old, little more than 40 per cent of the population are likely to survive until the age of 40. In South Africa a good third of the population is bound to die before 40. But in China and in Latin America 90–95 per cent survive their 40th birthday. For the rich countries and for the ex-communist countries, the UN Development Programme therefore looks at the probability of reaching the age of 60. A third of Russians are unlikely to get to that age, and throughout the whole of the former Soviet Union this fate befalls between a fifth and a third of the population. One among eight Americans will probably die before the age of 60, but only 6–9 per cent of Western Europeans and Japanese (UNDP 2007a: tables 3 and 4).

In spite of continuing, but maybe less than before, maltreatment as infants and small children, women of misogynous Asia now tend to live longer than men, a fairly recent development in South Asia, perhaps the other side of female foeticide. In the world as a whole, women live four years longer than men. Until the 1980s women in South Asia had shorter lives than men. That is no longer the case: in Pakistan a woman's life is now on average one year longer than a man's, in Bangladesh two and in India three. It is women of AIDS-stricken sub-Saharan Africa who now most frequently have their vital force drained, both in absolute terms, with a life expectancy at birth of 53, and relatively, living only two years longer than men, and in Mozambique, Zambia, Zimbabwe and Nigeria only one year more. In the rich countries, women live five years longer on average.

At the other end of the gendering of old age and premature death are the East Slavic countries of the former Soviet Union – Belarus, Russia and Ukraine – where women outlive men by 11–12 years, not because of any particular female longevity, but because of a traumatized post-communist male adulthood made extra vulnerable by its vodka culture. (Historical data from World Bank 1990: table 32; 2000: table 1.3; recent data from World Bank 2010: table 1. On post-communist mortality, see Cornea and Paniccià 2000; Stuckler et al. 2009.)

Your body carries your adult class into old age retirement. In the UK, for example, if you retire as an upper-middle-class bank or insurance employee, you are likely to live 7–8 years longer after your retirement at 65 than if your adulthood was spent as a brewery worker for Whitbread or as a Tesco shop assistant (*Financial Times*, 20–21/10/2007, p. 18).

In 1737 the French word *retraite* first appeared in its modern sense, of retirement from work with a pension (Gutton 1988: 185). In the course of the eighteenth century the practice of a retirement pension developed, primarily for military and civilian officers, but also for professional soldiers. The institution of caring for disabled soldiers goes back earlier and was enshrined in the grandiose Hôtel des Invalides in Paris. As a national insurance, pensions were first institutionalized in Germany in 1883, but as an actual mass phenomenon of pension payouts to veterans of the US Civil War from 1865. Benefit levels (in relation to average income) were higher for the American military pensions than they were for the new European workers' pensions, and around 1900 the number of beneficiaries was larger, or on par with, that of the pioneering European countries (Skocpol 1992: 109, 131ff).

However, a pension for ordinary people to live on is basically a post-Second World War Euro-American phenomenon, which still has to reach large parts of Latin America, not to speak of Asia and Africa. In Brazil, for instance, almost one person out of five above the age of 60 (the official retirement age) has no pension (Pochmann et al. 2005: table 3.9). In the early 2000s, the leftwing then mayor of Mexico City, Andrés Manuel López Obrador, initiated in the Federal District a modest pension and free basic medical care for everybody aged 70 and older. (His successor and party comrade Hebrard continues to cater to the needs of the elderly in a rather special way, distributing free Viagra to elderly men.)

A private capital investment pension system was introduced in Latin America by the military dictatorship in Chile in the 1980s. From the early 1990s, it was touted around the world by the World Bank, to which I managed to become a witness in Budapest in 1996, an event for which the bank had flown in slick, fast-talking Chilean bankers and had invited treasury officials, with a sprinkling of social policy experts, from Eastern Europe. (The rationale is set out in World Bank 1994.) The system seems to have fulfilled its primary purpose, of collecting vast sums of money from contributors for capital fund management. It did not address the issue of the absence of old age protection for the whole old age population, the crucial issue in the Third World with its formal–informal employment sector divide. After their rapid spread, in the swinging years of neoliberalism, private capital investment pensions are now largely discredited, even in Chile where the Bachelet government of 2006–10 made substantial efforts to install some equity for the aged.

Pension systems are being studied at length in China – in 1991 even this writer was consulted (by a reform committee of the Planning Commission) – but they are moving slowly. Only about 20 per cent of the working population there were covered by pensions insurance in 2003, while in India the equivalent figure was barely 10 per cent (Tao 2006: 518, 543; Anant et al. 2006: 211, 27). In China, it is mainly urban employees, who have pension insurance, spread very unevenly in a descending east–west provincial gradient. From the more socialist times, most of the retired from urban public employment receive a pension, though only 2 per cent of rural residents (Smeeding et al. 2008: 4). Only a small minority of rural residents, who make up more than half of all citizens, are covered by old age insurance, and it is a new system being experimented with, which is not yet paying any pensions (UNDP 2007b: 90, 55). The 17th Communist Party Congress (in 2007) magnanimously decided that the party will 'explore ways to set up an old-age insurance in rural areas' (UNDP 2007b: 41). In 2009 an extremely modest voluntary scheme was announced for very gradual introduction, which would provide a pension of about 15 per cent of rural working income (OECD 2010: 192).

Among old people in the early/mid-2000s, a rudimentary, what the WHO (2008: table 6.1) calls 'social', pension was received by 2 per cent in Vietnam, 13 per cent in India, and 32 per cent in Brazil. A household survey of Delhi in 2002 gives a reliable picture of the best circumstances of old people in India. At least half of them depended on transfers from their children, one in six received an ex-employee pension, and one in nine got a destitute person's public pension (Alam 2006: tables 4.1a–b). In 2004 the Indian government replaced a secure pension system for public employees with a 'defined contribution', i.e., a market-dependent scheme (Shenoy 2006: 85). Only in Europe, North America, Oceania, Japan and a few other countries such as Argentina and Uruguay do all or most old people receive a pension they can live on. Schemes are under way, in East Asia in particular, but are socially hampered by the World Bank (1994) plan to make pension insurance a major feeder into financial capitalism, universalizing the Chilean scheme, from which the military rulers cleverly excluded the armed forces, guaranteeing them a public pension. Such schemes of individual investment accounts run by private financial enterprises not only turn pensions from being a right to a risk borne entirely by the individual citizens; they also perpetuate in new forms the main vice of pension systems of the Third World, that they cater only to old people exiting the 'formal sector' labour market, i.e., public or big corporate employment.

Europe has uniquely generous pension entitlements. A substantial proportion of Europeans, East, West and South, in the 55–59 age group are retired. Only two-thirds of European males are still in the labour force by that age, compared to over 80 per cent in the rest of the rich world. A more differentiated global world emerges if we look at those aged 65-plus. If you don't get a pension, you have to go on

Table 4.9 Male labour force participation among the 65+ age group, 2005 (%)

Developed Europe	7
Eastern Europe	14
Developed Non-Europe	22
East and Southeast Asia	33
China[a]	(20)
South Asia	52
Central America & the Caribbean	44
South America	36
Middle East & North Africa	39
Sub-Saharan Africa	69
World	31

Note: [a]The Chinese rate pertains to both women and men.
Source: Kapsos 2007: table A4.2; for China: OECD 2010: table 7.2

working as long as you possibly can. For most people, retirement with a decent pension is a welcome period of leisure. It is a major achievement of the welfare states. But for some of us, in interesting but physically not very demanding jobs, the right to choose to go on working after, say, 65 or 67, would be an attractive option.

Unfortunately, even with a liveable pension, old age can mean significant relative poverty, incomparable to the historical poverty of ordinary old people, but certainly noticeable in consumer societies.

On the whole, pensions have reduced old age relative poverty very considerably in the rich world over the twentieth century, even into the early 2000s. The special cases where old age means less poverty have two different causes: old age working in Canada (frequent also in Turkey) and the communist pensions legacy in Eastern Europe, which, though not great by West European standards from the 1960s, still provides more economic security than post-1989 East European capitalism. The extraordinarily high rate of old age relative poverty in South Korea seems to be due to spectacular economic growth and de-agrarianization of the country without any accompanying pension rights, which only came into operation in 2008. The old poor in Korea are the ex-farmers and farm labourers left behind by a nouveau riche urban economy. Some similar processes seem to be at work in Brazil, compounded by long-distance urban migration, leaving the elderly poor in the northeast far behind. The very high rate of mul-

Table 4.10 Relative poverty among adults and old people, mid-2000s (% of the relevant population)

Country	<65 years	>65 years
Australia	12	22
Brazil	20	37
Canada	13	6
China	n.d.	17
France	7	8
Germany	8	10
Italy	12	11
Japan	12	22
South Korea	14	41
Mexico	18	27
Poland	12	3
Russia (2000)	19	14
Spain	11	17
Sweden	6	7
Taiwan	10	29
Turkey	14	15
UK	12	16
USA	17	25
OECD	9	13

Note: The poverty line is 50% of the median disposable national income, household adjusted. The OECD data refers to households with a head above retirement age.
Sources: for China: T. Smeeding et al. 2008: fig. 1; for OECD, Japan, Turkey: OECD 2008: tables 5.1 and 5.3; for the rest: Luxemburg Income Study, Key Figures

tigenerational living (on which more below) keeps Mexican old age poverty better in check than in Korea, where poverty levels are much lower and falling rapidly in the urban apartment towers. (In 1998 55 per cent of Korean 60-plussers were living with their children, in 2002 43 per cent; see Kim and Choi 2008.) Other Latin American countries in the Luxemburg income surveys – Colombia, Guatemala and Peru, the last two notoriously unequal – also have little extra old age poverty above the adult one.

The rather low rate of relative poverty in China, much lower than in Mexico, Korea and Taiwan, is not due to a better pension system, although old age non-market income is slightly more significant in China than in Mexico, but less than in Taiwan. A major reason is the urban–rural income gap (roughly 3:1), which means that urban pensions and other old age income go a long way when related to national income. At most, 1 per cent of 65+ women in cities have a disposable income less than half of the median national income, while 33 per cent living in the countryside have it. (Smeeding et al. 2008: tables 5 and 7; for a very different way of calculating relative urban poverty in China, see Saunders 2007). Another important reason is multigenerational living arrangements, to which we shall now turn.

Living arrangements

The increasing frailty and ailing of older people mean that age-specific living arrangements are needed, which of course does not necessarily mean that they materialize. There have evolved four major alternatives. The family, the next of kin, is the oldest and still the most important one. Charity, religious or secular, is another one, of ancient importance in virtually all the world religions, and in modern times manifested secularly above all by Anglo-Saxon philanthropy and charity institutions. It has nevertheless been secondary to other options. The third alternative is more recent, the welfare state, although it had its institutional, if by no means cultural, precursor in the dreadful English poorhouse or the French *hôpital*. For the solvent, there has always been a fourth way out: the purchase of help and service.

Europe west of a line from Trieste to St Petersburg (with some exceptions) was, as we noticed above, unique in the world in establishing the norm, more than 1,000 years ago, that a new couple should form its own household, separate from their parents. Elsewhere, the rule was at least to start out in a parental household, usually that of the father of the groom. Those ancient family patterns are still visible in today's living arrangements of older people. A normality of living your third age on your own, even if you are a widow(er), is overwhelming in Western Europe and its off-shoots overseas. In premodern agrarian society, a retiring parent(al couple) often made a formal contract with the adult child taking over, guaranteeing the elderly a cottage and a stream of basic supplies from the farm.

In other parts of the world, even in Latin America, a sizeable proportion of older people live with their children or other relatives. Among the 60+ of India, almost 90 per cent did so in the mid-1990s (Alam 2006: 95). This is not just family custom or choice though; many Indian elderly would prefer to live on their own, albeit close to their children. But if there is no system of liveable pensions, you are dependent on your family. This dependency may often lead to friction

Table 4.11 Elderly household structures in the world, c.2000 (% among the population over 65)

	Single	Couple only	Multigenerational[a]
Australia	34	52	14
Canada	29	50	21
China	1	19	81
Denmark	46	48	6
Germany	42	51	7
India[b]	4	8	88
Italy	26	43	30
Japan	19	39	41
Mexico	12	17	71
Sweden	46	51	4
Taiwan	12	30	59
UK	38	50	12
US	31	49	20

Notes: [a]This includes also other kinds of composite households than multigenerational ones, but in the developing world they are negligible.
[b]Data refer to 1994–5 and to people above 60.
Sources: India: Alam 2006: 95; Japan and Denmark: Murozumi and Shikata 2008: table 2; the rest: Smeeding et al. 2008: table 2

and abuse, so the Chinese government in 1996 (as we noticed above) and the Indian government in 2007 (*Le Monde*, 23/1/2009) have felt it necessary to pass legislation for the legal protection of the elderly.

Living arrangements in the non-European countries shown in table 4.11 correspond well to the tri-continental 1990s findings of the UN Demographic and Health Surveys: in Africa and Latin America, half of old people were living with an adult child; in Asia, excluding China and India, two-thirds; in Africa, 10 per cent or less were living alone (Bongaarts and Zimmer 2001: tables 1 and 3).

There are two major divisions here, one developmental – measurable in economic resources, such as GDP per capita – and one historico-cultural, manifesting different family patterns. In rich countries, the elderly have more means for living apart from their children than they do in poor countries. This is reflected not only in the contrast between the tri-continental and the West, but also between Mainland China, on the one hand, and Taiwan, South Korea and Japan, on the other. Moreover, recent rapid change, which we noted above already for South Korea, is occurring also in Taiwan, and on the Mainland, where, in 1995, 92 per cent of 65-plussers lived in multigenerational households, down to 81 per cent in 2002 (Smeeding et al. 2008: table 3). Family change is not exclusively dependent on economic growth. In Zambia, for instance, the old age situation seems to have been more affected by the politico-economic and AIDS crises. In the 1970s the government prohibited old age institutions, President Kaunda declaring it a 'sacred and noble duty' of the extended family to take care of its elderly. But after he had left office in 1991 the government conceded the need, and the places built by NGOs and churches were immediately filled (Cliggett 2005: 158).

But there are cultural patterns too, distinguishing not only Japan from Western Europe and North America, but also Southern from Northern Europe in more multigenerational living. Moreover, in Africa and Asia, but not in Latin America, the elderly are much more likely to live with their sons than with their daughters (Bongaarts and Zimmer 2001: 21), a manifestation of the predominance of patrilineal descent in African and Asian family systems. African long-distance labour migration, the complex circulation of children within a kin group, and AIDS are all manifested in African-Asian differences in relations between grandparents and grandchildren, more important in today's Africa.

Classical family systems are changing in their own ways. European single or couple-only living should not be interpreted as isolation. Most elderly are in frequent regular contact with children and other family members. A recent EU survey found that a third of 65+ people are caring for grandchildren or helping other family members every day (Eurostat 2008). Rather, it means autonomy of living.

Northern Europe, the Nordic countries and the Netherlands, have pioneered public services for the elderly – cheap home services of cleaning, shopping, cooking and paramedical care – making it possible for ordinary senior citizens to continue living a decent life in their own homes. Old age service has spread in Europe, to Germany and France in particular. But even in Europe, like the UK, much depends on the size of your wallet, or on your willingness to accept charity. Outside Western Europe, public social services for the aged are severely underdeveloped.

An Ideal Twenty-first Century Life-course

At the end of a hard, concentrated work shift, some dreaming from empirical experience may be legitimate. An ideal geo-social life-course in the twenty-first century might then include a safe birth followed by non-authoritarian parenting in Northwestern Europe, continued by a Finnish-style state schooling – top performing, independent of your parents' wealth, no cramming (Müller and Kogan 2010: fig. 4). Then, growing up into a free Northwestern European youth, with the ability to travel around the world, an Oxbridge university education, and ending in style with a memorable wedding anywhere in Asia, with a wonderful partner from a different culture from your own. After that, you would embark on an exciting, hard-working and highly rewarding adulthood in a big city of East Asia (or India). This would be followed by a serene retirement in some quiet, beautiful and well-connected place, like Geneva or Vancouver. Finally, you had better go to Scandinavia for elderly care.

Death and After

At the end of old age there is a funeral. It may be remembered that ostentatious weddings are an Asian speciality from Azerbaijan to Korea, but funerals, the terminals of our life-course, are, on average, most magnificently staged in Africa (Goody 1976: 10). In other words, to the previous section on a life-course in style might be added a Lagos Island or a Cape Town funeral.

After-life is a more complicated matter. It is certainly not very propitious in Europe, except in Poland, Ireland and a few smaller places, like Malta. It is much better to go west, to the Americas, where, headed by the USA and Chile, people are overwhelmingly believed to live after death. Or south, to Africa; or east, to Asia. A problem is that you might end up in hell rather than in heaven, a strong reality in Muslim countries and also in many Christian ones, like Zimbabwe, the Philippines, Mexico and the USA (Inglehart et al. 2004: tables F51–4). In Hindu India and in Buddhist Southeast Asia your sins are likely to carry you into a miserable next life on earth.

If you want to be venerated after you have left the surface of the earth, your best option is China and Vietnam, where house altars to family ancestors have been re-established at amazing speed, and where your birthday will go on being feasted (Taylor 2007; Chan et al. 2009). In Mexico you might get at least a small shot of tequila on the annual Day of the Dead.

Your chances of becoming a basically benevolent ancestral spirit are largest in indigenous Africa, in Vietnam, and increasingly in China, where you are more and more likely to be remembered and honoured on the annual Tomb Sweeping Day.

CONCLUSION: HOW WE GOT HERE, AND WHERE WE ARE GOING

Guidebooks usually have no conclusion. This one has, largely because thinking it and writing it have been a learning experience for the author. Drawing upon my previous research and on that of many, many others, this guide has tried to bring together a large number of different threads in an effort to begin to understand a whole world which is embracing us all, regardless of whether we like it or not. The emergence of humanity or humankind as the society we are living in makes it imperative for all of us to begin to learn how this world came about, what roads were travelled and with what enduring experiences. What accounts for its amazing diversity, and for its multifaceted connectivity?

It is neither a straightforward nor a short story. To narrate it with some adequate complexity would require skills and space surpassing those of Lawrence Durrell's multi-perspectival *Alexandria Quartet*. What a sociologist tends to do when faced with vast and intricate social webs is to try to discern and to systematize patterns of inter-relations and interactions, of connections and divisions, of forces and action and the ensuing repercussions. She or he is normally wary of simple mono- or oligo-causal theories, however sophisticatedly math-ematically modelled, and is usually very alert, like all good historians, to the important, and often lasting, impact of contingency and chance. On the other hand, that impact is not a random walk, a social sci-entist would argue, but is, often unknowingly, inserted into an ongoing flow of social dynamics, albeit seldom altering it. The victory of the Arab tribes over the Byzantine empire in the battle of Yarmuk in 634, Columbus's discovery of the Americas in 1492 or Yeltsin's defeat of Gorbachev in 1991, for instance, were contingent outcomes, but the Muslim expansion, the European conquest and the end of

Soviet communism which followed pushed a recognizable social dynamic in a particular, unforeseen but understandable direction.

How Did We Get Here?

Above, we identified a fivefold field of human social dynamic, of the mode of livelihood or production – driven by learning, by intercultural trade and by its specific social conflicts; of population ecology, i.e., the interaction of population development and its environment habitat; and, thirdly, of struggles for status, recognition and respect, which under human conditions have become existential and collective, and not just individual and sexual. In some form, those three dynamic drives are common to animal as well as to human populations and societies, a commonality which rather underlines their power. Uniquely human are culture and politics. The former means, above all, a capacity to use symbols and language and thereby to transmit experiences learnt and preferences, values, norms acquired. Cultures engender modes of persuasion and dissuasion. Politics entails, more than anything else, the capacity of collective organization for a goal and of collective power.

The way in which these variables worked themselves out and interacted in their different natural environments gave rise to a number of multidimensional human configurations, civilizations. At least five of them are major sociocultural areas today – and many smaller ones might be added – the Sinic, the Indic, the West Asian, the European (exported to most of the Americas) and the sub-Saharan African. These civilizations are still reproducing, though in mutated forms, their cosmologies with their characteristic conceptions of the meaning and the interrelations of this world, between this world and others, between the sacred, the secular and the taboo; as well as their family-sex-gender patterns and their values. They are influencing the curricula of their children and youngsters, and they largely decide if and for how long you will have a time of youth. They provide adult standards of high culture and models of action, through a classical language and a classical cultural canon (in the largely oral civilization of Africa more loosely defined as a family of customary traditions). They pattern your old age. They also bear upon our prospects after death.

But civilizations are only one layer of the ground on which we are standing, and their extension or contraction has been shaped by waves of globalization, in the broad sense of transpolity, transcultural, intercontinental but not necessarily planetary movements. The first such wave, from the early fourth to the early eighth century CE, defined the heartlands of the major civilizations, making Egypt and Syria Arabic, for instance, and created what we now call the world religions, from European Christianity to East Asian Buddhism. The second wave, in the late fifteenth and the sixteenth centuries, conquered the Americas for European civilization, religion and languages. Today's linguistic division of the Americas was soon imposed, Spanish in most of the region, Portuguese in Brazil, French and English in the north. It was also the first assertion of long-distance naval power, reaching into Asia as far as the Philippines, and ending the continental thrust of nomad warriors, whose last major exploit was the conquest of India by Babur, having escaped from Samarkand to Kabul, from where he launched his founding of the Mughal dynasty in India.

Then there was World War 0, the first, still unacknowledged, world war between Britain and France and lasting for more than half a century, from the mid-eighteenth century to 1815. It created North America (mainly) and Europeanized India Anglophone, and brought the surging British Empire to Singapore and Malacca, Ceylon and the African Cape. The French were not defeated on all fronts. The Code Napoléon, the French Civil Code of 1804, was exported to Latin America, including Louisiana, as well as to Latin Europe, and the in the end defeated French expedition to Egypt did leave long-lasting cultural ties between the elites of France and Egypt.

The fourth wave of globalization was adumbrated by the French conquest of Algeria in 1830 but really took off with the British 1840s victorious war to impose the imports of British-owned Indian-grown opium into China. It ended with the inter-imperialist slaughter of 1914–18. This was the wave that created the twentieth- and twenty-first-century divide of developed and underdeveloped, or 'developing' countries, which still largely governs the different life-trajectories of the world, in particular their chances of survival. It was the surge of capitalism in Europe, the USA and other European offshoots. Global trade stoked the engines of North Atlantic industrial capitalism, while the once rich and developed Asian world was defeated and underdeveloped. Africa got its contemporary lay-out of arbitrary boundaries and of official European languages.

For all its cutting military edge, of armoured steamships and machine guns, and in spite of its ending in a butchery of unprecedented size, it may still be argued, as it usually is in conventional presentations, that the fourth wave created an important drive of trade extension and of capital flows, sustained by new means of transport and communication. From a purely economic point of view, what followed after 1918 was de-globalization, with a decline in flows of trade, capital and people, recuperated only by the 1990s.

However, a new wave of globalized politics was starting, with the Communist International, which brought European revolutionary labour politics and ideology to China, Vietnam and other parts of Asia, later inspiring anticolonial movements in Africa as well as in other parts of Asia. With the rise of revolutionary political parties, the parameters of politics had changed. On the other side of the political spectrum, anti-communist politics became an international rightwing agenda, started by the ten countries' foreign interventions against the nascent Soviet Union in 1919–20, and officially consecrated, but in a skewed particular way, by the 1936 Anti-Comintern Pact between Germany, Italy and Japan. The Japanese attack on the US Pacific fleet at Pearl Harbor, on British Southeast Asia, and the German and Italian declarations of war against the USA created the first non-Eurocentric world war. After the joint defeat of the fascist powers, this globalized war mutated into a global Cold War, pitting the USA and its allies against the USSR and its allies.

While many of the main protagonists of this fifth political wave of globalization are now gone – the Comintern and the Soviet 'socialist camp' as well as the members of the Anti-Comintern Pact – legacies remain. Most importantly, perhaps, Europe was cut down politically, losing its colonial empires and its superpower status, while compensating itself by surprisingly successful economic development. Northeast and Southeast Asian economic 'miracles' are largely owed to the Cold War, to the social challenge of communism, inducing land reform, and to the American response, of accessible export markets and of huge regional spending during the Korean and the Vietnam wars, from Japan to Thailand. The lucrative sex trade in the Philippines and in Thailand is also a start-up gift of the US armed forces.

The Cold War experience keeps the current political elites of the EU divided, with the new anti-communist ones of Eastern Europe much more supportive of the USA and American wars, the Iraq war in particular, than their right-of-centre equivalents in Western Europe. There is also a noteworthy difference between the East and the West European interpretations of the Second World War, visible in the annual Baltic parades of veterans (and family) of the Waffen-SS, unthinkable further west.

The political fifth wave of globalization was not only one of world-wide antagonism. It also produced the first institutions of concerted global action, the League of Nations after the First World War and the United Nations after the Second World War, and their specialized organizations, the ILO from the old League, and the roster of UN institutions, from the WHO, the FAO, UNESCO etc., to the UNDP. They are all important institutions of knowledge production, of consciousness-raising, occasionally, as in the case of the WHO, of policy and its implementation.

The current, sixth wave of globalization is still with us. It was once, in the 1990s, characterized as the 'McDonaldization' of the world, which now sounds an almost obscenely flippant and US-centric (even if critical) view. It was driven by a new dynamics of capitalism, deriving from deindustrialization, the electronics revolution and finance. Whatever future historians will make of it, two features are likely to stand out. This was the wave which socially brought humanity together, concerned with the same issues – human rights, planetary environment and global capitalism – and massively connected, through satellite broadcasting and by self-communicating over the internet. Secondly, this was the wave which began turning the world away from the North Atlantic, back to its pre-modern Asian centres. Historical evidence shows that this sixth wave is not likely to be seen as *sui generis* or unique; nor should its epochal significance be ignored.

Modernity is another geological layer of contemporary culture. Outside its original aesthetic core application, modernity has in the last decades been invoked or decried in many different meanings. Above, we have used it not for more or less idiosyncratic descriptions/denunciations/homilies, but as an analytical tool for spotting crucial cultural change and its social ramifications. Modernity is then taken in the sense of a cultural orientation claiming autonomy from the authority of the past and directed towards creating a new future, never seen before.

Actually existing modernism has almost always coexisted with some selective respect for the past, perhaps nowhere more so than in Britain, the pioneer of modern empirical science and of industrial capitalism, with its preserved landowning aristocracy and its medieval courtly and university rites. Few modernists will deplore that this programme of the 1909 Futurist Manifesto was never implemented: 'We will destroy the museums, libraries, academies of every kind . . .' (Humphreys 1999: 11).

Nevertheless, no longer recognizing the confinement of ancestral wisdom was a major step of human development. As we noticed above, modernity has to be studied and ascertained sectorally – knowledge production, art, architecture, economy, politics. Taking political turns as socially pivotal, we can distinguish four major pathways to modernity, defined by their different constellations of forces for and against. Modernity was never an immanent evolution; its emancipation from the past was always an issue of contention and conflict. New means of livelihood were developing, changing constellations of collective power, and new sources of knowledge were emerging.

How much Europe owes its modern breakthrough to American discoveries and involvements, never envisaged by Aristotle and the other sages of antiquity, remains controversial. However, there is no serious contradiction to the assertion that modernity in Europe came out of indigenous battles, of the French Revolution, of seventeenth-century English revolutions. While few historians and historical sociologists today would dare to sum up these internal conflicts as bourgeois revolutions, their very internality made class a salient political concept in Europe in the wake of the French Revolution, reinforced by the European development of industrial capitalism. Class and articulate social ideologies, '-isms', have been significant features of European politics ever since, although they are now diminishing. Even 'New Labour' was still, in some minimalist sense, Labour. The line-up of the churches against it led triumphant European modernity to generate the most secularized part of the world, and internalist modernization meant that pre-modern social authorities were defeated more thoroughly than elsewhere.

To the 'New Worlds' of European overseas settlement, by contrast, the Other of anti-modernity, was always outside, in corrupt metropolitan Europe and among the 'savage' natives and slaves. Here, the question was not 'What rights should the people have?' but 'Who are the people?' From this there developed a quite particular hiatus between a universalist political discourse and its particularistic interpretation and implementation. The clergy was here on the side of independent modernity, and the Americas remain a bastion of modern religiosity. Class was always less salient within this universalist political rhetoric, and traditional authorities were, with some regional exceptions, much weaker than in Europe, which made a populist, in parts of Latin America plebeian (seldom armed), politics possible. Even today, the US political system, for instance, is more open and unpredictable than the European – that is, with respect to 'Who will govern?' as representative of the people, not to 'How will the country be governed?'.

The New World route to modernity was one of mass immigration, which was initially clearly defined in terms of race, but which is now, after the end of institutionalized racism, much more capable of managing current patterns of mass migration than old out-migration Europe, than the reactive modernizers are with their policies of defensive closure, or the ex-colonial states, overwhelmed by internal ethnic complexities. While the New World of the European settlers all share some important characteristics, among all the differences of their political divisions one country, above all, from the first half of the nineteenth century, the USA was set apart from the rest: the early, unqualified and unbroken success of its modernity, its internal government, its economy, its demographic ecology of population and space and its regional military force. Fuelled by an evangelical world mission, this state of unlimited self-confidence has seen world power as its 'Manifest Destiny' ever since the dawn of the twentieth century.

In the ex-colonial zone, where modernity developed from identification with the colonial aggressor to rebellion against him, the colonial division between masters and natives is still reproduced, even though it has been officially renounced. The new rulers take over the residences of the old, and their states use the official language, and either adopts or corrupts the administrative rules and practices of the colonial masters. Few African countries have adopted a pre-colonial language, although Tanzania is promoting Swahili, in Pakistan there is Urdu and in Bangladesh Bengali. But almost everywhere, mastery of the ex-colonial language is part of elite culture. The main exception is Indonesia, whose pre-colonial Malay lingua franca has been elevated to *Bahasa Indonesia*, the Indonesian national language. Anticolonial nationalist sentiment remains a very powerful discourse – deriving from the resentments of colonial humiliations, in spite of the fact that there were historically quite a number of positive identifications with the colonial rulers, in India particularly – and ex-colonial politicians are usually skilled in delivering it in several languages.

Class and social ideologies were correspondingly underdeveloped. While traditional indigenous religions gained credentials as a source of anticolonial resistance, missionary Christianity (in particular) and Islam were carriers of modern conceptions of education and medicine. No wonder, then, that the colonial road to modernity has reproduced religious beliefs and practices on a comprehensive scale, in Africa including evil magic and witches. As an external intrusion, colonial modernity never penetrated the conquered traditional societies very deeply and successfully. More often than not, they deliber-

214

ately refrained from trying, preferring to rule through local chiefs and *rajas*. In Africa, with its feeble states, this has today left considerable powers with pre-modern chiefs (Mamdani 1996), but also in some especially conservative ex-colonies, like Malaysia.

Reactive modernization from above, under acute Euro-American threat, was the fourth main route to modernity. Basically, it amounted to learning from the threatening barbarians in order to keep them out. In the nineteenth century, Japan was the only country which really succeeded, although a few other countries also managed to stave off colonizing threats and invasions – Siam, Afghanistan, Abyssinia – and, although encroached upon by many rapacious vultures, China and the Ottoman empire at least managed to avoid becoming colonies. In the twentieth century, the oil-rent states of Saudi Arabia and the Gulf constituted a second wave of reactive modernization, though it was very different because it was fully dependent on importing labour. It might be argued that the capitalist 'modernizations' pushed by the post-Mao leadership of China, and soon emulated in Vietnam, makes up a third wave of reactive modernization, driven by a fear that the Communist Party in national power will be undermined by national poverty.

Anyway, the historical legacy here is an integrated but dualized culture and society. Integrated, because that was what the success of reactive modernization meant; dualized between an adapted political economy, including its education system, and, on the other hand, preserved practices of authority and deference, of style and aesthetics and of beliefs and ritual.

Where Are We Going?

Will our history remain relevant? Where will the world dynamic take us?

With respect to the former question a fairly certain answer is 'yes'. This may of course be more easily uttered in Cambridge – where the Classics Department is much larger than that of Sociology – than elsewhere. But the new rapidly expanding Chinese cultural institutes in the world are named after Confucius, who was explicitly harangued by an upcoming Chinese leader at Davos in January 2010, and there even seems to be a popular Confucianism spreading in China, although an ill-timed launch of an officious film about him competed badly with Hollywood's *Avatar* in early 2010 (*International Herald Tribune* 29/1/10, p. 16; 2/2/2010, p. 2; Poceski 2009: 254). The early 2000

Indian government party, BJP, currently in opposition, promoted Indic civilization very actively, including the teaching of Sanskrit, and uses its long historical traditions profusely in its political rhetoric. Congress, the current leading government party, is secularist and less traditionalist, but not unhistorical.

Popular religiosity is not abating. Post-communism has given it a boost in Eastern Europe as well as in East Asia. In the West Asian/ North African Islamic civilization, Islamic traditions, with diverging interpretations, are strengthening. African civilization has always been more elusive, but there are no visible signs of any weakening. African family systems have been undermined by the prolonged economic crisis and escapist urbanization, but its distinctive features – polygamy, bride wealth, high fertility, expansive sexuality, extended effective kinship, patriarchy – are all still in existence. On the whole, I found in 2004 no tendency for the family-sex-gender systems of the world to converge.

The modern experience remains different throughout the world. Our nation-states were constituted in radically different ways, which continues to have an influence on our national identities. Europe will remain more secular than the Americas, for instance. Pre-modern this-worldly authority and deference will remain stronger in the ex-colonial zone and in countries of reactive modernization than it will in Europe or in the New Worlds of settlement. Class is still much more salient in Europe, as a reference of identity and organization, than it is in other parts of the world. The US mission to 'lead' the modern world is still uncontested among the American elite.

In brief, history will stay with us in the foreseeable future. But where are the dynamic winds blowing? We may sum up discernible perspectives and possibilities under five headings.

Firstly, we can see an end to the modernist emancipation from narrow natural constraints which lifted the parameters of human population ecology. Or, rather, we are experiencing its limits, and the risks and the costs of the hubris of stepping over them. At the same time, the possibilities of the human body seem to be widening.

The Asian green revolution has exhausted itself, and Indian agriculture, the livelihood of two-thirds of the Indian population, is under mounting pressure, from the continuing decline of already low land versus population ratios, depleted soils and scarcity of water. How Africa will feed its still rapidly growing population is anyone's guess, although a technological jump may make a big difference there, on still mostly abundant land, now being sold to foreign investors with their own food security interests, though. In 2008, the UN projected that the Nigerian population will almost double by 2050, to 289 million, and the Ugandan to treble, to 90 million. Climate change, of more turbulence as well as warming, is hanging as a cloud over the planet, but most threateningly over the poorest parts, as drought over the savanna belt of Africa, as flooding of the delta land of Bangladesh. The global climate has come onto the political agenda, but hardly as a target of global action. A minimalist muddling seems the most probable future course.

In other respects, demography is likely to get still more under human control, thanks to biomedicine. Human life-courses are likely to be extended, and fewer people will be thrown off course altogether as infants and young children. More kinds of cancer are likely to become more readily treatable, like breast and prostate cancer already. Fertility is no longer just controlled, but created. Genetic engineering and cosmetic surgery are likely to shape ever more human bodies.

Secondly, economically we are living in the aftermath – or suspension? – of the systemic Marxian dialectic of capitalism and its tendential collectivization of the means of production and the strengthening of labour. The everyday class conflict of capitalism and its dialectics are still a central feature of this century.

A safe bet for the next decade is that capitalism will remain the dominant mode of livelihood or production on earth. True, the direct reign of capital is more limited than is generally thought. As we noticed above in table 4.5 and in the elaboration of it, at most 40 per cent of the human working population operate within capitalist relations of work. There also exists self-employment, family helping (usually patriarchal), and public service. But the economic dynamic derives from capitalism, and the 2008–9 financial crisis saw much anger addressed at financiers and bankers, but little anti-capitalist protest, and no alternative ideology or movement. On the contrary, the underwriter of the relatively small-scale Latin American alternatives, *Chavista* Venezuela, was badly weakened by the fall of oil prices.

In the discernible future, the prospects of capitalism will be decided in China. The outcome cannot be called predetermined. The Communist Party state is still rhetorically committed to 'socialism', and it has the political capacity to turn the country onto a new path. But it will only do so under one of two conditions: either that a non-capitalist turn would be perceived as a more promising road of national wealth and/or power; or that social conflicts generated by capitalism would seriously threaten the unity and the power of the country. The first condition is unlikely to arrive in the foreseeable future. We saw above how the Marxian trajectory of an increasing lack of fit or 'contradiction' between the forces of production and the private capitalist relations of production was reversed, returning to more of an equilibrium in the 1970s. There are as yet no signs of private capital returning to shackle productivity and efficiency, although an Achilles heel is discernible – its doubtful capacity for switching to alternative sources of energy. In a longer perspective, capitalist relations of production may turn out to be in fatal conflict with ecologically sustainable forces of production.

The second condition remains as a threat, but it faces formidable obstacles. While there are lots of protests in capitalist China, they tend to be very localized, usually restricted to a single plant or village. Confronting the powers both of money and of the state, the protests have few resources of collective organization wider than the factory or the village. Legal claims, as well as the local assembly and petitions – or the occasional local riot – become an outlet. The working class of the heavy industry plants of the north did have a memory of the Maoist time when they were hailed as the rulers of the country, and those workers occasionally staged class-conscious protests, as in the city of Liaoyang in 2002, carrying portraits of Mao and singing the 'Internationale'. But they were cut down by industrial reorganizations, like the shipyard workers of Gdansk or the coal-miners of the Donbass. The young rural post-communist migrants who work the phenomenal sweatshops of the Pearl River Delta have no such cultural resources to draw upon (see further the extraordinary work by C. K. Lee (2007a) and also her edited volume (2007b)).

What could turn the tables would be a spiral of popular class protests and internal party strife, leading to a real communist coming out on top of the official Communist Party. Such a scenario is not inconceivable, although it would not per se initiate a new sustainable course. Gorbachev's leadership meant that democratic socialism was something that could grow inside the CPSU, but only as an idea, not as practice.

Some time in the future, capital accumulation and economic growth will probably be superseded by a means of livelihood primarily geared to other ends – say, to human security and happiness, to social and environmental harmony and to cultural development. But that time is far off in still poor China. Traction of some such perspective seems more likely to start in Europe and Japan, or maybe in parts of California.

But whatever the odds of post-capitalism, capitalism means class conflict, and a tendency to strengthen workers by its very success, concentrating and connecting them, freeing them from traditional deference. That part of Marxian analysis remains true of twenty-first-century manufacturing. The current rate of workers' exploitation in the export zones around the Third World, including Guangzhou, Shenzhen and the rest of the Pearl River Delta, are unsustainable in the medium run, and already forcefully challenged in early 2010 by the successful strikes at Honda and Foxcom.

The recent rise of inequality in most, if not all, parts of the rich world may not continue, but there are no significant social forces on the horizon that are very likely to push successfully for a reduction, with the possible short-term exception of bankers' bonuses. That is because it does not derive from a higher rate of exploitation, but from market processes of economic distanciation, privileging fortunately placed top performers, from televised Premier League footballers to business executives and financial traders (on different mechanisms of inequality, see Therborn 2006). Such processes can, of course, be countered, but that would require a strong communitarian integration, for which there is not much political will or force available at present. This is in spite of the fact that social science has produced robust evidence that the less egalitarian countries are paying a heavy price for their inequality (most recently, Wilkinson and Pickett 2009), in terms not only of the deprivation, unhappiness and humiliation of the disadvantaged, but also of fear, security costs, crime and violence experienced by the privileged. For the middle classes, communitarianism rarely reaches beyond their suburb, and the popular classes have become fragmented and demoralized with the turn to deindustrialization. The marginalized poor are on the margin politically as well as socially. If they protest, it is most frequently in the form of immigrant youth riots, which are easily cordoned off from the political mainstream

The 2000s have seen the middle classes turn to the streets in many countries. As they are gaining so much by other means, it is not very probable that there will be uprisings in China, or in India, Indonesia or Korea, where there already exist consolidated democratic channels of expression. But middle-class protest is likely to persist in West Asia and North Africa, and to come in Central Asia and sub-Saharan Africa. Serious attempts at tackling Latin American inequality, or policies that otherwise hurt middle-class interests, are also likely to return the middle classes to the streets, where they already have ample experience, from Santiago de Chile in the 1970s to Caracas and Tegucigalpa in the 2000s.

In the rich world, intra-capitalist power is hanging in the balance at the time of writing. There is a certain momentum for trying to rein in banking and finance, in particular to make the productive or the 'real' economy less dependent on financial gambling. But the gamblers have made powerful political friends, including among so-called left-of-centre politicians of the US Democrats and the British New Labour. Something will have to be given to apease popular anger, but the proportion of meat and verbiage is impossible to predict. By mid-2010, though, it seems that the iconoclastic moment of liberalism had subsided, and that with some precautions added we are heading back to capitalism as usual, nowadays meaning with the gamblers on top.

The world dynamics of capitalism turned out to be surprisingly divided in the 2008–9 financial crisis, contrary to the globalization discourse of borderless interdependence. While the rich world and its dependencies declined, the economies of China and India continued to grow vigorously, and that of Indonesia too, though less impressively. This divided outcome between the first and the third economies of the world in a global crisis is, as far as I know, unprecedented. It should not be treated as answering the question whether the USA will remain the dynamic centre of capitalism, though.

The expansion of finance has made US capitalism volatile and crisis-prone, and American manufacturing has taken a blow, losing its dominance of automobiles, for instance. However, American capitalism is not stagnating, and nor is it falling behind. Fuelled by unrivalled state military spending and intellectually fed by the best research universities of the world, the USA is still leading, and is unsurpassed in, the world in electronics, aerospace, biomedicine, consumer goods design and retailing. Its closest competitors are, on the whole, old sunset powers, like Japan in electronics and Western Europe in the other areas, not (yet) the enterprises of 'emerging markets'. It seems that the only technological area in which China is near the top is renewable energy and other green technology, a major branch of the future, where world hegemony is still undecided (*International Herald Tribune* 30–31/1/2010, pp. 1 and 5). The American leads are unlikely to continue for ever, but, with the possible exception of renewable energy technology – where the USA is hampered by powerful oil interests – there is no evidence of imminent decline.

Renewable energy is indeed an area in which a centralized, politically directed economy – if you wish, a kind of socialist economy – could very well succeed, where private relations of production may be less functional. There is a given public target – supply of renewable energy – and the fundamental technological innovations have been made, although they require further development and the outcome will largely depend on the size and focus of investment.

It is easier to predict something about European and Japanese capitalism. The EU Lisbon goal of becoming the world's most competitive knowledge economy will not materialize, neither this year as intended nor in any foreseeable future. While Western Europe has a number of advanced producers, from luxury cars and fashion to pharmaceuticals, its ageing population and its delimited public universities are most unlikely to lead the world knowledge production of the future. For the same reason, even more strongly hammered on a smaller and more aged country, largely closed to immigration, Japan will never become 'Number 1', as the hype of the 1980s predicted.

In the existential field, thirdly, we are witnessing a return of the suppressed modernist past, beneath the nuclear family, secularism and development, as well as an assertion of existential issues in geopolitics.

Issues of both gender and sex recognition and respect have surfaced. They are likely to remain contested, in spite of the widespread recent respectability of women's rights, of Gay Pride parades and homosexual marriage. The question of the place of religion in society was never laid to rest by modern secularism. It has returned with new vigour, in West and South Asia and in Eastern and Western Europe particularly. For different reasons, in the three former cases due to defeats or failures of secularist politics, of Arab nationalism, Congress socialism, communism, in Western Europe because of the arrival of a new religious force, immigrant Islam, and its xenophobic reception.

Victims of 'development' are coming out en masse, demanding apologies, restitutions or compensation, rights and respects. They range from poor children deported from the UK to the white empire and Aboriginal children taken from their parents to 'civilized' families to expropriated and/or marginalized 'First Nations' and tribal peoples throughout the world. In Indo-Latin America and in northeast India these have become frontline political problems. In India they sustain a large-scale insurgency, and in Latin America insistent Native Indian demands are being raised almost all over the hemisphere, from Mexico to southern Chile. Ethnic and ethno-religious recognition, status and respect are important in most Asian countries, from Turkey to the Philippines, and they can easily turn into explosive and viciously violent conflicts in most of Africa.

Existential strivings for recognition and respect, and corresponding contention rest also upon geopolitics. The question is to what extent and in what form they will become collective issues and conflicts. At the state level, they are preventing the return of a new Sinosphere as the centre of the most developed world. Although they are subsiding, including the lifting of the Korean ban on importing Japanese culture, the existential resentments among the main members of the Sinic civilization remain raw and alive. The Chinese have not forgotten the horrors of Japanese imperialism, the Koreans not those of Japanese colonial rule. Ancient Chinese superiority is recognized nowhere outside China, and least of all in Vietnam, where it reigned for a resentful millennium under the Chinese empire and where it attempted, unsuccessfully, to reassert itself militarily only three decades ago.

In West Asia, issues of recognition and respect are at the heart of the Zionist-Palestinian conflict. Will Palestinians accept a Jewish state in Palestine? Will the Zionists accept the right of all Palestinians to live in Palestine? So far, the answers around are, mostly but not universally, 'yes', and, almost universally, 'no', respectively. The odds are against the Palestinians, ground down by ruthless Israeli power, which is backed up, whenever need be, by the might of the US Treasury and war machine. But Israeli politicians are beginning to pay some attention to the fate of their old friend the once formidable apartheid regime in South Africa, maybe even to the unsustainability of its Bantustan programme.

The current Islamist–Western conflict is more likely to peter out than to continue, barring some new, unforeseeable event. It is not a civilizational clash, but a conjunctural, unintended consequence of the US anti-communist strategy in Afghanistan in the late 1970s–80s, which hoisted anti-modernist Islamist fighters as saviours of the world. Thinking they had defeated one superpower, they then thought they could at least push the other one out of Muslim lands. That did not work, as the US of course wanted to keep control of its oil supply. Decline might have started there, but it was halted by the spectacular attack of 11 September 2001, and even more by the American and 'Western' overreaction to it, with two massive invasions and big draconian concentration camps – Bagram, Abu Ghraib, Guantánamo – where humiliation was a systematic 'interrogating technique'. However, the far from incomprehensible rage and resentment against that are likely to cool over the coming years – unless there is a new invasion, which is not to be excluded. Both Yemen and Iran are currently close to the firing line. Unless stoked by recurrent American 'Western' and Israeli wars, violent Islamism is a generational phe-

222

nomenon, likely to fizzle out, like violent anarchism a century ago, or Western European new 'Communist Party building' 30 years ago. The idea – and the corresponding Islamophobic fear – that Islam will conquer the world will evaporate, like the hopes and fears of communism.

Fourthly, a global geopolitical power shift is clearly occurring, ending a North Atlantic centrality for a quarter of a millennium, so far peacefully, on bases of economics and demography rather than by violence and military might. New forms of politics are emerging, the future power of which is still unclear.

Will China rule the world, as the great British journalist Martin Jacques (2009) has argued with great verve and to a rave reception? Maybe, but hardly before my life has run its course, however long that may take (I was born in 1941). First of all, the world is becoming less ruleable, as Europe and the USA have already experienced in their African and Latin American backyards, respectively. Secondly, China still has a long way to go before acquiring a military and a technological edge on the rest of the world. Finally, the Christian Euro-American imperial vocation to 'civilize' or 'lead' the world is alien to Chinese civilization – but not, of course, the idea of being the dominant centre of the civilized world, to which others owe respect. But that the twenty-first century will be Chinese, in the qualified and almost all the time contested sense that the twentieth was the American century, is a plausible hypothesis.

At least as likely, though, is that the world stage will see the emergence of other major players. India is already there and unlikely to let go. Brazil is about to get big power status, long coveted, and boosted into the foreseeable future by its newly discovered huge offshore deposits of oil. Likely to arrive on the front stage rather soon is Indonesia, a populous resource-rich country, still searching for its political role in the world and still hampered by cultural decline during the long decades of military dictatorship. Sooner or later, Nigeria is going to make it, given the size of its population and its oil wealth. Already, any visitor to Africa can notice the Nigerian-South African connection, migratory, intellectual and of licit as well as illicit business. South Africa is recognized as a big regional power of Africa; Nigeria will be.

Without an unlikely incorporation of Russia, Europe looks bound for continuous political decline in the world. As a major world trader with, so far, a distinctive set of social rights, and with a political culture still not quite returned to the view of war as normal politics, not to speak of the idea of war as glory, the European Union could have a part of considerable global influence. As a kind of Scandinavia writ large, economically and culturally open, prosperous, efficient, generous and egalitarian at home, concerned, decent and harmless – and in its finest moments, as in the best years of Olof Palme, a loud voice of reason and moral outrage – abroad, an influential though powerless benchmark of aspiration to many, while despised by the powerful and the privileged.

Unfortunately, in my no doubt biased opinion, the scenario of Europe as the world's Scandinavia is not very likely. Its domestic political base has been seriously weakened, social democracy socially by deindustrialization and politically by the sub-imperialist, enhancing capitalism option of Tony Blair and 'New Labour', Christian democracy by Italian corruption and German neoliberal secularization. Social liberalism became marginalized after Keynes, the new Greens have turned out socially volatile, and the socialist and communist left has so far mostly denounced the European project.

The Eastern extension of the EU, an important and on its own terms rather successful project, has not added any progressive forces to the Union – on the contrary. On the horizon of 2010, the incorporated Eastern Europe does not harbour a single social democratic, Christian democratic, social liberal or environmentalist force of any significance, and the only left is the ostracized, little reformed Communist Party of Bohemia and Moravia. Instead, you have a variety of neoliberals, ex-communist and anti-communist, and cultural reactionaries with some social fillips, or without. In foreign policy, the new Eastern elites are proud to be auxiliaries of the Americans – all signing up for the invasion of Iraq, and then supplying symbolic troops both to Afghanistan and Iraq.

However, it is not to be excluded that in the coming years it may dawn upon some European leaders, that a 'special' servant relationship to the declining American empire is not the best European option of foreign policy.

Extra-European immigration is another unresolved issue of European integration. It is a sign of European success, a subcontinent of more than four centuries of out-migration becoming a magnet of immigration, expressed most graphically in Argentineans lining up in Buenos Aires to claim an Italian re-entry to a country their parents or grandparents were happy to escape a century ago. European countries have been taken by surprise by this attraction, which now has made classical countries of out-migration, from Sweden to Spain, having foreign-born populations similar to that of the US, about an eighth of the resident population. So far, the Western European welfare state has not been very successful in handling the novel issues of immigration. Some states, such as the Danish and the Dutch, once models of wellbeing, have become horror stories of xenophobia and harassment of Others.

Some of us will keep the possibility of a European Scandinavia as a hope and as a political goal, but darker scenarios look more likely to materialize (cf. Anderson 2009).

A fundamental question of the coming decades, to which I have no proper answer, is whether the USA will use its formidable, unrivalled military power to arrest its likely relative economic decline, and its decline of non-armed political power The British opium war model is no longer a viable US option, and hardly a Pearl Harbor-type attack on China. If the US should go to war with China, it seems most likely to be triggered by some conflict around Taiwan, or Tibet. The most probable mid-twenty-first-century outcome seems to be some fragile stand-off between an economically and demographically powerful China and a USA weaker in those respects, but much better armed and, perhaps, at least as influential ideologically.

Electronic channels of mobilization have changed the game of politics, how much and in what direction are still open questions. So far, their main effects have been system-opening, challenging or undermining regimes in power. Hitherto, their opening impact has surpassed the closures by new forms of surveillance. But a reversal in some parts of the world is not unimaginable.

Global civil society is likely to continue growing, scrutinizing and criticizing state players. The connectivity of humankind is likely to intensify, and a global public sphere to emerge. But, as the ineffective huge popular demonstrations against the Iraq war in 2003 showed, when big state leaders are set on a course of action they can rarely, if ever, be stopped, before their course runs into a quagmire, like the American war in Vietnam in 1968. States will continue to dominate global politics for a foreseeable future.

Finally, cultural modernism is being recentred and recycled, while postmodernism seems confined to the Euro-American left-of-centre. Centred mass communication is being challenged by masses of inter-personal electronic communication.

Modernism is now carried forward primarily by Asian developmentalism, flanked by African and Latin American ditto. The former is likely to take pride in the past of Asian civilizations, and twenty-first-century modernism generally is set to be much more ecologically conscious and existentially sophisticated than its predecessor. Global high culture and learning will become increasingly de-Europeanized and Asianized. In future decades, developmentalist modernism is likely to be challenged by aged populations of Europe and East Asia with their prior concerns of security and serenity.

While keeping their presence in social life, cultural legacies are likely to become increasingly fractured and hybridized. National cultures will be reshaped, reproduced, and repackaged. Transnational migration will not go away, but the capacity of national cultural assimilation is unlikely to keep pace. The range of interpersonal communication will continue its recent expansion, and deterritorialized virtual cultural communities will grow in importance. The relative weight of the two cultures, the territorial and the virtual, will probably not be decided on the cultural field, but by what will happen to the geopolitics of state power. Cultural clashes are most likely to persist, but, like hitherto, between smaller, more recent and more politicized units than civilizations. What clashes there will be is anybody's guess, but one likely candidate is between religious fundamentalism and secularized hedonism in West and South Asia, similar to but possibly more violent than the late twentieth to early twenty-first-century 'culture war' in USA. Mass values of sex and gender are likely to change. Militant political Islamism is likely to abate, after having shown that it has no solutions to the mundane problems of this world. The post-communist surge of organized religion in many, if by no means all, countries may subside, but there are no signs that the stopped forward march of secularism will resume.

Planetary imagination and pan-human consciousness are likely to persist, and to deepen with the Afro-Asian countryside drawn into electronic networks. But with much more of an Asian perspective, universalist values and a strong human rights culture are less likely to develop further. More probable is a strengthened awareness of the plurality of human values, and more a concern with their coexistence than with the diffusion and victory of the best.

That is about what a cautious academic may dare to say about the future. However, the contingency and uncertainty inherent in the human social world mean that a different outlook is not to be dismissed a priori, above all not a view more governed by values and commitment to action than to evidential probability. The radical youth who have listened to, and danced to, the catching tune of the World Social Forums, 'Another world is – possible', are neither wrong nor naive. They are the hope of the new century, because another world is needed.

REFERENCES

Alam, M. 2006. *Ageing in India*. New Delhi, Academic Foundation.

Allen, R. 2005. 'Real Wages in Europe and Asia: A First Look at the Long-Term Patterns', pp. 111–30 in R. Allen et al. (eds), *Living Standards in the Past*. Oxford, Oxford University Press.

Amnino, A. and Guerra, F. -X. (eds) 2003. *Inventando la nación. Iberoamérica Siglo XIX*. Mexico, Fondo de cultura económica.

Anant, T. C. A., et al. 2006 'Labor Markets in India: Issues and Perspectives', pp. 205–300 in J. Felipe and R. Hasan (eds), *Labor Markets in Asia*. Basingstoke, Palgrave.

Anderson, B. 1996. 'Language, Fantasy, Revolution: Java 1900–1950', pp. 26–40 in D. Lev and R. McVey (eds), *Making Indonesia*. Ithaca NY, Cornell University Southeast Asia Program.

Anderson, B. 2006. *Imagined Communities*. Rev. edn. London, Verso.

Anderson, P. 1974. *Passages from Antiquity to Feudalism*. London, NLB/ Verso.

Anderson, P. 1998. *The Origins of Postmodernity*. London, Verso.

Anderson, P. 2009. *The New Old World*. London, Verso.

Anderson, P. 2010. 'Two Revolutions', *New Left Review* 61 (new series), 59–96.

Appadurai, A. 2008. 'The Capacity to Aspire: Culture and the Terms of Recognition', pp. 29–35 in D. Held and H. Moore (eds), *Cultural Politics in a Global Age*. Oxford, Oneworld.

Appiah, K. A. 1992. *In My Father's House*. New York and Oxford, Oxford University Press.

Ashcroft, B. et al. (eds) 1995. *The Post-Colonial Studies Reader*. London, Routledge.

Augar, Ph. 2009. *Chasing Alpha*. London, The Bodley Head.

Aydin, C. 2007. *The Politics of Anti-Westernism in Asia*. New York, Columbia University Press.

Bairoch, P. 1988. *Cities and Economic Development*. London, Mansell.

Bairoch, P. 1997. *Victoires et déboires*. 3 vols. Paris, Gallimard folio.

Banister, J. 2005 'Manufacturing Employment in China', *Monthly Labor Review*, July, 11–29.

Barnes, I. 2008. *World Religions*. London, Cartographica Press.

Bartelson, J. 2009. *Visions of the World Community*. Cambridge, Cambridge University Press.

Bauman, Z. 1992. *Intimations of Postmodernity*. London, Routledge.

Bayly, C. A. 2004. *The Birth of the Modern World, 1780–1914*. Oxford, Blackwell.

Bayly, S. 2007. *Asian Voices in a Postcolonial Age*. Cambridge, Cambridge University Press.

Benjamin, T. 2009. *The Atlantic World*. Cambridge, Cambridge University Press.

Berman, H. 1980. *Law and Revolution. The Formation of the Western Legal Tradition*. Cambridge. MA, Harvard University Press.

Berners-Lee, T. 1999. *Weaving the Web*. San Francisco, Harpers.

Berry, A. and Serieux, J. 2006. 'Riding the Elephants: The Evolution of World Economic Growth and Income Distribution at the End of the Twentieth Century (1980–2000)'. New York, UN, DESA Working Paper 27.

Bhatt, E. 2006. *We Are Poor But So Many*. Oxford, Oxford University Press.

Blackburn, R. 1988. *The Overthrow of Colonial Slavery*. London, Verso.

Blackburn, R. 1997. *The Making of New World Slavery*. London, Verso.

Blossfeld, H. -P. et al. (eds) 2005. *Globalization, Uncertainty and Youth in Society*. London, Routledge.

Bodde, D. 1981. *Essays on Chinese Civilization*, Princeton, NJ, Princeton University Press.

Bongaarts, J. and Zimmer, Z. 2001. 'Living Arrangements of Older Adults in the Developing World: An Analysis of DHS Household Surveys'. New York, UNFPA Working Paper 148.

Boserup, E. 1970. *Women's Role in Economic Development*. London, George Allen & Unwin.

Bourguignon, F. and Morrisson, C. 2002. 'Inequality Among World Citizens, 1820–1992', *American Economic Review* 92, 727–44.

Brading, D. 1998. 'Patriotism and the Nation in Colonial Spanish America', pp. 13–45 in L. Roniger and M. Sznajder (eds), *Constructing Collective Identities and Shaping Public Spheres*. Brighton, Sussex Academic Press.

Braudel, F. 1963/1987. *Grammaire des civilisations*. Paris, Arthaud.

Breman, J. 2003. *The Labouring Poor in India*. Oxford, Oxford University Press.

Breman, J. 2004. 'The Informal Sector', pp. 402–25 in V. Das (ed.), *Handbook of Indian Sociology*. Oxford, Oxford University Press.

Breman, J. 2007. *The Poverty Regime in Village India*. New Delhi, Oxford University Press.

Briggs, A. and Burke, P. 2005. *A Social History of the Media*. Cambridge, Polity.

Brown, J. 2006. *Global South Asians*. Cambridge, Cambridge University Press.

Callahan, M. 2009. 'Riddle of the Tatmadaw', *New Left Review* 60, 27–64.

Cassen, B. 2003. *Tout a commencé à Porto Alegre*. Paris, Mille et Une Nuits.

Castells, M. 1996–8. *The Information Age*. 3 vols. Oxford, Blackwell.

CEPAL/ECLA. 2008. *Anuario Estadistico de América Latina y del Caribe*. Santiago de Chile, CEPAL/ECLA.

Chan, A., Madsen, R. and Unger, J. 2009. *Chen Village*. 3rd edn. Berkeley, University of California Press.

Chanda, N. 2007. *Bound Together*. New Haven, Yale University Press.

Chang, Ha-Joon. 2008. *Bad Samaritans*. New York, Random House Business Books.

Chang, L. T. 2008. *Factory Girls*. London, Picador.

Chaudhuri, K. N. 1985. *Trade and Civilization in the Indian Ocean*. Cambridge, Cambridge University Press.

Chaudhuri, K. N. 1990. *Asia Before Europe*. Cambridge, Cambridge University Press.

Chen, S. and Ravaillon, M. 2008. 'The Developing World Is Poorer Than We Thought, But No Less Successful in the Fight against Poverty'. World Bank Policy Research Working Paper 4703.

Chesnais, J.-C. 1992. *The Demographic Transition*. Oxford, Clarendon Press.

Chronic Poverty Research Centre 2004. *Chronic Poverty Report 2004–5*. Manchester, Chronic Poverty Research Centre.

Chua, A. 2003. *World on Fire*. London, William Heinemann.

Clark, P. 2009. *European Cities and Towns 400–2000*. Oxford, Oxford University Press.

Clarke, S. 2008. 'Globalization and the Uneven Subsumption of Labour Under Capital in Russia', pp. 32–51 in M. Taylor (ed.), *Global Economy Contested*. London, Routledge.

Cliggett, L. 2005. *Grains in the Grass*. Ithaca and London, Cornell University Press.

Coaldrake, W. 1996. *Architecture and Authority in Japan*. London, Routledge.

Coedès, G. 1966. *The Making of Southeast Asia*. London, Routledge & Kegan Paul.

Coedès, G. 1968. *The Indianized States of Southeast Asia*. Honolulu, East-West Centre Press.

Collins, R. 2006. *A Short History of Africa*. Princeton, Markus Wiener.

Cooke, Fang Lee 2005. *HRM, Work and Employment in China*. London, Routledge.

Cornia, G. A. and Paniccià, R. (eds) 2000. *The Mortality Crisis in Transition Economies*. Oxford, Oxford University Press.

Cousins, L. S. 1985. 'Buddhism', pp. 278–343 in J. Hinnells (ed.), *A Handbook of Living Religions*. London, Penguin.

Croll, E. 2006. *China's New Consumers*. London, Routledge.

229

Curtin, P. 1984. *Cross-Cultural Trade in World History*. Cambridge, Cambridge University Press.

Curtin, P. 2000. *The World and the West*. Cambridge, Cambridge University Press.

Dale, S. 2010. *The Muslim Empires of the Ottomans, Safavids, and Mughals*. Cambridge, Cambridge University Press.

Dalrymple, W. 2009. *Nine Lives*. London, Bloomsbury.

Darwin, J. 2007. *After Tamerlane*. London, Allen Lane.

Das, S. 2010. 'Caste, Ethnicity, and Religion: Linkages with Unemployment and Poverty', pp. 354–67 in S. Thorat and K. Newman (eds), *Blocked by Caste. Economic Discrimination in Modern India*. New Delhi, Oxford University Press.

Das, V. 2004. 'Introduction', pp. 1–16 in V. Das (ed.), *Handbook of Indian Sociology*. Oxford, Oxford University Press.

Datt, R. 2002. 'Industrial Relations: The Menacing Growth of the Phenomenon of the Lockout', pp. 179–200 in R. Kumar (ed.), *Indian Labour in the Post-Liberalisation Period*. Kolkata, K. P. Bagchi & Co.

Davis, M. 2006. *Planet of Slums*. London, Verso.

Deaton, A. S. 1976. 'The Structure of Demand 1920–1970', pp. 89–131 in C. Cipolla (ed.), *The Fontana Economic History of Europe*, vol. 5:1. London, Collins/Fontana.

De Grazia, V. 2005. *Irresistible Empire*. Cambridge, MA, Belknap Press.

Demélas, M. -D. 2003. *La Invención de la política*. Lima, IFEA & IEP.

Diop, C. A. 1967/1993. *Antériorité des civilisations nègres: Mythe ou vérité historique?* Paris, Présence Africaine.

Dobson, W. and Hufbauer, G. C. 2001. *World Capital Markets*. Washington, DC, Institute for International Economics.

Dunn, J. 2005. *Setting the People Free. The Story of Democracy*. London, Atlantic Boks.

Eckert, C. J. et al. 1990. *Korea Old and New*. A History. Seoul, Ilchokak.

Eisenstadt, S. 2006. *The Great Revolutions and the Civilizations of Modernity*. Leiden-Boston, Brill.

Eurostat. 2008. Europe Memo/08/752.

Felipe, J. and Hasan, R. 2006. 'Labor Markets in a Globalizing World', pp. 63–142 in J. Felipe and R. Hasan (eds), *Labor Markets in Asia*. Basingstoke, Palgrave.

Fernández-Armesto, F. 2000. *Civilizations*. London, Macmillan.

Fernández-Armesto, F. 2008. *The World: A Brief History*. 2 vols. Upper Saddle River, NJ, Pearson Prentice-Hall.

Fleck, S. 2009. 'International Comparisons of Hours Worked: An Assessment of the Statistics', *Monthly Labor Review* May, 3–26.

Fogel, J. 2009. *Articulating the Sinosphere*. Cambridge, MA, Harvard University Press.

Fourastié, J. 1979. *Les Trente glorieuses*. Paris, Fayard.

Gereffi, G. et al. 2005. 'The governance of global value chains', *Review of International Economy* 21:1, 78–104.

Githiora, C. 2008. 'Kenya: Language and the Search for a Coherent National Identity', pp. 235–51 in A. Simpson (ed.), *Languages and National Identity in Africa*. Oxford, Oxford University Press.

Glasius, M. and Timms, J. 2005. 'The Role of Social Forums in Global Civil Society: Radical Beacon or Strategic Infrastructure?', in H. Anheier et al. *Global Civil Society 2004/5*. Los Angeles and London, Sage.

Glenny, M. 2008. *McMafia*. New York, Alfred Knopf.

Goody, J. 1976. *Production and Reproduction*. Cambridge, Cambridge University Press.

Goody, J. 1993. *The Culture of Flowers*. Cambridge, Cambridge University Press.

Goody, J. 1998, *Food and Love*. London, Verso.

Goody, J. 2010. *Renaissances*. Cambridge, Cambridge University Press.

Graebner, W. 1980. *A History of Retirement*. New Haven and London, Yale University Press.

Graevenitz, G. von (ed.) 1999. *Konzepte der Moderne*. Stuttgart-Weimar, J. B. Metzler.

Grewal, D. S. 2008. *Network Power*. New Haven and London, Yale University Press.

Guilmoto, C. 2009. 'The Sex Ratio Transition in Asia', *Population and Development Review* 35(3): 519–50.

Guimaraes, N. A. 2009. *Desemprego, uma construção social. São Paolo, Paris e Tóquio*. Belo Horizonte, Argumentum.

Gumbrecht, H. U. 1978. 'Modern, Modernität, Moderne', pp. 93–131 in O. Brunner et al. (eds), *Geschichtliche Grundbegriffe*. Stuttgart, Klett-Cotta.

Gutton, J. -P. 1988. *Naissance du vieillard*. Paris, Aubier.

Haavio Mannila, E. and Rotkirch, A. 2010. 'Sexuality and Family Formation', pp. 465–97 in S. Immefall and G. Therhorn (eds), *Handbook of European Societies. Social Transformations in the 21st Century*. New York and Berlin, Springer.

Hadiz, V. 2001. 'New Organizing Vehicles in Indonesia: Origins and Prospects', pp. 108–26 in J. Hutchinson and A. Brown (eds) *Organising Labour in Globalising Asia*. London, Routledge.

Hanlon, P., Walsh, D. and Whyte, B. 2006, *Let Glasgow Flourish*. Glasgow, Centre for Population Health.

Harle, J. C. 1986/94. *The Art and Architecture of the Indian Subcontinent*. New Haven and London, Yale University Press.

Hatton, T. and Williamson, J. 2006. *Global Migration and the World Economy*. Cambridge, MA, MIT Press.

Hattstein, M. and Delius, P. 2005. *Islam. Kunst und Architektur*. Netherlands, Könemann.

Haynes, J. (ed.) 1998. *Religion in Global Politics*, New York, Longman.

Heinsohn, G. 2008. *Söhne und Weltmacht: Terror im Aufstieg und Fall der Nationen*. Munich, Piper.

231

Hempel, J. 2009. 'How Facebook Is Taking Over Our Lives', *Fortune*, 2 March, 35–41.

Hertel, T. and Zhai, F. 2004. 'Labor Market Distortions: Rural–Urban Market Inequality and the Opening of China's Economy'. Washington, DC, World Bank Policy Research Paper 3455.

Hobsbawm, E. 1987. *The Age of Empire, 1875–1914*. London, Weidenfeld & Nicolson.

Höllinger, F. and Haller, M. 2009. 'Decline or Persistence of Religion', pp. 281–301, in M. Haller et al. (eds), *The International Social Survey Programme 1984–2009*. London, Routledge.

Hourani, A. 1983. *Arabic Thought in the Liberal Age, 1798–1939*. Cambridge, Cambridge University Press.

Howland, D. R. 1996. *Borders of Chinese Civilization*. Durham, NC, Duke University Press.

Huang, Y. 2008. *Capitalism with Chinese Characteristics*. Cambridge, Cambridge University Press.

Huard, P. and Durand, M. 1954. *Connaissance du Viêt-Nam*. Paris, Imprimerie Nationale.

Humboldt, A. von. 1966[1822]. *Ensayo político sobre el Reino de La Nueva España*. Mexico, Porrua.

Humphreys, R. 1999. *Futurism*. London, Tate Publishing.

Huntington, S. 1996. *The Clash of Civilizations and the Remaking of the World Order*. New York, Simon & Schuster.

Ibn Khaldun. 1967[1377]. *The Muqaddinah. An Introduction to History*. London, Routledge & Kegan Paul.

Ichijo, A. and Uzelac, G. (eds) 2005. *When is the Nation?* London, Routledge.

Iliffe, J. 2007. *Africans*. 2nd edn. Cambridge, Cambridge University Press.

ILO. 2007. *Key Indicators of the Labour Market*. Geneva, ILO.

ILO. 2008a. *Global Employment Trends*. January. Geneva, ILO.

ILO. 2008b. *Global Wage Report 2008/09*. Geneva, ILO.

ILO. 2009. *Global Employment Trends*. January. Geneva, ILO.

ILO. 2010. *Global Employment Trends*. Geneva, ILO.

IMF. 2009. *World Economic Outlook Update*. July.

Inglehart, R., Halman, L. and Welzel, C. 2004. 'Introduction', pp. 1–20 in R. Inglehart et al. (eds), *Human Beliefs and Values*. Mexico, Siglo XXI.

International Sociology. 2001. Special issue on Civilizations, 16:3.

Jacques, M., 2009. *When China Rules the World*. London, Allen Lane.

James, C. L. R. 1938. *The Black Jacobins*. New York, Vintage Books.

Jodhka, S. 2006. 'Agrarian Structures and Their Transformations', pp. 365–87 in V. Das (ed.), *Handbook of Indian Sociology*. Oxford, Oxford University Press.

John, J. and Narayanan, P. 2006. 'Elimination of Child Labour: Why Have We Failed?', pp. 180–200 in Council for Social Development, *India Social Development Report*, Oxford and New Delhi, Oxford University Press.

Jones, G. 2007. 'Delayed Marriage and Very Low Fertility in Asia', *Population and Development Review* 33(3), 453–78.

Joshi, S. 2001. *Fractured Modernity*. New Delhi, Oxford University Press.

Kaldor, M. , Kumar, A. and Seckinelgin, H. 2009. 'Introduction', pp. 1–25 in A. Kumar et al. (eds), *Global Civil Society 2009*. Los Angeles and London, Sage.

Kapsos, S. 2007. 'World and Regional Trends in Labour Force Participation: Methodologies and Key Results', ILO, Economic and Labour Market Papers, 2007/1.

Kaser, K. 2000. *Macht und Erbe*. Vienna: Böhlau.

Keay, J. 2000. *India. A History*. London, Hammersmith.

Kennedy, H. 2007. *The Great Arab Conquests*. London, Weidenfeld & Nicolson.

Khilnani, S. 1998. *The Idea of India*. New York, Farrar Straus & Giroux.

Khondker, H. H. 2006. 'The National, the Religious, and the Global in the Construction of Global Identity in Bangladesh', pp. 81–106 in G. Therborn and H. H. Khondker (eds), *Asia and Europe in Globalization*. Leiden, Brill.

Kiernan, V. 1969. *The Lords of Human Kind*. London, Weidenfeld & Nicolson.

Kim, Jin Wook and Choi, Young Jun. 2008. 'Private Transfers and Emerging Welfare States in East Asia: Comparative Perspectives', Luxemburg Income Study Working Paper 507.

Kiple, K. 2007. *A Movable Feast*. Cambridge, Cambridge University Press.

Kosellek, R. 2002. *The Practice of Conceptual History*. Stanford, Stanford University Press.

Kumar, A. et al. (eds) 2009. *Global Civil Society 2009*. Los Angeles and London, Sage.

Kuznesof, E. 2005. 'The House, the Street, Global Society: Latin American Families and Childhood in the Twenty-first Century', *Journal of Social History* 38:4, 859–72.

Lam, W. 2009. 'Hu Jintao's Great Leap Backward', *Far Eastern Economic Review* Jan/Feb, 161.

Lapidus, I. 2002. *A History of Islamic Societies*. 2nd edn. Cambridge, Cambridge University Press.

Lawrence, S. & Ishikawa, J. 2005. 'Trade Union Membership and Collective Bargaining Coverage: Statistical Concepts, Methods and Findings', Geneva, ILO Social Dialogue Indicators, Working Paper 59.

Lee, C. K. 2007a. *Against the Law: Labor Protest in China's Rustbelt and Sunbelt*. Berkeley, California University Press.

Lee, C. K. (ed.) 2007b. *Working in China*. London, Routledge.

Lett, E. and Banister, J. 2009. 'China's Manufacturing Employment and Compensation Costs: 2002–06', *Monthly Labor Review*, April, 30–38.

Lewis, B. 1964/1994. *The Shaping of the Modern Middle East*. New York and Oxford, Oxford University Press.

Li Yongping and Peng Xizhe. 2000. 'Age and Sex Structure', in Peng Xizhe and Guo Zhigang (eds), *The Changing Population of China*. Oxford, Blackwell.

Li, Zhisni 1994. *The Private Life of Chairman Mao*. London, Arrow.

Lindert, P. H. 2000. 'Three Centuries of Inequality in Britain and America', pp. 167–216 in A. Atkinson and F. Bourguignon (eds), *Handbook of Income Distribution*, vol. 1. Amsterdam, Elsevier.

Liu Yanbin, 2007. *China's Labor Market and Proactive Employment Policy*. OECD seminar, www. oecd. org.

Livi-Bacci, M. 2007. *A Concise History of World Population*. 4th edn. Oxford, Blackwell.

Logan, W. 2000. *Hanoi. Biography of a City*. Sydney, UNSW Press.

Lyotard, J.-F. 1984. *The Postmodern Condition*. Minneapolis, University of Minnesota Press.

McKeown, A. 2004. 'Global Migration, 1846–1940', *Journal of World History* 15, 185–9.

McNeill, J. R. 2000. *Something New Under the Sun*. London, Penguin.

McNeill, J. R. 2010. *Mosquito Empires*. Cambridge, Cambridge University Press.

McNeill, W. 1979. *Plagues and Peoples*. Harmondsworth, Penguin.

Maddison, A. 2001. *The World Economy. A Millennial Perspective*. Paris, OECD.

Maddison, A. 2007. *Contours of the World Economy, 1–2030 AD*. Oxford University Press.

el Magd, N. A. 2008. 'Website Ignites Political Action', *Guardian*, 1 May, 20.

Mamdani, M. 1996. *Citizen and Subject*. Princeton, Princeton University Press.

Markovits, C. 2000. *The Global World of Indian Merchants, 1750–1947*. Cambridge, Cambridge University Press.

Marmot, M. 2004. *Status Syndrome*. London, Bloomsbury.

Marmot, M. 2005. 'Social Determinants of Health Inequalities', *The Lancet* 365(9464), 1099–104.

Marr, D. 1981. *Vietnamese Tradition on Trial, 1920–1945*. Berkeley, University of California Press.

Martin, D. 1997. *Reflections on Sociology and Theology*. Oxford, Clarendon Press.

Mason, P. 2007. *Live Working or Die Fighting*, London, Harvill Secker.

Mason, R. H. P. 1969. *Japan's First General Election, 1890*. Cambridge, Cambridge University Press.

Mayer, K. U. (ed.) 1990. *Lebensverläufe und sozialer Wandel*. Kölner Zeitschrift für Soziologie, Sonderheft (special issue), 31.

Mazrui, A. and A. M. 1998. *The Power of Babel*. James Currey.

Mbembe, A. 2001. *On the Postcolony*. Berkeley, University of California Press.

Mensch, B., Grant, M. and Blanc, A. 2006. 'The Changing Context of Sexual Initiation in sub-Saharan Africa', *Population and Development Review* 32(4), 699–727.

Meyer, J. et al. 1997. 'World Society and the Nation-State', *American Journal of Sociology* 103(1), 144–81.

Micklethwait, J. and Wooldridge, A. 2009. *God Is Back*. London, Allen Lane.

Milanovic, B. and Yitzhaki, S. 2002. 'Decomposing World Income Distribution: Does the World Have a Middle Class?', *Review of Income and Wealth* 48:2, 155–77.

Milanovic, B. 2008. 'Even Higher Global Inequality Than Previously Thought: A Note on Global Inequality Calculations Using the 2005 International Comparison Program Results', *International Journal of Health Services* 38:3, 421–9.

Mitchell, L. 2009. *Language, Emotion and Politics in South India*, Indiana University Press.

Mitford, N. 1955. 'The English Aristocracy', pp. 158–68 in S. Spender et al. (eds), *Encounters*. London, Weidenfeld & Nicolson.

Morrisson, C. 2000. 'Historical Perspectives on Income Distribution: The Case of Europe', pp. 217–60 in A. Atkinson and F. Bourguignon (eds), *Handbook of Income Distribution*, vol. 1. Amsterdam, Elsevier.

Mosley, L. 2007. 'The Political Economy of Globalization', pp. 106–25 in D. Held and A. McGrew (eds), *Globalization Theory*. Cambridge, Polity.

Mudimbe, V. Y. 1988. *The Invention of Africa*. London, James Currey.

Mukherjee, R. 2002. 'Agricultural Labour in the Indian Economy', pp. 259–72 in R. Kumar (ed.), *Indian Labour in the Post-Liberalisation Period*. Kolkata, K. P. Bagchi & Co.

Müller, B. and Haller. M. 2009. 'Social Identities in Comparative Perspective', pp. 175–96 in M. Haller, R. Jowell and T. Smith (eds), *The International Social Survey Programme, 1984–2009*. London, Routledge.

Müller, W. and Kogan, J. 2010. 'Education', pp. 217–89 in S. Immerfall and G. Therborn (eds), *Handbook of European Societies*. New York, Springer.

Murozumi, M. and Shikata, M. 2008. 'The Structure of Income in Elderly Households and Relative Poverty Rates in Japan from the Viewpoint of International Comparisons'. Luxemburg Income Study Working Paper 483. www.lisproject.org.

Nagaraj, R. 2007. 'Labour Market in India'. OECD Seminar on Labour Markets in Brazil, China, and India. www.oecd.org.

Nanda, A. R. and Ali, A. 2007. 'Health Sector: Issues and Challenges', pp. 18–32 in Council for Social Development, *India Social Development Report*, Oxford and New Delhi, Oxford University Press.

National Sample Survey Organization. 2003. *Household Consumer Expenditure and Employment-Unemployment Situation in India. NSS 58th Round*. Delhi, Government of India.

Newsweek. 2010. Issues 2010. Special edition.

Nigerian National Bureau of Statistics. 2006. Census of 1991.

Nisbett, R. 2003. *The Geography of Thought*. London and Yarmouth Maine, Nicholas Brealey.

OECD. 1999. *Historical Statistics 1960–1997*. Paris OECD.

OECD. 2000. *Economic Outlook*. Paris OECD.

OECD. 2006. *OECD in Figures, 2006–2007*. www.oecd.org.

OECD. 2007a. *OECD Employment Outlook*. Paris, OECD.

OECD. 2007b. *OECD Economic Survey of India*. Paris, OECD.

OECD. 2008. *Growing Unequal?* Paris, OECD.

OECD. 2009. *OECD in Figures*. Paris, OECD Observer Supplement 1.

OECD. 2010. *OECD Economic Surveys. China*. Paris, OECD.

Okafor, O. C. 2009. 'Remarkable Returns: The Influence of Labour-Led Socio-Economic Rights Movement on Legislative Reasoning, Process and Action in Nigeria, 1999–2007', *Journal of Modern African Studies* 47:2, 241–66.

Okri, B. 1991. *The Famished Road*. London, Vintage.

Oommen, T. K. 2009. 'Indian Labour Movement: Colonial Era to the Global Age', *Economic and Political Weekly* XLIV(52), 81–9.

Osterhammel, J. and Peterson, N. P. 2005. *Globalization. A Short History*. Princeton, Princeton University Press.

Panikkar, K. M. 1960. *Common Sense About India*. London, Victor Gollancz.

Parish, W., Laumann, E. and Mojola, S. 2007. 'Sexual Behavior in China: Trends and Comparisons', *Population and Development Review* 33(4): 729–56.

Peleggi, M. 2007. *Thailand, The Wordly Monarchy*. London, Reaktion Books.

Peng Xizhe and Guo Zhigang (eds) 2000. *The Changing Population of China*. Oxford, Blackwell.

Poceski, M. 2009. *Introducing Chinese Religions*. London, Routledge.

Pochmann, M. et al. 2005. *Atlas da exclusão social*, vol. 5. Agenda não liberal da inclusão social no Brasil. São Paolo, Cortez editora.

Poe, D. Z. 2003. *Kwame Nkrumah's Contribution to Panafricanism*. London, Routledge.

Pollock, S. 1996. 'The Sanskrit Cosmopolis', pp. 197–247 in J. E. M. Houben (ed.), *The Ideology and Status of Sanskrit*. Leiden, Brill.

Pollock, S. 1998. 'India in the Vernacular Millennium: Literary Culture and Polity in South Asia, 1400–1750', *Daedalus*, Summer, 41–74.

Pollock, S. 2006. *The Language of the Gods in the World of Men*. Berkeley, University of California Press.

Pomeranz, K. 2000. *The Great Divergence*. Princeton, Princeton University Press.

Porter, R. 2000. *The Creation of the Modern World*. New York and London, Norton.

Poston Jr, D. L., Mao, M. X. and Yu Mei-yu. 1994. 'The Global Distribution of Chinese around 1990', *Population and Development Review* 20(3), 631–45.

Potts, L. 1990. *The World Labour Market. A History of Migration*. London, Zed Books.

Przeworski, A. and Vreeland, J. 2000. 'The Effect of IMF Programs on Economic Growth', *Journal of Development Economics* 62, 385–421.

Rahman, T. 2000. *Language and Politics in Pakistan.* Oxford, Oxford University Press.

Rao, A. 2009. *The Caste Question. Dalits and the Politics of Modern India.* Berkeley, University of California Press.

Ratha, D. and Xu Zhimei. 2008. *Migration and Remittances Factbook.* Washington, World Bank.

Ray, R. and Qayum, S. 2009. *Cultures of Servitude.* Stanford, CA, Stanford University Press.

Reid, A. (ed.) 1997 *The Last Stand of Asian Autonomies.* Basingstoke, Macmillan.

Richta, R. et al. 1969. *Civilizace na rozcesti.* Prague, Rudé Pravo.

Riley, J. C. 2005. 'Estimates of Regional and Global Life Expectancy, 1800–2001', *Population and Development Review* 31(3), 537–43.

Roberts, R. and Kynaston, D. 2001 *City State.* London, Profile Books.

Rock, M. 2001. 'The Rise of the Bangladesh Independent Garment-Workers Union (BIGU)', pp. 27–47 in J. Hutchinson and A. Brown (eds), *Organising Labour in Globalising Asia.* London, Routledge.

Rodrik, D. 1997. 'What Drives Public Employment?' Cambridge, MA, National Bureau of Economic Research, Working Paper 6141.

Rogan, E. 2009. *The Arabs.* London, Allen Lane.

Rosenau, P. M. 1992. *Postmodernism and the Social Sciences.* Princeton, NJ, Princeton University Press.

Rossi, I. and Rossi, M. 2009. 'Religiosity. A Comparison Between Latin Europe and Latin America', pp. 302–12 in M. Haller et al. (eds), *The International Social Survey Programme 1984–2009.* London, Routledge.

Roy, O. 2004. *Globalized Islam.* London, Hurst & Company.

Roy, O. 2008. *La Sainte Ignorance.* Paris, Seuil.

Roy, O. 2010. 'The Allure of Terrorism', *International Herald Tribune*, 11 January, 6.

Runciman, W. G. 2009. *The Theory of Cultural and Social Selection.* Cambridge, Cambridge University Press.

Sarotte, M. E. 2009. *1989: The Struggle to Create Post-war Europe.* Princeton, NJ, Princeton University Press.

Sassen, S. 2001. *The Global City.* Rev edn. (1st edn 1991). Princeton, NJ, Princeton University Press.

Saunders, P. 2007. 'Comparing Poverty Among Older People in Urban China Internationally', *The China Quarterly* 190, 451–65.

Schama, S. 2006. *Rough Crossings.* London, BBC Books.

Schwarz, H. and Ray, S. (eds) 2000. *A Companion to Postcolonial Studies.* Oxford, Blackwell.

Scholte, J. A. and Timms, J. 2009. 'Global Organisation in Civil Society. The Effects on Poverty', pp. 80–95 in A. Kumaret et al. (eds), *Global Civil Society 2009.* Los Angeles and London, Sage.

237

Seidman, S. (ed.) 1994. *The Postmodern Turn*. Cambridge, Cambridge University Press.

Sen., A. 2005. *The Argumentative Indian*. London, Allen Lane.

Shavit, Y. and Blossfeld, H.-P. 1993. *Persistent Inequality*. Boulder, CO, Westview Press.

Shane, S. 2010. 'In Terror Scares, Evidence of a Diminished Enemy', *International Herald Tribune*, 14 January, 1, 4.

Shenoy, P. D. 2006. *Globalization. Its Impact on Industrial Relations in India*. Geneva, ILO and New Dawn Press.

Sherlock, S. 2001. 'Labour and the Remaking of Bombay', pp. 147–67 in J. Hutchinson and A. Brown (eds), *Organising Labour in Globalising Asia*. London, Routledge.

Shimazu, N. 1998. *Japan, Race and Equality: The Racial Equality Proposal of 1919*. London, Routledge.

Silver, B. 2003. *Forces of Labour*. Cambridge, Cambridge University Press.

Simpson A. 2008 (ed.) *Languages and National Identity in Africa*. Oxford, Oxford University Press.

Singh, Y. 2002. *Modernization of Indian Tradition*. Jaipur and New Delhi, Rawat.

Sklair, L. 2001. *The Transnational Capitalist Class*. Oxford, Blackwell.

Skocpol, T. 1992. *Protecting Soldiers and Mothers*. Cambridge, MA. Belknap.

Smeeding, T. et al. 2008. 'Elderly Poverty in an Ageing World: Conditions of Social Vulnerability and Low Income for Women and Men in Rich and Middle-Income Countries', Luxemburg Income Study, Working Paper Series 497. www.lisproject.org.

Smith, D. 2003. *Hinduism and Modernity*. Oxford, Blackwell.

Smith, S. A. 2008. *Revolution and the People in Russia and China*. Cambridge, Cambridge University Press.

Speir, C. 1973. *Phases of Indian Civilization*. Delhi, Cosmo Publications.

Spence, J. 1990. *The Search for Modern China*. New York and London, Norton.

Srinivas, M. N. 2002. *Collected Essays*. Oxford, Oxford University Press.

Srinivasan, S. and Bedi, A. S. 2009. 'Tamil Nadu and the Diagonal Divide in Sex Ratios', *Economic and Political Weekly* XLIV(3), 56–63.

Stewart, K. 2009. 'Poverty, Inequality and Child Well-being in International Context: Still Bottom of the Pack?', pp. 267–90 in J. Hills et al. (eds), *Towards a More Equal Society?* Bristol, Policy Press.

Stuckler, D., King, L. and McKee, M. 2009. 'Mass Privatisation and the Post-Communist Mortality Crisis: A Cross-National Analysis', *The Lancet* 373(9661), 399–407.

Sugyarto, G., et al. 2006. Labor Markets in Indonesia: Key Challenges and Policy Issues', pp. 301–66 in in J. Felipe and R. Hasan (eds), *Labor Markets in Asia*. Basingstoke, Palgrave.

Summerfield, G. 2006. 'Gender Equity and Rural Land Reform in China', pp. 137–58 in J. S. Jaquette and G. Summerfield (eds), *Women and Gender*

238

Equity in Development Theory and Practice. Durham and London, Duke University Press.

Tao, R. 2006. 'The Labor Market in the People's Republic of China', pp. 503–58 in J. Felipe and R. Hasan (eds), *Labor Markets in Asia.* Basingstoke, Palgrave.

Taylor, M. 2008. 'Power, conflict and the production of the global economy', pp. 11–31 in M. Taylor (ed.), *Global Economy Contested.* London, Routledge.

Taylor, P. (ed.) 2007. *Modernity and Re-enchantment. Religion in Post-revolutionary Vietnam.* Singapore, ISEAS.

Taylor, P. J. 2004. *World City Network.* London, Routledge

Taylor, P. J. 2009. 'Measuring the World City Network: New Developments and Results', GaWC Research Bulletin 300, www.lboro.ac.uk/gawc/rb/rb300.html.

Tezanos, J. F. (ed.) 2009. *Juventud y Exclusión Social.* Madrid, Sistema.

Therborn, G. 1984. 'The Prospects of Labour and the Transformation of Advanced Capitalism', *New Left Review* 145, 5–38.

Therborn, G. 1989. 'Reform and Revolution. Reflections on Their Linkages Through the Great French Revolution', pp. 197–222 in J. Bohlin et al. (eds), *Samhällsvetenskap, ekonomi, historia.* Göteborg, Daidalos.

Therborn, G. 1992 'The Right to Vote and the Four Routes to/through Modernity', pp. 62–92 in R. Torstendahl (ed.), *State Theory and State History.* London, Sage.

Therborn, G. 1995. *European Modernity and Beyond.* London, Sage.

Therborn, G. 2004. *Family in the World, 1900–2000.* London, Routledge.

Therborn, G. 2006. 'Meaning, Mechanisms, Patterns and Forces: An Introduction', pp. 1–60 in G. Therborn (ed.), *Inequalities of the World.* London, Verso.

Thorat, S. and Newman, K. (eds) 2010. *Blocked by Caste. Economic Discrimination in Modern India.* New Delhi, Oxford University Press.

Tilkidjiev, N. (ed.) 1998. *Middle Class as a Precondition of a Sustainable Society.* Sofia, AMCD.

Tokman, V. 2004. *Una voz en el camino. Empleo y equidad en América Latina: 40 aõs de búsqueda.* Santiago de Chile, Fondo de Cultura Económica.

Topan, F. 2008. 'Tanzania: The Development of Swahili and a National and Official Language', pp. 252–66 in A. Simpson (ed.), *Languages and National Identity in Africa.* Oxford, Oxford University Press.

Trocki, C. 1997. 'Chinese Pioneering in Southeast Asia, 1760–1840', pp. 83–102 in A. Reid (ed.), *The Last Stand of Asian Autonomies.* Basingstoke, Macmillan.

Tryhorn, C. 2009. 'Nice Talking To You, Mobile', *Guardian*, 3 March, 16.

Tu Wei-ming. 1990. 'The Confucian Tradition', pp. 112–37 in P. Ropp (ed.), *Heritage of China.* Berkeley, University of California Press.

UN. 2008. Department of Economic and Social Affairs, Population Division, www.esa.un.org/migration.

UNDP. 2007a. *Human Development Report 2007/2008*. Geneva, UNDP.

UNDP. 2007b. *Human Development Report China 2007/2008*. Geneva, UNDP.

UNESCO. 2005, *International Flows of Selected Cultural Goods and Services, 1994–2003*. Paris, UNESCO.

UNFPA. 2007. *The State of World Population*. New York, UNFPA.

UNFPA. 2008. *The State of World Population*. New York, UNFPA.

UNFPA. 2009. *The State of World Population*. New York, UNFPA.

UN Habitat. 2007. *The State of African Cities*. Nairobi, UN.

UN Habitat. 2008. *The State of the World Cities 2008/9*. Nairobi, UN.

UNICEF. 2005. *The State of the World's Children*. Geneva, UNICEF.

UNICEF. 2006. *The State of the World's Children*. Geneva, UNICEF.

UNICEF. 2008. *The State of the World's Children*. Geneva, UNICEF.

US Congress 2008. Congressional Budget Office, Issue Brief 17.4.

US Department of Health and Human Services. 2008. *Health*, United States.

US Department of Labor. 2008. *A Chartbook of International Labor Comparisons*.

Venkata Ratnam, C. S. 1994. 'Changing Role of Trade Unions in a Period of Transition', in P. Sinha et al. (eds), *Trade Unions in a Period of Transition*. Delhi: Friedrich Ebert-Stiftung.

Wallech, S. 1992. ' "Class versus Rank": The Transformation of Eighteenth-Century English Social Terms and Their Theories of Production', pp. 269–91 in M. C. Horowitz (ed.), *Race, Gender, Rank*. Rochester, NY, Rochester University Press.

Wallerstein, I. 1974. *The Modern World System*, vol. I. New York, Academic Press.

Waterman, P. and Timms, J. 2004 'Trade Union Internationalism and Global Civil Society in the Making', in H. Anheier et al. (eds), *Global Civil Society 2004/5*. London, Sage.

Weber, E. 1979. *Peasants Into Frenchmen: The Modernization of Rural France, 1870–1914*. London, Chatto & Windus.

Welch, A. T. 1985. 'Islam', pp. 123–70 in J. Hinnells (ed.), *A Handbook of Living Religions*. London, Penguin.

Westad, O. A. 2005. *The Global Cold War*. Cambridge, Cambridge University Press.

WHO. 2008a. Commission on Social Determinants of Health, 2008. *Closing the Gap in a Generation*. Final report. Geneva, WHO.

WHO. 2008b. *World Health Report*. Geneva, WHO.

Wilkinson, R., and Pickett, K. 2009. *The Spirit Level*. London, Allen Lane.

World Bank. 1990. *World Development Report*. Washington, DC, World Bank.

World Bank. 1994. *Averting the Old Age Crisis*. New York, Oxford University Press.

World Bank. 2000. *World Development Indicators*. Washington, DC, World Bank.

World Bank. 2002 *Globalization, Growth, and Poverty*. Washington, DC, World Bank.

World Bank. 2005. *World Development Indicators*. Washington, DC, World Bank.

World Bank. 2007a. *Purchasing Power Parities ICP*. Washington, DC, World Bank.

World Bank. 2007b. *Remittances Trends*. Washington, DC, World Bank.

World Bank. 2007c. *World Development Report*. Washington, DC, World Bank.

World Bank. 2008. *Migration and Development Brief 5*. Washington, DC, World Bank.

World Bank. 2009. *World Development Report*. Washington, DC, World Bank.

World Bank. 2010. *World Development Report*. Washington, DC, World Bank.

Wrong, M. 2000. *In the Footsteps of Mr Kurtz*. London, Fourth Estate.

Yadav, N. 2006. *Gender, Caste and Class in India*. New Delhi, Pragun.

Xiang Biao. 2008. 'Ethnic Transnational Middle Classes in Formation: A Case Study of Indian Information Technology Professionals', pp. 341–68 in A. Saith, M. Vijayabaskar and V. Gayathri (eds), *ICT and Indian Social Change*. New Delhi and London Sage.

Zea, L. 1965. *El Pensaminento Latinoamericano*. 2 vols. Mexico, Pormaca.

Zeng Yi. 2000. 'Marriage Patterns in Contemporary China', pp. 91–100 in P. Xizhe and G. Zhigang (eds), *The Changing Population of China*. Oxford, Blackwell.

INDEX